The Spirit of The Herbfarm Restaurant

The Spirit of
The Herbfarm
Restaurant

What was Paradise?
But a garden,
an orchard of trees,
and herbs, full of
pleasure, and nothing
there but delights.

The Herbf

The Spirit of
The Herbfarm
Restaurant

A Cookbook and Memoir: With More Than
100 Recipes, Tips, and Techniques from
America's First Farm-to-Table Restaurant

WRITTEN BY RON ZIMMERMAN
FOREWORD BY DR. SINCLAIR PHILIP

Skyhorse Publishing

Skyhorse Publishing books may be purchased in bulk at special discounts for sales promotion, corporate gifts, fund-raising, or educational purposes. Special editions can also be created to specifications. For details, contact the Special Sales Department, Skyhorse Publishing, 307 West 36th Street, 11th Floor, New York, NY 10018 or info@skyhorsepublishing.com.

Skyhorse® and Skyhorse Publishing® are registered trademarks of Skyhorse Publishing, Inc.®, a Delaware corporation.

Visit our website at www.skyhorsepublishing.com.

10 9 8 7 6 5 4 3 2 1

Library of Congress Cataloging-in-Publication Data is available on file.

Cover design by Ron Zimmerman & Kai Texel
Cover photo credit: Steve Hansen

Print ISBN: 978-1-5107-8012-5
Ebook ISBN: 978-1-5107-8027-9

Printed in China

IN SEARCH OF THE PERFECT MEAL

UNTIL THE INDUSTRIAL REVOLUTION OF THE NINETEENTH century, most people ate the foods of their fields, forests, rivers, and sea. In areas of warmth, they planted grapes on the valley slopes where crops wouldn't flourish. In these places farmers made wine. They fermented their own harvests. Monks made wine, refining their choice of vines and techniques century by century.

Farther north was beer country. Vines didn't thrive in the short and cool summers. So beer was born from local barley, millet, oats, and wheat. Similarly, different crops grew better in different climates where people used varied methods of preserving and cooking.

These are the things that created local cuisines.

When the circumstances of opening my own restaurant came together, I wanted it to be a throwback to eating locally while creating contemporary dishes. To do this, we started with our own farm and worked with foragers and smallholders. Each week we created a "show" in nine acts that I hoped would remind people that we, too, are part of nature. There were no à la carte choices. The chef-selected menu flowed in an ordered sequence from appetizer to "entrée" to dessert. Beverages (wines from the Pacific Northwest) were paired to each course without additional charges.

We instigated the unorthodox convention of charging guests prior to their arrival at the restaurant. This meant that no bill was ever presented and guests could leave at their leisure. We had no tipping. The result was, as I'd hoped, a welcoming evening just as if we'd invited you to dinner in our home.

This format was to achieve our main goal:

> For a few short hours we hoped to make your life as perfect as you'd always hoped it would be.

To judge by our guests, we succeeded.

For my Mom & Dad, Bill & Lola Zimmerman
and Carrie Van Dyck, wife and loving partner,
for believing in The Herbfarm dream with me.

It's the same story the crow told me
It's the only one he know
Like the morning sun you come
And like the wind you go.

— *Jerry Garcia*

View at dusk of mighty Mount Rainier from The Herbfarm restaurant.

The Herbfarm Restaurant, Woodinville, WA. Photo by Chris Weber

Enter to the grand fireplace in the salon and the Founder's dining room.

A stroll through the hallway to the main wine cellar leads to the restrooms

Contents

Foreword

THE SPIRIT OF THE HERBFARM RESTAURANT is Ron Zimmerman's life in recipes, an ode to herbs and regional, seasonal cuisine, and the history of a famous restaurant. It is the tale of a brilliant and adventuresome man in the form of his stories and recipes.

Ron and I met in early 1980s while he and Carrie were frequent visitors to the Sooke Harbor House, a seaside inn and restaurant located in Sooke, British Columbia, which my wife, Frederique, and I owned and ran. Ron was a very charming, likeable person with a shy chuckle and a soft sense of humor. He was wildly imaginative, enquiring, creative, and analytical.

We had more in common than most people I know. We both focused our interest on local, wild, native foods. We both loved the mystique, history, and traditions around the world of wine. We were both researchers always striving for deeper knowledge and understanding of food history and culture while also striving to re-create or maintain native traditions. We spent many an evening in front of the fireplace, sipping our way through philosophical discussions of ingredients, cooking techniques, and restaurants until the wee hours of the morning. Much to our wives' chagrin!

We were great friends and dined together often over the years, even with Julia Child the year that The Herbfarm served its first meal in a garage in Fall City, Washington. According to this book, my restaurant had a big influence on Ron and similarly, The Herbfarm had a substantial influence on mine.

I was a scuba diver and would procure shellfish for our dining room. Ron, also a fisherman, would trap crayfish for his restaurant. He was trapping crayfish during the last year of his life for the photograph and recipe on page 126 of Asparagus Soup and Crayfish with Nodding Onion.

The Spirit of The Herbfarm Restaurant also serves as an introduction to many of the best wild foods of the Pacific Northwest because Ron, like me, liked to forage for a variety of wild ingredients from berries to miner's lettuce, from Salicornia to edible mushrooms.

Mushrooms! Yes! From the days of our first meeting, I learned that Ron had an abiding affinity for mushrooms. Ron once wrote, "The Pacific Northwest woods offer one of the best selections of esculent mushrooms in the world—a mycologist's dream."

The Herbfarm's longest-running themed menus are the A Mycologist's Dream menu and the Truffle Treasure menu. As each year's menus were created, Ron ensured that the foods and herbs he used would enhance mushroom flavors. He had repeatedly and systematically experimented to find the best herb and mushroom pairings. In the nineties, these were the exciting days of the early, emerging culinary use of Oregon black and white truffles. You will find delicious fungal recipes inside this book.

The Herbfarm is said to have the distinction of being the first farm-to-table restaurant in the United States. It is the only AAA 5-Diamond-rated restaurant west of Chicago and north of San Francisco and has been lauded in *Gourmet* magazine and *Martha Stewart Living*, *USA Today*, and the *Financial Times*. *Travel & Leisure* magazine rated it one of the top 50 restaurants in the world. *National Geographic* called it "The number one destination restaurant in the world."

A serious researcher, Ron became one of the preeminent authorities in our region on the theory and practice of Pacific Northwest Cuisine. Many classes on growing and cooking with herbs and local foods were offered at The Herbfarm each year. One of the classes I taught there featured pinto abalone, sea urchins, gooseneck barnacles, limpets, and other wild northwest delicacies. The classes promoted local food leaders and chefs including Bruce Naftaly, Thierry Rautureau, Tom Douglas, Dr. Denis Benjamin, Susan Herrmann Loomis, Caprial Pence, John Doerper, Jon Rowley (the champion of Olympia oysters and Copper River Salmon), Sally Jackson and her local cheeses, Kathy Casey, and too many others to mention here.

In 1991 during the IACP Conference, Ron presented a master class offering a serious overview of Pacific Maritime Cuisine and the Rules of The Herbfarm kitchen. "A cuisine is not just food. It is the way we know and understand the world," Ron said. He spent much of his life promoting a deep appreciation for this way of cooking, eating, and contemplating the world.

Ron and Carrie organized many educational forays for their staff to visit local farmers, fisherfolk, and cheese makers as well as other local restaurants. They encouraged their staff to discover new ingredients and explore them to their depths. Not surprisingly, in the end, their key staff took on ownership of The Herbfarm when Ron and Carrie retired.

Once I started reading this book, I found I could hardly put it down. This is a landmark book! The Herbfarm is, after all, my favorite restaurant in the United States. Thank you, Ron Zimmerman, for the gift of this cookbook-memoir. You took the last year of your life to share the wealth of your knowledge contained within. This book is a shining testament to your culinary contributions; you were a pioneer and an inspiration to North American Cuisine.

In a way, this book is also about Carrie Van Dyck, Ron's wife and business partner. Carrie carried out a large share of the staffing, business, and educational work of the farm and restaurant. Her persistence, intelligence, and superior organizational skills used in support of Ron were essential to the completion and publication of *The Spirit of The Herbfarm Restaurant*.

It is a great honor for me to write this foreword. This book is replete with herbal cooking tips systematically analyzed by flavor groups and food affinities. It highlights the best common and out-of-the-ordinary foods of our region, both domesticated and wild. Ron was always generous, and this book shows his generosity with his knowledge. Twenty percent of the profits from this book are to be contributed to the scholarship in Ron's name, which provides support for students who want to continue the studies of local, seasonal creations in the Pacific Northwest.

So . . . happy cooking to you.

—Dr. Sinclair Philip
former co-owner, operator, and wine director of the
award-winning Sooke Harbour House Hotel and Restaurant

A Tribute to Ron Zimmerman

WHAT RON KNEW—intuited really, in that special way of his—is that even fonts have flavor. I know that sounds crazy, but it's true: every font, like Helvetica or Palatino or Bookman, tastes a little different to our senses, and in design you pair your fonts like choosing a wine, and you lay out a page of a book or a menu like you plate an entrée.

We all know that Ron loved telling stories through food, but most people don't realize how much he loved design: fonts, and color, and patterns, and borders.

Fifty years ago, out of college and basically broke, he called IBM and somehow talked them into leasing him a $10,000 Selectric Composer, like a typewriter on steroids. Suddenly he was a designer, a typographer, a layout artist. He built an early career on his way with words—not just writing them or saying them or typing them, but designing them.

By 1987, he was one of the first desktop publishers in the world, beta-testing a little piece of software called PageMaker. And he continued pursuing both a love of food with his love of great design . . . continued it to his last days, working on this book, not just writing but painstakingly designing every page.

To Ron, words and fonts and pictures were all ingredients. And he loved mixing them, experimenting, tasting, adjusting, automating, and ultimately sharing them with friends. Ron knew that the heart of great design is expressing a story, and he and Carrie designed a life, an adventure, an amazing story shared with us, and with the world.

—David Blatner, president, CreativePro Network

A Memoir . . . and a Cookbook

PART I
What the Rain Said: Smoke

IT WAS DARK. It was late. Or more probably, very early.

I'd lost all sense of time.

I sat hunched in a weathered Adirondack chair. The yellow barricade tape draped inches before me blocked the gravel drive. Seeping smoke marred the January drizzle, smudging everything with its corrosive stink.

At least it was quiet now.

■

Just hours before, my wife Carrie and I had left our rural farm and restaurant for the first time in more than two hard weeks. We'd headed out to celebrate surviving a series of seasonal disasters with a Chinese dinner in a nearby town. First, an unrelenting windstorm had threatened to shred our greenhouses. We'd made repairs at three o'clock in the morning. Then the same gale-force winds brought a cedar tree crashing down on the restaurant's office roof. Heavy snowfall cut power to our rural valley. The weight of the snow collapsed three of our greenhouses. We'd had to cancel our sold-out New Year's Eve dinner—our last chance to put money in the bank before the doldrums of January and February set in.

Worst of all, the restaurant's basement and wine cellar were flooding. In the autumn, we'd built a second prep kitchen on the back of our little farm restaurant. We were in the process of creating a private dining venue in the cellar. We'd moved most of our wine from the basement into a rented truck with an electric heater. The hole the contractor drilled in the basement's concrete floor had turned into a fountain as ceaseless

My mother and father had been married seven years, and when I arrived they counted my fingers and toes, deemed me a keeper, and took me home to live in a tent.

Dad was still building our house by himself—using only hand tools—when he wasn't working as the short-order cook and guide at our small fishing resort on the Rogue, just a bit inland from Gold Beach. When the first phase of our new home was finished, we moved inside and no longer needed the cold outhouse.

The next six years were my baptism in a place and an era that, to this day, still owns my imagination. In those years, timber was replacing salmon as king. The country roads reverberated with belching logging trucks loaded with giant Douglas firs and western red cedar. At night the coastal lumbermills burned waste sawdust in their conical steel "teepee burners," which, to my child's eyes, glowed menacingly red hot in the darkness.

The Rogue River itself is legendary. Prolific Western writer Zane Grey, author of the wildly popular *Riders of the Purple Sage*, fly-fished the waters and kept a cabin as a writing retreat upriver at Winkle Bar. Salmon and steelhead drew anglers from throughout the world. Though the fish runs were diminishing, the numbers still supported canneries at the river's mouth. When I was five, Dad proudly took me to a cannery with my first salmon—a twenty-one-pound king that might have pulled me off our river dory if my dad hadn't hooked it on his waiting gaff. It remains the biggest salmon I ever caught.

Soon our family grew to four. My brother Bob arrived one December, twenty months after me. In pictures of that time, I look delighted to have a baby brother to play with.

Living in Gold Beach, our family ate an abundance of fish and game, those wild and natural foods free to those who ventured into the woods and water to collect them. Because dad fished the Rogue, we ate a lot of salmon—fresh, canned, or smoked. Dad also liked to pickle chunks of the fish with onions and spices, which he put up in mason jars for the winter pantry. He brought home intact skeins of salmon eggs and fried them whole, basted with butter and served in slices.

To supplement the salmon, Dad hunted deer and ducks. We raised chickens for eggs as well as for table. Behind the chicken coop was a tree stump, where Dad's sharp hatchet would make quick work of separating a chicken's head from its body.

The head stayed on the stump while the headless body ran wildly all about. Mom, who had to scald and pluck the birds, never forgot the smell of wet hot feathers. She also learned to cook the live Dungeness crab that were abundant around the dock in Gold Beach. The first time she cooked a crab, she threw away the legs, assuming they had no meat, a memory that made her laugh years later. Her early years on a Nebraska farm hadn't prepared her for the watery bounty of the Oregon coast.

Once a year, we'd pile into our black Kaiser Willys Jeep for the trip down the coast and back up through the Siskiyou Mountains to Medford, Oregon. Mom and Dad brought back pears and peaches, which Mom canned in quantity for the off-season. She also put up the carrots, beans, and rhubarb we grew in our large garden. Since few people had home freezers or root cellars, canning was the best way to preserve the harvest for leaner months. "Putting food by" was central to my early household, the necessary corollary of thrifty hunting, foraging, and agriculture. As a boy, I assumed that everybody in America ate this way.

From Farm Fields to Goldfields

My mother, Lola Kammer, came of sturdy Pennsylvania Dutch stock, from those adventurous souls who had sailed here from Switzerland and the German Palatine some three hundred years before her birth. The youngest of six children, Lola spent her formative years on the family's farm in Brule, Nebraska, a town of three hundred near the old Oregon Trail and smack in the middle of the United States. There was little around but farmsteads, prairie grass, and other self-sufficient families, all of whom worked the land and kitchen from dawn to dusk.

As a product of farm life and the Great Depression, Lola grew up fast and seemed older than her years. She cared for the chickens, geese, and turkeys; tended the kitchen garden; and learned honest frugal cooking with food she saw born, living, and dying on the farm.

Not long after her eighteenth birthday and high school graduation, Lola's father, George, strode out one morning to work his land. When he didn't return, his wife Katherlyne donned her coat and set out to find him. She discovered George dead in the field he had tilled for forty years.

Now with no man to run the farm, Katherlyne sold the land and bought a house in town. As there was little work to be had during those Depression years, and seeing little future in Brule, Lola took a train to California to live with an older sister. There she took a job in a men's boardinghouse, doing household chores and helping make and serve the boarders' meals. One of the boarders was a mischievous young man whose pranks included sneaking a goldfish into another lodger's water at the communal dinner table. The prankster was Bill Zimmerman.

My father was born in a log cabin in Fairbanks, Alaska. His father, Franklin Zimmerman, had grown up on the family farm in Harvel, a hamlet of two hundred in southern Illinois across the Mississippi from Saint Louis. Franklin's folks did well raising chickens, sheep, ducks, cattle, and horses as well as tending acres of field crops—what looks like a successful operation on the engraved postcard my grandparents had made and saved. Today the farm is still in the family, now monocropped to thousands of acres of soybeans.

When he was of age, Franklin set off to the University of Chicago, where he earned a degree in mining engineering. A month after his graduation, on the morning of the 17th of July 1897, telegraphs throughout the world furiously relayed electrifying news. The steamship *Portland*, just in from Alaska, had docked at Schwabacher's Wharf in Seattle laden with "A Ton of Gold!" Within days nearly 100,000 men were making plans, some already heading to Seattle. The Klondike—the world's last great Gold Rush—was underway.

Among those men hearing the news and heading west by train was twenty-two-year-old Frank Zimmerman. He'd pieced together a grubstake from his family and partnered with his buddy "Brunky." The pair provisioned in both Seattle and Victoria, buying everything from nails and dried beef to shovels and pickaxes and the requisite pistols and mules.

Arriving in Skagway, the duo set out to relay their year's worth of supplies over the notorious Chilkoot Pass, a ballbuster known to defeat men and mules alike. At a lake on the other side, they built a raft, then waited for the spring thaw to begin the 550-mile river trip to Dawson City. The long litany of hardships endured by the fortune seekers in reaching the goldfields has often been told. But Frank and Brunky were young and fit: Chilkoot Pass earns but a single line in Franklin's diary.

In Alaska, Franklin married Anna Mary. He made and lost a fortune. He and Anna Mary had three children. The eldest, John Franklin (Frank), would die in Naples during the Allied invasion of Europe. Bill, the youngest by many years, missed his big brother deeply all his life.

Just as Lola's father had gone afield never to return, so Franklin went out one day to check up on his mine. When he didn't come back, a search party found him dead under a half-ton of rocks.

At the age of twelve, my father Bill was fatherless. Anna Mary, Bill's mother, relocated the household to Arcadia, California, just as the Great Depression took hold. With the family's fortunes now greatly diminished, young Billy stepped up. He bought wholesale crops and sold fresh corn, oranges, and vegetables from a roadside stand. With a cheap single-shot .22, he hunted the undeveloped scrub of Arcadia, toting home jackrabbits to supplement the table fare. He ushered at the Santa Anita racetrack where he saw the legendary Seabiscuit—the little horse with a big heart—run. Later he worked in the warehouse of Sears Roebuck, whose giant Wish Book catalog was like the Amazon of its time. In the sprawling warehouse, he wore roller skates to traverse the vast space. Fast on his wheels, Bill quickly became known as "Whiz," an acronym for William H. Zimmerman.

Deprived by fate of the college experience his father had enjoyed, Bill went to night school and studied engineering. A practical problem solver, Dad took a position at Rohr Aircraft designing the tooling for American Army aircraft. His success at Rohr landed him at Lockheed, where he stayed until the move north with Lola to Gold Beach.

Woods, Water, and Gardens

My parents had always had green thumbs. When we owned the fishing resort on the Rogue River, they terraced the hillside below our home for a large garden. From this plot, we reaped Golden Bantam corn (Dad's lifelong favorite), Blue Lake Beans, spring peas, carrots, Kennebec potatoes, turnips, and salad greens. The grand prize each June was the Hood strawberry, a strawberry's strawberry, firm, deep red to the core and dripping with sweet juices.

Despite its gifts, the Rogue proved capricious. Our fish camp resort was tucked up on riverfront land dotted with centuries old myrtle trees, a beautiful spot. Though the property had survived at least three hundred years of floods and flows, water started to eat away at the embankment. With alarming speed, the land sloughed off and washed downstream. In desperation, my folks moved the buildings to the other side of the North Bank Rogue River Road. But the river that spawned their dream ended it. We moved north. Dad had accepted an engineering job at Boeing in Renton, Washington.

When we moved to the then-wilds of Bellevue east of Seattle, my folks brought along their lifelong knack for gardening. My brother Bob and I spent hours hoeing the corn, weeding carrots, and searching for any wily zucchinis that had escaped our notice. These monsters grew so large that each, scooped out and filled with tomato, hamburger, and oregano stuffing, delighted and fed the entire Italian family that lived down the hill from us.

At the back of our property, Dad built us kids a ten-by-twelve-foot cabin. This rustic little cottage sported a shake roof, two windows, and board-and-batten siding. In the corner, he installed a small wood-burning iron stove set on a footing of bricks. The stove heated the room on chilly days. Best of all, its flat top encouraged cooking.

Our cabin became a clubhouse for the local kids where we'd gather to plan elaborate backyard "Olympics" or set off on forays as "the Rangers" into the adjoining woods where we studied plants and animals. The outings would even include quizzes I created, which, if passed, would earn certificates and badges that I made with such titles as "Curator of Mammals" or "Master of Trees."

One summer, Bob and I decided to see if we could go two weeks living in the cabin. We cooked vegetables from the garden, fried up eggs and pork chops, and slept every night on the hard 2x4 bunks. We only went in the house to use the bathroom, though Mom insisted after a few days that we at least take a shower.

I don't know if my parents purposely raised us to be independent. Maybe they were just mirroring how they had been brought up. Parents were less afraid and kids had more freedom then. Mom would scold us for watching TV during the day. "Turn off the TV!" she'd insist. "Go outside and play. Just be home in time for dinner."

We could do almost anything we wanted with little or no permission or supervision. My brother and I would disappear into hundreds of acres of forest where no adult ever ventured. I was free to ride my one-speed Schwinn bicycle anywhere it would take me. A patch of loose gravel sent my bike out of control one day. Crashing through a ditch and into an embankment, I was thrown several feet and momentarily knocked out. I awoke to find a lacerated right knee. The wound probably should have had a few stitches, but I walked the bike home, cleaned up, and taped the knee. I've still got the scar, but my folks were none the wiser.

Mom would shoo us away from the TV and out into the world, but she expected us to be home for dinner. Our family ate promptly at 5:30 each day except for those occasions when we ventured to Seattle's Chinatown to join my folk's friends, Roland

and Trudy, at the Twin Dragons Restaurant. ("Order one dish per person plus one for the table," Dad would knowingly tell the diners on each visit).

At home, we all ate everything—no special diets or substitutions allowed. Mom and Dad expected us to clean our plates. If the occasional dish didn't appeal, my parents would remind us of "all the starving children in India"—the parental guilt trip of its day.

Outdoors with Bob and Bill

I have always been fascinated by wild plants and edible native foods. I was in the fifth grade and we were living in Bellevue, Washington, when my teacher, Mrs. Clark, discovered I had a knack for identifying native trees. She turned portions of the class's occasional outdoor nature walks over to me. In junior high, I joined the school's Outdoor Club. These teachers preferred peaks and mountaineering to nature walks. In the club, they taught first aid, the "ten essentials," how to rope up for safety, how to hold an ice axe, and how to tie knots.

The head of the Outdoor Club would invite the most eager members on weekend trips. We climbed Mt. Anderson and Mt. Townsend in the Olympic Mountains, sinking knee-deep in crusted spring snow. Our grand adventure was a multiday summer challenge where we traversed and camped the breadth of the Olympic Mountain range, climbing from Sol Duc Hot Springs to the High Divide and then twenty brutal miles down the Hoh River on a trail crossed by giant storm-fallen trees.

In our teens, my younger brother Bob and I became inveterate hikers, exploring the woodlands and peaks of the North Cascades. We vowed to embark on our trips come rain or shine. When it rained, our main outfits involved shorts and simple ripstop nylon ponchos. There was no point in wearing pants while hiking, as the wet bushes crowding the tails would soon soak our pant legs. At night, we'd make the the ponchos into our impromptu shelter.

Much of the food we ate on these outings was dried, put up in bags, and sold out of a small second-floor Seattle space with squeaky wood floors. The place smelled of old canvas, wax, and leather. This was the first REI store. A lean, tall man sold us lengths of stiff Goldline climbing rope from Austria. That tall man, Jim Whittaker, would later be the first American to summit Mt. Everest. As the years passed, Bob and I provisioned numerous adventures. Many of these involved some sort of living off the land, a skill set that improved with time. For oceanside dinners, my brother Bob and I pried blue mussels the size of a child's shoe off rocks on the Olympic Peninsula coast. Since these blue bivalves lived in the Pacific surf, their meat was tougher and more deeply flavored than the farmed mussels of Puget Sound. The tiny wild strawberries on the sandy bluffs were ambrosia; blackcap raspberries a treat. I experimented with fern fiddleheads and dug wild onions from sandy headlands.

I usually carried flour and often a sourdough starter into the mountains. With these fundamentals, I could bake bread before a fire using a nifty folding aluminum reflector oven. Sometimes I'd purposely challenge myself, traveling food-light and counting on landing fresh fish for dinner. I kept a can or two of tuna or sardines at the bottom of my backpack just in case the fishing flopped.

When I started college, Bob and I explored the Sierra Nevada, John Muir's beloved "Range of Light." On one trip, we swung through Napa Valley. I was just getting fascinated with wine. Napa then was not an outpost for lifestyle millionaires. No stretch limos delivered bachelorette parties. Nor was Napa Valley the inland sea of Cabernet vines spotted with wineries it is today. Whole swathes of the valley still raised fruits and nuts, and you couldn't tell a winemaker from any other farmer. Everybody who grew things dressed in coveralls and drove well-worn old pickups.

In those days, Italian Swiss Colony was an old and charming co-op for families of Italian heritage. Charles Krug had been around since 1882. Louis Martini arrived in the valley twenty years later. Martini fermented its grapes in open-top concrete fermenters and aged the wine in giant redwood tuns. These were later torn out in favor of more "modern" techniques. The cooperage shrank from silo size to sixty-gallon French oak barrels. Ironically, many wineries today have gone back to concrete for fermentation, even to aging in larger wood barrels. Plus ça change . . .

In the tasting area at Louis Martini, one could purchase bottles of green Hungarian, Pinot Chardonnay, Zinfandel, Chablis, or Burgundy. These generic names had little in common with their French equivalents. In fact, Martini's "Burgundy" contained exactly zero Pinot Noir grapes, those great red grapes responsible for the real thing.

"Do you think I should buy the 1958 Cabernet Sauvignon?" I asked my brother more than once. This was when French first-growth Bordeaux went for $13 and a night's stay at a Motel Six cost $6. Finally, I took the the leap. Thus began years of wine collecting and drinking from my own wine cellar. From the reserve library selections listed on a chalkboard at Martini that day, my prize buy was a single bottle of the 1958 Louis Martini Special Reserve Cabernet Sauvignon—a splurge at $4.00. My cellar was founded on that bottle, which I took home for safekeeping. By the time I drank it, forty years later, the cellar at The Herbfarm restaurant held over 17,000 bottles.

My college buddy—later my business partner—Bill Nicolai and I made the first (perhaps still the only) nude ascent of Mount Rainier, stopping frequently on glaciers where he'd curl into a shivering ball to warm himself before the last push. My summit photo shows him triumphant, his face wide with a huge grin, ice axe held high and his privates severely shrunken by the cold. Despite, or maybe because of the handicap of Bill braving the mountain in just his boots and birthday suit, we made the climb in just four hours and twenty minutes, a very fast ascent for its time.

The next to-the-last climb of my mountaineering years was the twelfth ascent of Mt. Sir Sandford, the highest and most formidable mountain in the Canadian North Selkirks. The mountain had foiled many attempts for over a century, including some by Swiss mountain guides. The weather was notoriously fickle and the mountain paired snow and ice work with difficult, high-angle rock pitches. Four of us, including Bill, fully clothed this time, reached the summit, an area the size of a dining room table perched atop a two-thousand-foot fatal drop down the sheer southwest face.

Back at our base camp in a meadow across the valley, we celebrated our success, confident we'd be flown out via helicopter. Then the weather turned. The chopper didn't come for days.

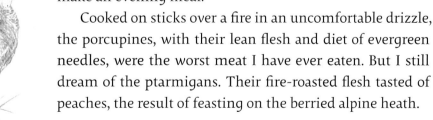

Low on food, we started to eye the local residents. A pair of porcupines wandered into our camp. Brian Berry, our expat American guide, dispatched them with his ice axe. We concluded that the local ptarmigans had never seen humans since they lacked the proper measure of suspicion. With judicious rock throwing, a direct hit would send up a puff of feathers and make an evening meal.

Cooked on sticks over a fire in an uncomfortable drizzle, the porcupines, with their lean flesh and diet of evergreen needles, were the worst meat I have ever eaten. But I still dream of the ptarmigans. Their fire-roasted flesh tasted of peaches, the result of feasting on the berried alpine heath.

Meanwhile, I Learned to Write

In high school and college I worked in a HVAC and sheet metal shop. That money along with savings from teenage jobs such as yard work, crafting and selling fishing tackle, picking berries, and managing a hilly paper route rife with mean dogs, paid for much of my five years at the University of Washington. I imagined I might become a doctor and majored in zoology. My Japanese lab partner, Aiko, taught me to cook squid over a Bunsen burner for lunch.

As a young college graduate, I lived rent-free in a small loft over a stand-alone garage in Seattle's north end, trading vegetable gardening and cooking for my keep. I was struggling to make money. So a *Mother Jones* article, "Make $12 an Hour Typesetting at Home," galvanized my attention. IBM had created a machine that could typeset professional, proportional letter spacing with real type fonts. The device looked like an oversized Selectric typewriter with added dials. I called IBM and said I'd read about their "Composer."

A few days later, a car pulled into the driveway and two men in dark-blue suits carried my typesetting machine into the old garage. I was stunned they would even consider me a client. I had no income, and these machines sold for a staggering $10,000. But after signing a few papers, they left me the typesetter and a thick stapled book of perforated coupons to tear off and send in with each monthly payment. And I was in the typesetting business.

I typeset and created "camera-ready" artwork, cranking out countless ads for *Popular Photography* and other magazines. With a former college roommate, I enlisted the magic machine to start *Raven's Mask* poetry magazine and published a few small books of verse as Bonefire Press. Both undertakings, predictably, lost money and folded.

■

I started spending my nights at my friend Bill Nicolai's three-machine, one-product sewing shop, where I inspected the stitching and seams of the finished tents. I created a brochure for the tent, which we handed out in the summer at the University Street Fair. That commenced an eleven-year partnership with Bill Nicolai and Bill Edwards nurturing and growing Early Winters, an outdoor recreational company. Together we took Nicolai's singular product, a double-walled alpine-style mountaineering tent immodestly named the Omnipotent, from a hippie-dippy operation into one of the most innovative firms in the outdoor field. We rose on the luck that no other American manufacturer was interested in a new and unnamed fabric that had a flexible white membrane of expanded polytetrafluoroethylene.

We had just brainstormed a streamlined, lower-priced coated nylon tent we dubbed the Potent, the idea being that the heat of the human body inside the tent would draw in air near the foot and release the moisture-laden exhalations through a protected upper vent. We gave a sample of our aerodynamic three-pound tent to Ian Hibell, the world's greatest long-distance cyclist who would take our new baby on an epic trek from the Arctic Circle to the tip of South America. A few weeks after Ian set off, however, he returned our prototype Potent with an attached note saying, "I'd stay drier and would rather sleep outside in the rain than in your so-called Potent. And, by the way, where I come from in England 'Po' means outhouse, and that's what I think of your tent!"

Joe Tanner changed all that. He arrived at our shop one hot summer's day, the little bell above our front door announcing a visitor. A balding man in a modest brown suit, Joe Tanner carried a briefcase that he opened to show us a few yards of a then-unnamed fabric that's now widely known as Gore-Tex®.

Pat Pace, our lead sewing machine operator, stitched up the Potent design using the new fabric. We tested it on a short mountain trip. And it worked.

I renamed the three-pound tent the Light Dimension and set about writing copy as well as creating a brochure, cover letter, order form, envelope, and a $20-off coupon. For me, developing the product and the pitch always go hand in hand. We mailed the package to everyone who had ever expressed interest in the Omnipotent.

Then we waited. At first, nothing. And we waited. And we waited.

Then one day the door jingled and the postman staggered in with a mailbag full of orders. He dumped out the envelopes on a fabric cutting table. We were in business—and way over our heads.

Our three sewing machines couldn't keep pace with the orders. As the numbers mounted, I started stapling them to the wall with only the name and address showing. Soon I'd covered that wall. And then another. It was time for triage. I tagged each order with a round sticker. Green meant all is well. Yellow meant they were anxious. And red meant someone had called—mad as hell—and was ready to cancel. While we juggled the tent orders, Bill Edwards designed the world's first Gore-Tex wind-and-rain parkas, which we quickly promoted in our catalog.

Chasing the Light

The arrival of the first Gore-Tex samples launched a new chapter of
the Early Winters story. I installed my IBM Composer in the shop's
office and started creating and mailing brochures. Soon enough, we
found ourselves running a thriving mail-order catalog business.

We decided we'd shoot our catalogs on location. And we wanted
to feature real people, not professional models, using our gear in
the real outdoors. To find the models for our first full-color shoot, we turned to Seattle
radio station KZAM, where DJ Jim Stutzman announced our "big opportunity" on the
air. Among those responding to our ad for real-life models was an attractive dark-haired
young woman. A native New Yorker, she imagined we'd be overwhelmed by applicants.
She hitched a ride on the back of a motorcycle and got there earlier than we did.

Bill Edwards and I arrived late with photographer Hiroshi Iwaya and the brand-
new Polaroid SX-70 instant camera he hadn't used yet. More applicants arrived and
filled out our rather eccentric questionnaire—*Would you rather star in a rock and
roll band or cross the Alps in a balloon?* Haphazardly, Bill grabbed some Gore-Tex
parkas for the trial shots. First model up was the early arriver, Carrie Van Dyck, who
had to pose in an extra-large and quite unflattering jacket. Pretty sure she hadn't
made the cut, Carrie came back later in the day and asked to be photographed in a
better-fitting garment.

"It's okay," we assured her. "You've already got the job."

Hiroshi shot exceptional photos on that excursion.
Our white van, packed with samples, trailed a huge
rental RV with the models inside on the meandering
3,000-mile trek. Cell phones weren't invented yet, so the
vehicles kept in touch with walkie-talkies that had limited range. Sometimes we'd drive all night to be in place
for sunrise shoots, then work until the sunset "golden
hour" before calling it a day. Nights, we alternated motels
with outdoor camping.

Carrie had a knack for organization. She became the
glue binding the pieces and kept us on a tight schedule. Our photo shoots eventually
took us to the Oregon and California coasts, Catalina Island, Yosemite and the high
Sierra, Mount Rainier, the White Mountains, the Mojave Desert, Navajo Country,
the Montana Rockies, the glaciated Bugaboo mountains in eastern British Columbia,

Monument Valley and dramatic red-rocked national parks. We chartered Robert Guggenheim's yacht to shoot a catalog in British Columbia's Barkley Sound. When the boat's generator fizzled out, we docked in Port Alberni for repairs.

As I rested on my bunk with the porthole cracked, I heard footsteps approaching on the dock.

"Americans!" one man said. "We'll get 'em!"

They came back a bit later, boarded our vessel, grilled the captain, and put the yacht and us under house arrest for lacking the requisite paperwork. The Royal Canadian Mounted Police demanded $50,000 to release the boat. Luckily, the Chief of Police in Victoria let us go. My brilliant plan B was for Carrie to scuba dive and wrap netting around the props of the RCMP boat, so we could make a run for American waters in the middle of the night. Already then, she was a key player in my schemes. We spent our three days of detention drinking beer and shooting pool in a smoky Indian bar. Finally free to leave, we went back to Barkley Sound, where Carrie dove for rock scallops—maybe the sweetest food I'd ever taste. Photographer Hiroshi discovered the sea urchins of the bays and showed us how to open the round echinoderms to feast on the delicate uni roe.

As we gained experience on these forays, we grew confident we could shoot outdoor photos anywhere. We also discovered that the whackiest questions on the application proved useful. Prospective models who would "rather star in a rock 'n' roll band" liked to party hearty. They were out of energy by day four of shooting. Not so Carrie. Because of her organizational talent and her work ethic, we called her back from New York for subsequent trips. Eventually, we hired her full-time and she moved to Seattle as our photo trip coordinator.

I didn't know then that she would one day become my wife and my partner at The Herbfarm.

The Flavor of the World

As the Early Winters mail-order business flourished I began traveling for the company, to China, to Korea, to Japan. But France remained my culinary Holy Grail. The country pulled me like a lodestone.

In the late 1970s, some generous but now-unknown person had given me a copy of Roy Andries de Groot's *The Auberge of the Flowering Hearth*. De Groot's tale begins with nightcaps in an oak-clad New York bar opposite Central Park where, as was his wont, he gathered with friends to sip his favorite liqueur. "What is this Green Chartreuse?" one friend asked. The bar's bottles, some decades old, offered few clues on their yellowing back labels.

The question, though, nags de Groot for some weeks. He has few insights—and certainly no solid answers. A journalist by trade, he decides to pitch a story. With some prodding, his publisher underwrites a sojourn across the Atlantic to discover the mysteries of the herbal liquor. De Groot's quest takes him to France. It draws him to the high mountain air of the Alps. He manages a visit to a thousand-year-old Carthusian monastery, a stone redoubt under Le Grand Som, the great mountain peak where, it is said, the monks, who take vows of silence, first developed the secret formula of Chartreuse some three hundred years earlier. It had taken one of the brothers twenty-seven years to perfect the recipe.

Needing a base of operations, de Groot takes board at a little inn. In this cozy stone auberge, the owners—two women—cook tirelessly each day entirely with what's at hand, the foods native to their high and wild valley.

Glinting trout from the crystalline streams. Grouse fattened on berried alpine heath at the timberline. Chamois from impossibly high rock ledges. Wild mushrooms emergent from the forest duff. Fearful boars from the depths of the woods. And garden vegetables plucked mornings from the ground or vine. All in season. All tuned to an unending cycle, the comings and goings of the rhythms of life shaped by centuries in their high and remote valley.

I was so enchanted by this refined but primal tale I wanted to travel to France, to experience firsthand those transcendent mountains above Chambery. To find that hidden valley under the granite gaze of Le Grand Som's dominating summit. To see, partake of, to revel in what I imagined to be a lost culinary Eden.

My timing was bad. When I finally got there the women, Ray and Vivette, had retired. The auberge was shuttered. The magical bonhomie of the table and its time existed only in the pages of de Groot's book and in the memories of what grateful guests survived.

The Inn of the Flowering Hearth was closed for business. But my dream of re-creating it in a new world was planted deep.

■

My fifteen trips to France over subsequent years served up stews and peasant fare at time-worn truck stops as well as multicourse evenings of refined dishes paired with fine wines at the storied tables of Michelin three-stars. I both devoured and took notes on the many details of Michelin-starred perfection and filled notebooks with sketches and ideas. It was a time when nouvelle cuisine and classic Escoffier coexisted in harmony, the former lighter and fresher with more elaborate presentations, the classic haute cuisine packed with plate-licking richness and flavor. Fame is capricious in the restaurant business. While some of the dishes like Pierre Troisgros's inimitable Salmon with Sorrel Sauce live on, the brilliance of chefs Louis Outhier, Paul Haeberlin, Olivier Roellinger, Roger Vergė, Marc Meneau, Alain Chapel, and even Georges Blanc merit homage, too.

Among the top toques of that epoch, the leader was Frėdy Girardet, whose three-star outpost was not in France but rather in Switzerland, the hills above Lausanne. Girardet's training was grounded in classic techniques, yet his cooking stripped away everything not central to liberating or elevating his ingredients. He cooked *à la minute*, often using pan juices to build and finish a sauce just before plating. On a good night, he'd riff on the ingredients like a jazz musician improvising a run. He called this inventive cooking cuisine spontanėe. Chefs traveled from all over the world to dine at Chez Girardet. Chicago's renowned chef Charlie Trotter took his whole staff to Europe with the express intent of learning from this master with his broad open smile.

On a tour of France with Carrie, Bill Edwards, and Carrie's mom, Eva, who spoke fluent French, we hoped to dine at "Girardet" as well. The restaurant had no open reservations, but they dutifully added us to the waiting list. Eva would find a pay phone at every stop and check on our status. "Non, non, Madame," they'd say. "No one has canceled." Sadly, on the last day, the Girardet reservationist said, "Oui, Madame! We can take you at nine tonight." By that time, however, we were three hours away and had to decline.

Our disappointment soon revealed a silver lining. Rolf Schiess, a longtime friend of Eva's in Zurich, suggested we contact Chez Norbert. It was Carrie's birthday and she was new to foie gras. When we arrived, we told the maître d' of Carrie's newfound appetite. The chef rose to the occasion, producing a multicourse fête with a variation of the fatted liver in every dish. It was a glad and jolly evening topped off with a cassette recording of Frank Sinatra singing "Happy Birthday." What we learned that night was that great dining should also be fun.

Twelve years later, when Carrie and I heard that Girardet would retire on his sixtieth birthday, we booked our flight to Geneva.

The red-eye touched down in radiant late-morning sun. Though I don't believe it was part of our plan, we phoned La Maison de Marc Veyrat on Lake Annecy for a luncheon reservation. Chef Marc Veyrat—always recognizable by his traditional broad-brimmed black Savoyard mountain hat—earned his Michelin stars "botanically cooking" with the native mountain plants and herbs of the region. This was years before Scandinavian chefs popularized the practice. I was eager to taste Veyrat's finds, which I imagined were akin to the 130 herbs in Green Chartreuse but deployed in food, not drink.

The restaurant glowed, its interior of ancient timbers and repurposed farm tools all waxed and polished to conjure a farmhouse fantasy. The bread cart was fashioned from a wooden baby cradle and overflowed with yeasty choices. Our luncheon, on the hot stone patio next to the lake spanned four hours. The tuxedoed waiters sweltered but never faltered. Though enjoyable, some of the dishes, like a local whitefish, fell short. But the mysterious liquids served in rustic coddled egg cups were revelatory. I particularly liked Veyrat's use of wild gentian, a little-known herb my parents were growing then.

By now we were exhausted. We headed north, passing the fountains of Geneva and golden fields of sunflowers. In the morning, we explored the area around Lausanne and even drove into the hills to make sure we could find Girardet's hallowed restaurant.

Dinner that night is a haze in my memory. We had a wonderful table that looked out into the main dining area. The cassoulet of truffled cardoons was perfection, as was duck with leeks and Beaujolais served tableside. Some of the dishes, like the plate of colored vegetables cut into diamonds and arranged as a tight and perfect mosaic, were not spontaneous but carefully premeditated. And delicious.

Our dinner at Girardet wasn't the best meal of my life, anticipation being sometimes more vivid than the real thing. But the food aside, I had achieved a life goal. When Fredy Girardet came to our table, he was kind and gracious. In our fractured French and his limited English, I told him that his life's work was an inspiration to me. And Girardet really did retire at sixty. I heard that he later regretted his decision. Hard and consuming as restaurant work can be, it animates our existence.

I'm thankful that we made the pilgrimage.

The Times They Are a-Changin'

Early Winters was on a roll.

After eight years of doing the bulk of the catalog creating myself, I hired Laura Flaherty, Pam Heath, and Deborah Wilner to relieve me of catalog writing and production chores. Laura took over as marketing manager in 1981. Together, Laura and I trained our team of writers and artists to produce the ever-increasing number of catalogs that supported the business. We all traveled to take marketing seminars or attend catalog conventions.

I continued honing my skills by attending New York University marketing classes. I often flew to Los Angeles for two-day seminars from the Center for Direct Marketing, where a young Christopher Kimball was the assistant. Kimball went on to start *Cook's Magazine* and America's Test Kitchen. In due time, I was invited to sit on marketing panels at conferences and was lucky enough to become friends with many of the greats in the business.

For two consecutive years, *Inc. Magazine* named Early Winters one of the "Fastest Growing 100 Companies in America." They invited us to Harvard for a weeklong summer colloquium on business management. *Catalog Age* magazine awarded us gold as the nation's best sporting goods and recreational publication. I was on the Speakers Forum of the Seattle Direct Marketing Association. In 1984, at the national direct marketing conference in Chicago, Dick Hodgson named me the best catalog copywriter in the United States. In later years, the DMA also tapped The Herbfarm for having the best catalog in America.

Nicolai and I were invited to join the board of Outward Bound on a five-day paddleboat junket navigating the rapids of the Middle Fork of the scenic Salmon River in Idaho, also known as the "River of No Return." On the expedition were the CEOs of John Deere, Rockwell International, the Headmaster of the Phillips Academy, John Emerick of Norm Thompson Outfitters, and Apollo astronaut Eugene Cerman. Afterward, Cerman sent me a NASA spacesuit helmet, a keepsake to this day.

My most-important fellow traveler on that trip was John Emerick's brother-in-law, Jim Willenborg, a brilliant San Francisco tech wizard who became a friend and adviser, who helped The Herbfarm out more than once in a time of need.

■

With the success of Early Winters, I could splurge. So I bought Mark Twain's dining table. I'd recently relocated from an eccentric rooming house in the University District to a lovely house on Seattle's Queen Anne Hill, and I wanted the Twain table to be the centerpiece of my new dining room. I had culinary plans. (Note: This is the table on the front cover of this book!)

For some years, Bill Edwards and I had immersed ourselves in wine and dining. In Chicago, we taxied to suburban Wheeling for dinner at Jean Banchet's Le

Français. A dashing bigger-than-life French chef, Banchet eschewed the Continental cuisine that typically branded a restaurant as "fine dining." He was part of a new wave of culinary enlightenment in America. Food lovers traveled from all points to partake of his menu. On our visit, I ordered pheasant soup as a first course. When the food came, the waiter theatrically planted a stuffed pheasant on my charger, then slapped his brow. "Oh, my mistake! You ordered the *soup!*"

The whole pheasant was whisked away, to be replaced by a perfect consommé.

Sometimes great dining can be playful, too.

■

In the early 1980s, Carrie and I dined at Barry Wine's The Quilted Giraffe. The restaurant was located in a large house in New Paltz, eighty miles north of New York. Their "Beggar's Purses" of crepes stuffed with sour cream and caviar were tied into baglike bundles. Each was meant to be eaten in a single bite. With success, the Wines moved their restaurant to a townhouse in New York City, and later to a shimmering art deco space on the ground floor in the AT&T tower. Just a block from André Soltner's lauded Lutèce (a hard reservation; a disappointing meal), the Quilted Giraffe's food was far more avant-garde and ambitious than anything in America at the time. Barry Wine diverged completely from classical French and Italian, even offering the first Kaiseki menu in a non-Japanese restaurant. Wine's presentations became more elaborate. The *New York Times* gave the restaurant four stars four times. The city's artists, celebrities, and power brokers (including a young Donald Trump) flocked there to see and be seen. The Beggar's Purses were still on the menu but were now a $75 supplement. They arrived on silver pedestals, women being advised to "close your eyes and take the whole thing in your mouth."

My take was that yes, presentation added to the experience. But it's equally important to be careful about what you say.

■

In Seattle, the breakthrough restaurant was Robert Rosellini's The Other Place. Rosellini partnered with Jon Rowley, a Reed College French major who fished Alaskan waters in the summer and traveled, researched food, and ate in Europe in winter. For a while, the two ran a small game farm, raising exotic fowl for the restaurant. But Rowley's most important lessons were sea-driven. He wondered why the food in Europe tasted so much better than here. He studied oysters in France and learned from Scandinavian fishermen how to bleed fish immediately as they were pulled from the sea. Instead of working with days-old fish, Rowley and Rosellini cut out the middlemen and significantly shortened the time from harvest to dinner plate. (See page 264 to learn more about Rowley and umami.)

Rowley would go on to champion the tiny native Olympia oyster, the Shuksan strawberry, and, after a two-thousand-mile quest, perfect peaches discovered at Frog Hollow Farm in California. He started the Pacific Coast Oyster Wine Competition to suss out perfect wine companions to raw oysters, typically a non-oaked Sauvignon Blanc.

But Jon's most enduring culinary contribution was getting fishermen in Alaska to bleed, clean and ice their Copper River catch right away. This made it possible to catch three hundred pounds of fresh fish and fly it overnight to Seattle. The quality was sensational. Chefs loved it. The arrival of the first Copper River Salmon became an annual spring rite in Seattle. Newspapers and TV crews converged on the airport to welcome the catch.

Heading up the kitchen at the Other Place was a young Bruce Naftaly. A baritone singer at UC Berkeley, Naftaly came to Seattle to study voice. To pay for his lessons, he took a summer job as the dishwasher at the restaurant. Within the year, having learned at the side of Chef Dominique Place, Bruce became head chef. His acute sense of taste and smell allowed him to create sauces that were "just so" for each dish. Bill Edwards and I would dine at Rosellini's, partake of sommelier Tony Kirchner's excellent selection of wines, and often order a fish dish. Bruce's black cod with a fennel cream sauce stands to this day as one of the great delights of my dining life. Naftaly went on to own Le Gourmand, a twenty-four-seat restaurant on the outskirts of Ballard, as well as other restaurants. His quiet determination to use locally sourced proteins and native plants—and his willingness to share his knowledge—inspired me to the point of emulation.

Another essential Seattle restaurant of that era was the Brasserie Pittsbourg in Pioneer Square, styled after a Parisian brasserie down to the mosaic floor tiles, pressed tin ceiling, and butcher-paper table coverings. The masterminds of this beautiful eatery were the French chef François Kissel and his no-nonsense wife Julia. The restaurant was always crowded at lunch, and the food was dished up cafeteria-style at a brass-railed counter. The menu changed daily and included such authentic French fare as veal chop with kidneys, sweetbreads, Provençal leg of lamb studded with garlic, and beef tenderloin with tarragon béarnaise sauce. My lunchtime go-to was François's large rolled omelet stuffed with mushrooms, spinach, and béchamel sauce. His salad dressing was legendary.

As a teacher at The Herbfarm, François would inevitably have a cigarette hanging from his lips as he talked and cooked. We were early advocates for banning smoking in restaurants. François was the only person who ever got away with smoking in our dining room.

■

As my parents had never been "back East," Carrie and I arranged an autumn junket, hoping we'd pick up a few tips for their herb farm.

After a flight to the "other" Washington, we took in all the major sites, from the Lincoln Memorial to the Declaration of Independence. Then it was off to the storied Inn at Little Washington, tucked into a little Virginia town at the foot of the Blue Ridge Mountains. Owner-chef Patrick O'Connell has tended this American treasure for over forty years. We enjoyed tea on the patio, then settled into one of the twenty-three rooms, each with different decor. The richly embellished decor is the life work of Joyce Evans, a London stage and set designer.

Patrick O'Connell's dinner preparations were worthy of the Inn's AAA Five Diamond and Michelin three-star status. The next morning, the hotel's house breakfast hit just the right notes, and we left Patrick's dream, happy to have my folks experience such a place.

In Boston, we toured Paul Revere's house, where my folks persuaded the groundskeeper to let them collect some hollyhock seeds. After a season of propagating them, they would begin selling "Paul Revere's Hollyhocks." We lunched in Faneuil Hall. I had my first baked scrod at Legal Seafood.

In Connecticut, we trekked to Covington to experience Caprilands, the most-storied herb farm in America. Willed into existence by the grande dame of herbs, Adelma Simmons, the fifty-acre plot had been an education to the New York chef David Bouley and the thousands who visited over the years. Mrs. Simmons was a generous five feet tall on her good days. Her signature outfit was a full-shoulder cape and matching felted beanie. Each day she gave visitors a "lecture" about a different plant. Seated on folding chairs in an old barn, I awaited her lecture, hoping it would focus on a culinary herb. But she talked that day of the artemisia family, popular with butterflies, but mostly bitter and inedible except for tarragon. Our optional Caprilands lunch in the all-black eighteenth-century house featured a tossed salad, a rice dish, a forgettable entrée, and a fruit cobbler. Later, when I was the vice president and on the Board of the International Herb Association, I came to know Adelma well. Though ninety years old, she always capped off each evening with at least one martini. By that time we'd opened The Herbfarm Restaurant, serving three-hour luncheons in six courses.

"I always wished I could charge what you do!" Adelma said, and winked. That was just before her second martini arrived. I would write and illustrate her obituary for *The Herb Companion*.

In New York, Carrie and I took my folks to the Statue of Liberty, Ellis Island, and on a stately horse-drawn hackney ride through Central Park. I put them up at the Hotel St. Moritz in a corner fireplace suite overlooking the park that was, ironically, only a few steps from where Roy Andries DeGroot began his Green Chartreuse quest in the Oak Room of the old Plaza Hotel.

We ended the trip with dinner at Cellar in the Sky, a small venue within the much larger restaurant, Windows on the World, perched atop the World Trade Center. This was a prix fixe multicourse dinner with wines chosen by educator and sommelier Kevin Zraly. The food was excellent. The Spanish guitar player added just the right atmosphere. Dad drank all of his wine and maybe some of Mom's. He grew quite jolly. "I could get used to this," he exclaimed every few minutes. "This is so wonderful that I want to kiss the chef!" I thought his exuberance was a bit loud, and I squirmed in my chair. But a man from the adjacent table for eight came over as their party left. "Pardon me," he smiled, "we're the board of directors for Windows on the World," he said. "Your father, he just made our night!"

■

As wonderful as Cellar in the Sky, Le Français, or The Quilted Giraffe may have been, among all North American restaurants where I dined, the Sooke Harbour House became my most admired. Located not in the United States but in British Columbia, on Vancouver Island's southern coast, the restaurant and inn exuded magic.

Frédérique and Sinclair Philip acquired the inn in 1979. They met in France while earning advanced degrees in economics. She was from Nice; he was from Vancouver. After ten years of living in a small village in France, and with a taste for *la belle vie*, they returned to Canada.

Carrie and I met Sinclair and Frédérique at the Sooke Harbour House a few months before opening our own restaurant. At the time, the inn had five upstairs rooms with a shared bath down the hall. The Philip family lived on-site in the basement. The place was still pretty much like the white clapboard farmhouse of 1929. The view was unbeatable. Sitting on a bluff just to the right of Whiffen Spit, the dining room and grounds afforded a sweeping cinematic view of the Strait of Juan de Fuca. Washington State's Olympic mountain range rose up in the distance, often hazed blue by the sea-salted air. Seals, orcas, and otters plied the waters near the stony, wave-lapped shore.

Gulls, eagles, and blue herons patrolled the sky. Sinclair, who sometimes went scuba diving for seafood, oversaw the development of the kitchen's cuisine. Frédérique ruled as general manager, her artistic sensibilities evident at every turn.

Eventually, the inn would have twenty-eight luxurious rooms. Each spacious getaway had a wood-burning fireplace, a deck or patio, and a soaking tub for two. All of the woodwork was crafted of native cedar, and each room had its own theme, expressed in decorative art, small details, and assorted amenities.

As wonderful as all this was, it was their kitchen that transformed Canadian coastal cuisine. When I was in college, my roommate, the poet Frank R. Maloney and I would putter north in my VW Bug to Vancouver's Horseshoe Bay to have what we considered the best fish and chips in the world. Occasionally we dined elsewhere in British Columbia, where the sodden fare was usually served with canned carrots and peas. Sinclair and the chefs at the Sooke Harbour House would change all that.

The clarity and purity of their food was exhilarating. The kitchen used fresh vegetables, native plants, and edible flowers from their own grounds or farms within twenty-five miles. Dishes were light-handed. Many were conjured from unusual ingredients: gooseneck barnacles, octopus, skate, venison, rock crab, kelp, kid, and rabbit loin. It championed the local. Distant fish, exotic fruits—even lemons—were banned from the kitchen, which meant that the chefs needed to kick it up with extra knowledge and creativity.

Because he lived downstairs when we first met, Sinclair could spend ample time with guests. On more than one occasion, the 2:00 or 3:00 a.m. clockface would find us lingering over a glass of wine in the comfy seats before the dining room's crackling fireplace. We bonded during long discussions of native edibles, of indigenous food and cooking techniques, or pondering what exactly constitutes a cuisine.

Many chefs came through that Sooke Harbour House kitchen. They became disciples, started their own places, and spread the gospel across Canada. Sinclair worked with ethnobotanist Dr. Nancy Turner to rediscover the foods and cooking practices of the region's First Nations. He became an expert mushroom and seaweed forager and was an active member of Slow Food Canada. A steadfast champion of Canadian wines, Sinclair and the Harbour House would win *The Wine Spectator*'s Grand Award for building one of the best cellars in the world.

When the soon-to-be Herbfarm went to a year-round service, Carrie and I had less time to get away. But we did take our staff members there on field trips and would even host a special dinner in the future.

■

In the early 1980s at Early Winters, Bill Edwards and I continued to share wine and dine adventures. We ventured to Alice Waters's Chez Panisse. The set menu changed every day, and our meal that first time featured sautéed pigeon breasts with figs in Sauternes. Alice was the mother of the fresh and local movement in California. From her kitchen would come a number of influential chefs including Jeremiah Tower (Stars), Paul Bertolli (Oliveto), Dan Barber (Blue Hill), April Bloomfield (Spotted Pig), and Joyce Goldstein (Square One).

Bill and I had signed up for an Orvis Fly Fishing School in Robert Mondavi's Napa Valley Chardonnay vineyard. It was here that we first tasted wine grapes plucked from the vine. And it was here that an investor in Dick and Peter Graff's Chalone Vineyard invited us to the remote winery high on the Gavilan Bench well south of San Francisco.

We stayed in the guesthouse, the sturdy beams of which were carved with grape clusters. The secret of the house was in the broom closet just off of the kitchen where a trapdoor opened to reveal a steep ladder. Climbing down, we entered a time warp. The cool rock-walled cellar was an archive of rare European imports and an irreplaceable collection of California wines stretching back to 1939. To be honest, after a big dinner with lots of wine, I was tempted to pinch one of those older bottles. I felt as if a genie in each bottle, eager to reveal its story, was beckoning me. Sadly, the guesthouse later burned, and the collection was lost forever.

■

To christen Mark Twain's table, I hosted a Great White Burgundy Tasting at my house. Every course was matched to a hallowed wine of admirable vintage. I researched, typeset, and produced a booklet of tasting notes for my guests.

The grand home fête was to be a wine-centric evening I dubbed "The Dionysian Dinner." I was so caught up in the project that I had a local press print a two-color menu cover while I typeset the evening's dishes on vellum inserts—a format we'd later use at

The Herbfarm restaurant. My culinary skills—and my confidence in them—had grown through observation and practice. I invited guests from as far away as San Francisco. The menu set the format that we'd follow when we opened The Herbfarm restaurant, even though that April evening, none of us knew that Carrie and I would be in the restaurant business in just two short years.

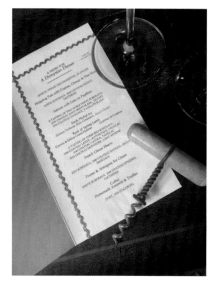

Dinner opened with an aperitif and a liver paté quenelle fashioned into a little hedgehog with pine nut spines. I baked spring salmon in paper pillows with a buttered lime-zest sauce. My mother had suggested three herbs from her Fall City Herb Farm for the intermezzo ice: lemon verbena, rose geranium, and sweet cicely. Mother knew best. It was a fantastic combination of botanical flavors. Next came racks of spring Ellensburg lamb with sides; French cheese hearts, homemade prune and Armagnac ice cream; and petits fours. The food was every bit and bite up to the standards of a very good French restaurant.

But the pièces de résistance were the wines we drank that night. For months I had vetted a collection of top French wines from notable vintages. In an era before wealthy Asians discovered top Bordeaux and Burgundies, such bottles were still accessible to most wine enthusiasts. The litany of grand crus—from a 1934 Chateau Filhot Sauternes and '66 Lafite Rothschild to an astonishingly fresh 1900 Rausan-Segla Margaux—made for a memorable and magical evening among friends.

Soon thereafter, my five-year lease on the Queen Anne house expired. The owners, who lived on the East Coast, had assured me they would not be returning west. I had the first right of refusal for buying the house. But we couldn't reach a deal. Carrie and I packed up my household and put it all, including Mark Twain's table, in storage. I moved into her brick house on Seattle's Phinney Ridge. Years would pass before we saw the Twain table again.

The Fishers Arrive. We Explore

One of the downsides of explosive growth like Early Winters' is an ever-increasing need for capital. *Inc Magazine's* rankings of the "Fastest-Growing American Private Companies" read like eulogies for firms that no longer exist. The same would become true of Early Winters, but not before we were bought out by Orvis.

Early Winters was no longer a seat-of-our-pants operation. We planned, budgeted, and attacked complex problems with the help of that new miracle, the spreadsheet. As VP of marketing, it was my job to help visualize new products, create catalogs (we now had a marketing staff of fifteen), evaluate the margin contribution of items based on their page space and location, and "prospect" for new customers.

Carrie dreamed of making her first trip to Europe. In London, we were joined by her mom, Eva, from New York. Renting a right-hand-drive car, we puttered through London's sullen suburbs before the countryside opened to sheep-filled fields and thatched villages. I was in the country to meet John Russell, the gracious Managing Director of Orvis UK, headquartered at Nether Wallop Mill on the Salisbury Plain. "You up for a little fishing?" Russell announced more than asked. He fitted us out with lightweight Orvis rods. Of our trio, only I had ever handled fly gear. John introduced us to our ghillie for the day. He guided us to one of Orvis' private two-mile fishing beats on the legendary chalk stream, the River Test.

At first, the fishing was slow. Carrie did well, though, casting a credible line. Eva demurred and watched. The ghillie walked the women back to the car when they got cold. When I was left to myself on the "Ginger Beer Beat" of this world-famous river, the fishing suddenly got hot. I hooked and landed brown trout with nearly every cast. It was the best trout fishing of my life. No one else was there to wtiness those moments. Just me and the river.

That night we dined with the Russells at the Sheriff House. The chef came to the dining room to announce the night's fare. "Tonight's salmon trout is from the little stream behind the restaurant," he reported. I looked from the dining table to the skinny ditch. But after the magical moments on The Test, anything seemed plausible.

■

In Reims, the center of Champagne production, flitting clouds patterned sunlight across the still-dormant vines. The air was chilly. I imagined monks tending these vineyards year after year for centuries. It was here that a blind monk, Dom Pérignon, first put a cork in a bottle of still-fermenting wine of Pinot Noir and Chardonnay. The carbon dioxide trapped in the bottle created a delightful fizz. Upon first trying his new invention, Dom Pérignon is reputed to have jumped up, exclaiming, "I think I'm drinking stars!"

And stars it was that night. Helped greatly by a robust dollar exchange, we found ourselves at Domaine Les Crayerés in marbled suites overlooking the parklike grounds. Black swans glided effortlessly on a pond.

The main dining room was paneled in lustrous wood. For our dinner that night, the sommelier paired each course with a different style and weight of Champagne. The variation among the wines was eye-opening. Between Champagnes based on Chardonnay (Blanc de Blancs), Pinot Noir (Blanc de Noirs), and Pinot Meunier (the unseen backbone hidden in Champagnes such as Krug Grande Cuvée), the beverages introduced my tongue to a flavor gamut spanning light elegance, through floral rosé, and into more robust Pinot Noir for the heavier foods.

When we finally got our liquor license at The Herbfarm, one of my first projects was curating a selection of Champagnes. Our little Champagne menu booklet quoted the blind monk, saying simply: "I think I'm Drinking Stars."

The next day we packed up and it was on to Dijon where we taste-tested some of the mustards that take the city's name. I'd always taken mustard for granted. But Dijon was a treasure chest of flavors, the mustards as varied as wines. Some were formulated from yellow mustard seeds, some with white, and others from black seeds, which I was surprised to learn, were at the heart of what we think of as "Dijon Mustard."

Leaving Dijon, we motored past the hallowed vineyards of Burgundy. When driving south, all of the famous vineyard parcels on la Grande Route des Vins lay on the gentle slopes of the hills on the right. We spent the night in the charming village of Beaune, the heart of Burgundy. The next day we descended underground at the Hospices de Beaunes to the Marche aux Vins, the cellar below the old abbey. Under the walled town are miles of stone tunnels and cellars holding millions of bottles, some of which were hidden behind fake walls during World War II.

The Marché was dark. Wine barrels were turned on end and each held a burning candle and an open bottle. We poured small samples into our souvenir "tastevins," flat silver cups that sommeliers once wore on chains around their necks. This made an excellent introduction to fine but basic Burgundy wines. And, of course, we had to stop to have our picture taken at the stone stela marking the most-storied vineyard in the world: Romanée-Conti. I wondered how many visitors had stolen vine cuttings here in the middle of the night only to find that the purloined Pinot Noir cuttings never achieved the original's greatness when planted at other sites.

Our French journey took us south. I genuflected as best I could as we passed the great hill of Montrachet before turning toward Lyon and following the Rhône south into the light of Provence. There we dined at Louis Outhier's L'Oasis in La Napoule on the coast of the Ligurian Sea. Though it was now the time of the year when the blustery mistral blows up from Africa, bold topless women sat outdoors, taking the sun, eating their lunches, lounging on the seaside stones.

At this time, L'Oasis was recognized as one of the best restaurants in the world. It didn't disappoint. We had a wonderful dinner there and then a long luncheon the next afternoon at Roger Vergé's enchanting old mill, Le Moulin de Mougins.

Fresh Start

The call came midmorning. Nicolai, Edwards, and I were to go uptown to the thirty-third floor of one of the city's prestigious glass and steel towers.

When we arrived we were ushered into a large glass-walled conference room where attorneys from the law firm Perkins Coie revealed that—as of ten o'clock—Early Winters had entered Chapter 11 bankruptcy.

We hadn't been consulted or tipped off.

The company was disbanded as quickly as peeling layers from an onion.

By the fall I was on my own.

Like all unemployed business specialists, I morphed into a "consultant." I worked on solving circulation problems for national catalogs, but I knew that to find a full-time catalog marketing position at my level of expertise I'd have to move to Chicago, Atlanta, or Los Angeles.

But I didn't want to leave the Pacific Northwest just to make the big bucks.

So I began making plans to start all over again.

■

On January 6, 1986, Carrie and I approached my parents about throwing in our lot with theirs at what was then called the Fall City Herb Farm. Mom had begun the business in 1974, casually offering some extra chive plants in a wooden wheelbarrow parked on the shoulder of the country road. As the honor jar filled with money, Bill decided that Lola needed a greenhouse for this newfound retirement business. The entire Zimmerman family helped build it, wood-framed, sheathed in taut plastic, with a pea-gravel floor.

A couple of years later, Dad and a neighboring carpenter, Bernie Bevis, replaced the garage doors of the farm's tractor shed with small-paned bay windows. Cedar walls and bunches of hanging herbs and dried flowers lent charm to the interior. The farm was branching out. The nursery now had a retail shop and enough room to store and package herbs. My parents added more greenhouses over the years and increased their inventory of live plants. The number of display gardens expanded from six to twelve. A flier I wrote for them in the mid-1970s lists 260 different live-plant varieties, a number that would grow to over 600.

The Fall City Herb Farm had no rivals in the region. Carrie and I could see it was positioned to take advantage of a general cooking trend invading American home kitchens to eschew processed foods in favor of fresh, local ingredients. Few published recipes explored the fresh side of culinary herbs, though that was soon to change. Angelo Pellegrini—Italian immigrant, champion of close to the earth cooking, home winemaker, culinary author, and English professor at the University of Washington—had published a basil pesto recipe in 1946 in *Sunset Magazine,* and that helped make basil a bestseller at the farm. But for years, fresh herbs were mainly relegated to garnishing food, as with a sprig of curly parsley.

◾

Carrie and I wanted to combine our talents to make my parents' farm a world-class operation. We explained this to them over margaritas while on vacation in Mexico. We'd expand the retail shop, the farm nursery, and offer food and crafting classes taught by staff and local experts. To help sell herb plants I'd create and mail two product catalogs and two thirty-two-page activity books each year.

"Oh, and by the way, I'd like to start a charming little restaurant on the farm serving six-course luncheons with beverages always included," I said. "We'll put in a beautiful vegetable garden just steps from the back door. The luncheon, including wine, will include a hosted herb garden tour as well as the chef's daily explanation of the menu. All of the food will be truly local. The meals will have themes that match the seasons. Every day we'll print a souvenir menu booklet the guests can take home. The Herbfarm as a cooking school and restaurant will give people a reason to drive twenty-five miles from Seattle."

After another basket of chips and salsa and a last round of margaritas, we were all on the same team. Dad said, "I'll dip into our savings to help get us started." And that was a good thing, because Bill Edwards and I had discovered that we'd signed personal loan guarantees when creating the Early Winters flagship Pike Place Market store. When Orvis left town, I was left on the hook for $65,000.

Part II
Designing a Small Restaurant

"**W**E'LL NEED TO** take out the front of the building." Bernie Bevis eyed the two garage doors. "This space would look nice with a stepped out front made of small-paned bay windows. The entry door can go here." He paused just where the restaurant entrance would be. With his hands, he drew his vision in the air. "We'll build a pony wall inside the entry and put in a leaded glass window. It'll be a small but welcoming space."

Bernie was a one-man general contractor. Give him a project and he made it better. A friend of my parents, Bernie had built the original two-car garage. Wisely, he and Dad had decided on a huge load-bearing center beam that eliminated typical garage trusses. This gave us an airy vaulted space we were now going to make into our little restaurant. With maybe sixteen weeks to transform the Fall City Herb Farm into The Herbfarm, it was time to get started.

Drawing on my previous business experience, I approached the project in per-haps overzealous detail. Vision statement: check. Project budget: check. Colors and decorating ideas: check. List of possible dishes and sample menus: of course. Chef's responsibilities: done. I'd even created detailed spreadsheets costing out likely opening dishes down to the penny.

Some of my spreadsheets showed negative profit, but we plowed ahead anyway. Somehow, we'd make it all work.

These were my thoughts on the look of the room, circa January 1986.

The Herbfarm Luncheon/Demonstration Center
Atmosphere: The restaurant will be a charming herb farm in the country. The decor will be French Country–ish: a blending of old and country in an almost reverse chic way. Modern elements will be integrated as a nice counterpoint to the rustic.

Color Ideas: Weathered wood, slate, terra-cotta, beiges and creams, dusky blue, saffron, and dark green accents with some orange popping here and there. Fresh bouquets of cut and potted flowers to brighten the theme.

Materials: Distressed wood, tile or stone floor, textured plaster, stenciled patterns.

Accents: Variable lighting, dried herbs and plants, dead tree branches, lots of fresh flowers, antiques, pieces of old buildings, patinaed kitchen and farm tools, hanging kitchen pots.

Tabletop: Three-quarter-length white under-cloths covered with half-length dark green cloths with tiny, repeating floral patterns. Over this, an ecru crocheted place-mat. Place plates (chargers) of white or green. High-quality tableware set in advance of the meal. Wine stems and glasses set for the coming of the tea cart. Bistro glasses for water. Flowers or herbs in a pot or small crock on each table.

Music: Guitar and piano jazz, Ella Fitzgerald vocals, French drinking songs and bistro music, mild seafaring chanteys; eighteenth-century English a cappella ballads.

Luckily, a lot of this didn't happen.

Seafaring chanteys? Drinking songs? What was I thinking? Stone floors? Nice look but chilly and apt to make the space too noisy. When guests dined on six courses over

two-and-a-half hours, they deserved to eat in peace, be comfortable, even coddled. Clamor was out.

I admired the work of the architect Christopher Alexander (*A Pattern Language*). Alexander was an outlier who was pooh-poohed by many fellow architects. His "patterns" were human-centered and timeless. Each was an empirical observation of how everything—from chairs to rooms and buildings and even sections of a city had been refined over centuries to fulfill the human need for functionality, comfort, *and* beauty. Trends and fashions come and go as we race to the "new." But truths and patterns proven by generations persist over time.

I did my best to keep Alexander in mind as we worked. The windows weren't just holes in the wall. They framed outdoor activity and calm farm beauty. The main dining and kitchen area had natural light with windows on two sides of every room. The front gave curious farm visitors glimpses of the action inside, while café curtains assured privacy for seated dining guests. We inserted diamond-shaped wooden trellising into the three two-by-four-foot skylights. This created a dappled effect, like pools of filtered sunlight on a forest floor.

To design the layout for our tiny open kitchen on the south side of the dining room, Carrie and I turned to our friend Bruce Naftaly at Le Gourmand. After we'd enjoyed dinner there one night, he locked the door and we set to work. Bruce believed that most kitchens are designed by people who don't cook. He was going to help us create one for people who cook for a living. We pushed his dining tables around to mock up the location of the major kitchen elements. The range with a custom burgundy hood would go on the back wall, centered on its tiled counter. The hand sink would be next to the dirty dish drop-off with a pass-through to the scullery. In the dining/demonstration kitchen, we needed a two-compartment prep sink. Beneath the front counter, we put a small commercial refrigerator and on top of it, a section of countertop that could be lifted to access a commercial two-burner gas range for cooking classes. Sink, stove, and refrigerator created a triangle, with space built in to safely pass an open oven door.

We sketched up this plan and delivered it to Bernie.

■

One night after a dinner in the Pike Place Market, Carrie and I were walking past what was still the world's first and only Starbucks. The lights were on and the door was propped open. Remodelers were hard at work inside. A handsome under-the-counter commercial dishwasher languished on the sidewalk. I poked my head inside and asked about it.

"It's in fine shape but it doesn't fit our new layout," the manager told us. After a few rounds of bargaining, Carrie and I left as the new parents of the very first Starbucks dishwasher. The machine could clean and sanitize dishes in under two minutes per cycle. It served us steadfastly for the next ten years.

We became fixtures on the auction circuit for dead restaurants. Each of these establishments had once been someone else's dream. Mostly we bought small things like mixing bowls, countertop mixers, spatulas, china, stemware. Our biggest haul was at an auction at the end of Pier 70 on the Seattle waterfront.

We won the bidding on a lot of fourteen tables and scored three or four stage lights that Bernie could mount on the big dining room beam and gentle with gel filters. We bought our dining chairs that night—thirty-six sturdy captain's chairs which we painted a semigloss sand color. Bernie cut birch plywood to fit the seats and Carrie covered the wood with foam and layers of padding, then upholstered the lot in dark burgundy velvet. She consulted her own discerning posterior to refine the seats until she'd found the perfect hard-to-soft balance. We replaced the canvas chair backs with a heavy dusky rose jacquard fabric. These had to be redone several times until the fit was sufficiently taut. Comfortable chairs were a must for a three-hour dining experience.

We also needed a way to keep ice creams and sorbets frozen. We bought an old-fashioned display freezer with a slide-open top. Most urgently of all, we needed to find our stove —the right stove. We couldn't build our front counter before we did—and our initial cash supply was dwindling fast. Carrie and I drove north to a restaurant supply place in Mt. Vernon in search of an affordable used range. Miraculously, by the front door sat a new dark green enameled commercial Garland six-burner gas range with a single gas oven. This beautiful piece of enameled art was on sale for $995.

SOLD!

We'd found the heart of our kitchen.

Meanwhile, Bernie and Bob Hise were finishing the interior build-out. (Bob had been my right-hand graphics artist at Early Winters and lived next door to Bernie.) We salvaged weathered barnwood from a couple of Early Winters' offices and repurposed the wood as wainscoting. To top the wainscoting, Hise handpainted a wooden chair railing that wrapped around the room. The silhouettes of a goose and a bunny, interspersed with a stylized nasturtium leaf, told a story in pictures. This pattern became the logo for The Herbfarm for the next forty years. A creamy crown molding topped the walls. Bernie plastered the walls to my vague specs, calling the slightly rustic look a "light

Mediterranean knockdown." We dabbed and rubbed the walls with three congenial pastels. Opposite the entrance, we set a simple iron fireplace and mantel, painted a dark sand color. Over the fireplace went a gilded three-by-five foot mirror I'd had custom-made in Boston when I lived on Queen Anne. At The Herbfarm, it looked sharp with a pair of side sconces and a big floral display in the middle.

We still had one wall in need of that certain something.

Tucked away in a dark corner at the auction of Lander's restaurant, Carrie spied a pitch-pine hutch. We bought it for a song and used it as the builder intended a century before—as a compact display-and-storage combo. It was a perfect look and fit for the space.

Sound-absorbing carpets, curtains, and tilework underway, everything nodding to our palette of rose, green, and beige. With the Thulian pink under cloths and tiny patterned green tablecloths, the whole scene had the charm of a summer garden. A few wooden farm tools—polished with wax to a sheen—completed the spell.

The aesthetics were in place.

In April, I asked Bruce Naftaly to help me learn to cook for larger groups. He took me behind his own scenes for a week. We poached twenty-four portions of rockfish in court bouillon, prepped vegetables, and made sauces. He let me make profiteroles and fill them with pastry cream just before serving. After a week of intense instruction, I felt up to almost anything.

Part III
Opening Daze

"**E**ACH LUNCHEON BEGINS** with a walk in the herb gardens (weather permitting) and will feature 5 or 6 tasting courses," I wrote on March 28, 1986. "The menu will change to follow the seasonal availability of the freshest Northwest seafood, vegetables, and game. We'll cook with no ingredients from outside of our region."

Below this, I had typed up a typical sequence of dishes for the information packet I gave each person who applied to be the chef with me. Though we never served this particular menu, it was an example of the dishes a guest *might* be served in our three-hour prix fixe, six-course dining experience.

Menu

Colorful Nasturtium Blossoms Stuffed with Herbed Local Goat Cheese.
Pink Swimming Scallops in Their Fluted Shells with Chervil and Shallots.
Apple and Rose Geranium Ice Intermezzo.
Chevrons of Boneless Farm Chicken Stuffed under the Skin with an Herb, Onion, and Garden Vegetable Mousse.
Herbfarm "Walk-in-the-Woods" Wild and Gathered Salad.
Miniature Raspberry Custard Tart with a Glass of Norfolk English Herbal Punch.
Choice of Ten Herbal Teas or Coffee from a Rolling Cart.

"Of utmost importance," I continued, "is that The Herbfarm luncheon is for the pleasure of our guests. Treat each patron as you would a guest in your own home. You will not be simply preparing great food, but are a host enhancing the quality of the farm and the dining experience."

There followed a profusion of possible dish ideas, of which these are but a few:

Starters: Herb Leaf Fritters. Pasta Salad with Shellfish and Basil Cream. Smoked Penn Cove Mussels with Sour Cream and Spring Onions.

Soups: Chilled Heritage Tomato Soup with Mint. Lovage Soup. Cream of Fiddlehead Ferns with Cilantro.
First Courses: Salmon with Lemon Verbena. Seafood Sausage with Dill Sauce. Grilled Columbia River Sturgeon with Nasturtium and Spiced Fruits.
Entrées: Rack of Spring Lamb with Herbs and Mustard. Sturgeon with a Rosemary-Honey Glaze.
Entrée Accompaniments: Pickled Nasturtium Buds or Pickled Apricots. Asparagus Tempura with Herb Vinegar. Just-From-the-Garden Peas with Mint.
Intermezzos: Cucumber Ice. Apple-Mint Ice in a Small Hollowed Apple. Sweet Cicely Sorbet with Candied Pansies.
Salads: Picked-This-Morning Red & Gold Tomatoes with Basil. Herbfarm "Walk-In-the Woods" Salad.
Finishing Touches: Angelica Tart with Crystalized Flower Garnishes. Tiny Sugar-Coated Shortbread Farm and Woodland Animals. Various Breads, Butters, and Drinks.

■

In response to our newspaper ads, twenty-five people applied for the kitchen position. All the phone and mail inquiries—no internet then—went to our Phinney Ridge house, where the living room had morphed into a sprawling office. The home kitchen remained intact for a while before succumbing to my art and drafting table needs. An upstairs guest bedroom became the accounting department.

Of the twenty-five chef applicants, we winnowed the list to three. Each cooked a meal for us.

We tapped Bill Kraut, who'd had his own restaurant, the Americana Café. He was humble, smart, and had a bright honest smile. His kitchen skills were honed, but I believed that we could kick them up a notch. Bill was an avid reader, kept up with the news, knew music and loved comic books, and eagerly absorbed the lore and lure of herbs and their history.

For whatever reason, I was inclined toward a prix fixe for the six-course luncheon with beverages included, this modeled on our visit to Caprilands. Carrie and I had a back-and-forth debate about the price. Should it be $12.50 or $12.95?

In the end, we opened at $12.95 (yep, Carrie won this round!).

For the summer 1986 season, we printed and mailed several thousand two-color twenty-four-page information and activity guides. These described the eighty-eight classes and demonstrations that Carrie had set up, including a July 4th weekend "Llama Fest" with rides for kids, packing demonstrations for backwoods campers, and wool-spinning for knitters. The digest-sized guide touted the new luncheon program with a garden tour and a "fixed-course menu mirroring the changing seasons."

Now, all we needed was practice. Carrie's mom flew out from New York. She quickly befriended my folks Bill and Lola, as well as Bette Stuart, Fall City's answer to Martha Stewart. To fill up the room, we invited some Early Winters alumni and tapped our nursery and store staff. Our friends and family "guinea pigs" were invited to critique the first meal.

At this point, both Bill and I realized we'd need some sort of bread. And we lacked a distinctive beverage. Though we had inquired about a wine license, the liquor inspector told us that cooking schools weren't eligible without a permit that needed to be renewed every day. We'd have to work on that.

For the beverage, we looked back to the eighteenth-century Shaker communities of the American northeast. Shaker women blended cool well water with vinegar, ginger, and some form of local sweetener. These jugs of "switchel," as they called it, were for the men during the late summer haying season. It refreshed even when the day was hot. We took the idea and named our version "Herbfarm Haymaker's Switchel." (See recipe on page 150.)

For the bread, we decided on a rosemary buttermilk biscuit, fragrant and cloud-light. Bill had just the right touch. We served them hot from the oven. With a liberal slather of one of our daily-made herbal butters, those biscuits were divine. Early guests still ask if we'll ever serve them again.

Why not try them at home?

Herbfarm Rosemary Buttermilk Biscuits

Makes 12–16

2 cups	All-purpose flour
1 Tbsp	Baking powder
1 Tbsp	Sugar
1 tsp	Salt
8 tsp	Butter
¾ cup	Buttermilk
1	Whole egg, beaten
2 Tbsp	Fresh rosemary, chopped

Preheat oven to 425°F

Sift the dry ingredients together. Cut butter into dry ingredients and mix until lumps are pea size. Do not overwork. Stir in buttermilk, egg, and rosemary. Turn out onto a floured breadboard. Knead a dozen times. Roll dough into golf-ball-sized balls, cut with a biscuit cutter, or drop generous spoonfuls (as seen in photo) onto an ungreased cookie sheet and bake for 12 to 15 minutes.

■

Two days before we opened to the public, Carrie took our guinea-piggers into the gardens for the first of the 5,300 tours that lay before her. She wove stories, picked herb leaves for everyone to smell, introduced them to "Rudy" the potbellied pig (later rechristened "Hamlet"), and walked the guests past cooing doves nesting comfortably in their rustic côte under a big cedar.

The tour moved inside through Bernie Bevis's entry vestibule. Once the guests were seated, the show began. Carrie passed through the room with a basket of warm biscuits. Barb "BJ" Force, our first server, filled guests' glasses with water then placed a full decorative Spanish bottle on each table for refills. The second glass was filled with our switchel.

The first course was "Hen on a Hill," a chicken liver paté wrapped in a blanched leaf topped with a chicken-shaped crouton. Next a soup of lovage, a little-known herb at the time with the flavor of strong dark celery. The palate cleanser was a rose geranium ice, pink but not too sweet.

The main course that day was Jon Rowley's Copper River King salmon. We bathed it in a reduction of shallots, tarragon, lime, and off-dry white wine with hints of wild ginger. Beside the salmon, we placed shredded carrots and zucchini touched with cumin.

While we served the dishes, the staff passed between the tables with baskets of living herbs so guests could see and smell the raw material used in the day's fare.

Next came our "Salad from the Meadow's Edge," twenty-five to thirty leafy and floral ingredients that Carrie would pick each morning. I stuffed large snail shells with smoked trout wrapped in Swiss chard leaf. Set on the edge of the plate, the snails looked ready to eat the salad. The salad was dressed with a vinaigrette we'd spent considerable time perfecting. Atop the salad, undressed, sat a crown of edible blossoms.

For dessert, we presented our guests with a large glass of fruit balls tossed with local honey and three kinds of julienned sage leaves. A small glass of an herbal elixir capped off the meal, except for the coffee and tea service.

When we removed their green cabbage plate chargers after the dessert, diners found a small form listing the day's courses. We asked them to rate the dishes on a scale of 1 to 10. Comments were welcome, too. I tallied the questionnaires on a spreadsheet immediately after service. Any preparation that didn't score eight or better was either fixed or removed from that week's menu. With this instant feedback, we improved our food day by day. We used these forms for the next ten years.

With some "first-day" nervousness, we cut the ribbon to the new restaurant. It was Sunday, May 25, 1986, halfway through Memorial Day weekend. We pinned festive herbal boutonnieres on all our female guests. After months of planning and years of gathering ideas from restaurants around the world, the tour and the meal both went flawlessly. It was sunny. The skylights cast a dreamy dapple over the room when the guests departed. The doves cooed across the graveled drive. A chicken strutted by, its head bobbing in time to an unheard chicken tune. All was calm. Life was good.

And then all hell broke loose.

The First Reviews

On June 13, less than three weeks after the opening, Stephen Paul of the *Journal-American* reviewed the restaurant. "Copper River Salmon was the main course and was so moist that I will no doubt be ruined for any other salmon for the rest of my life," he wrote. "Add the charming ambiance of the dining room, created by Zimmerman's soon-to-be better half, and you begin to see why this already polished gem awaits to dazzle you." This in a paper I'd delivered to people's doors back in the day.

On June 18, Ann Lovejoy's review in the *Seattle Weekly* filled half a page. "One of the best surprises is the development of the new Herbfarm luncheon program, a first-class restaurant tucked into what was once a garage but is now a little haven of gourmandery," she wrote. "The presentation throughout the meal was unfailingly attractive. The salmon is a hard act to follow, but Herbfarm has yet another delight up its capacious sleeve. Out come wonderful English country house plates holding simple mixed greens: several sorts of French lettuce, buttery smooth and crunchy together. This is the foundation upon which a Meadow's Edge Salad is assembled. Herbs, flowers, wildings, and seedling vegetables of extreme youth and delicacy are strewn from several little bowls, each holding an ingredient. The enchanting result is dressed simply with a balsamic vinaigrette which enhances without overwhelming the various tastes and textures."

On July 23, *The Herald* ran a full-color page and a half on the farm, gardens, and restaurant. When asked about the new restaurant, Dad said "Ron and Carrie have been riveted on success since. If there's one thing Ron understands, that's perfection."

Pacific Northwest magazine's Jessica Maxwell dined, then wrote: "The Herbfarm is more than a restaurant: it's a paean to Northwest botanical bravado. Here, in a jungle of exotic transplants and herbs, Ron Zimmerman and his wife, Carrie Van Dyck, serve up a thrice-weekly culinary gala—the Herbfarm Lunch, May through October."

Our phone lines were inundated. The restaurant was booked many months out. "We'd be happy to put you on a waiting list in case there's a cancellation," our staff offered over and over again. The waiting list was gigantic.

One fine July day that first summer, an Asian American father and daughter were dining at one of the front tables. Suddenly there came a clamor of what I guessed was Mandarin. The man was weeping. The daughter soon joined in. The man covered his face with his hands and tried to wipe away the tears. I approached the table and gently asked if everything was okay.

"After many years, my father has just regained his sense of smell and taste," the daughter told me. "He says it is because of the salad, because of the herbs in it."

Word got around. One morning, I was at the front counter chopping herbs for the noon meal. It was early and the place was empty, no visitors in the gardens or gift shop. Then I looked up, to find maybe half a dozen people peering at me over the café curtains.

I stepped outside and asked if I could help.

"My father has no smell," one daughter said. "Nothing helps. We have brought him here to take the cure."

The days we didn't serve meals, we baptized our new kitchen with a host of culinary classes. Our teachers were authors, chefs, and restaurateurs. Our friends Tony and Ann Kirschner of the Shoalwater Restaurant at the Shelburne Inn regaled students with the inside dope on their most popular dishes. Susan Herrmann Loomis, food editor, author of fourteen cookbooks, and avowed Francophile, hosted a series of insightful classes. Chef Bruce Naftaly took the students on a picking tour of our gardens, then cooked a seven-course meal from scratch with recipes to take home. For Father's Day, dads could, for a mere $4.00, learn about the mushrooms of the Northwest and sample several kinds as cooked by a pro from the Puget Sound Mycological Society. Lorren Garlichs, chef at the Captain Whidbey, covered wild and domestic berries from soup to desserts.

Tom Douglas, who now commands a restaurant empire, was then a young chef working at Café Sport in the Pike Place Market. He filleted a whole fish, demonstrated making fish stock from the bones, and poached the fish in the stock with fresh herbs. Many other days were filled with local instructors teaching herbal vinegars and dressings, flavored butters, salads, and jam and jelly making.

Then it came to a full stop.

■

During the feasibility study for the cooking school, the Eastside office of the King County Health Department told us that cooking classes needed neither permit nor license. On the 6th of August, health department inspector Bob Baird surveyed the facility and checked items off the list on his clipboard. The kitchen was clean and up to code. Then I mentioned that "guests are really enjoying our luncheons here on the farm."

After a long pause, Baird said, "You mean people are *eating* the food?"

"Yes, of course," I said, suddenly conscious of what I might actually be saying.

"Well, if you had the permits, you could demonstrate cooking, But no one is allowed to eat what you've cooked."

My heart did a near stop.

"I have to shut you down," he said. "You'll need to get a Cooking School Permit. Before that, you'll have to get your zoning changed, too. And by the way, you need to install a urinal in the men's room."

We had no choice but to cancel all reservations. It had been a gratifying seventy-three-day ride. The rest of the farm—nursery, gift shop, and special events— continued. The restaurant became a lovely stage for classes on herbal medicine, basket making, and gardening workshops.

When I asked my neighbor Fred Koba who ran the U-pick berry farm across the street. about the process, he said, "It took me eight years and $25,000 to change my zoning."

Fred was a patient man, and a resigned one.

While confined during World war II in their Army-constructed mini-city surrounded by barbed wire and guard towers, Fred's family lost their home and land on Bainbridge Island. The community of Japanese-owned Bainbridge Island farms had been the world epicenter of Marshall strawberry cultivation. The Marshall is considered the finest strawberry on earth but has an extremely short shelf life. It has to be enjoyed no more than two days after harvest. The berry was so celebrated that—at the behest of the King of England himself—Bainbridge Island's Japanese farmer community arose in the cool before dawn to pick flats of Marshalls. These were hand-carried on Puget Sound's fastest steamer to a royal banquet in Vancouver.

Here in Fall City, Fred and his wife, Nancy grew market berries and sold them to jam and jelly makers. When I was in junior high, I'd get up at dawn to join Fred's army of berry pickers. Fred hired all comers. From twelve-year-old kids to the crinkled, leather-faced man from skid row who'd lost his glass eye and smelled of whiskey. We'd all get down on hands and knees and pick berries five hours a day. Our pay was fifty cents a flat, not bad if you were a kid. Now Fred had to sell directly to the public or cease farming. He applied to build a year-round farm store to stay in business.

Short story long, that's why he had to get his zoning changed.

"Koba's report was not encouraging," I told Carrie.

We canceled our classes and I contacted the managers of Building and Land Development as well as the Department of Public Health. One kind bureaucrat took a fancy to us and helped with our dilemma. She walked our paperwork through the bureaucracy, saving weeks or months. The county amended the code by adding "Specialty Instruction Schools" to the list of permitted uses. This not only allowed our students to cook and eat at The Herbfarm, it made it possible for other county residents to teach what they knew best—dance, karate, horsemanship, and the like. We'd been shut down through August and September, but come October, the six-course educational luncheon experience could resume.

A Wedding on the Farm

On September 20th of that first Herbfarm year, Carrie and I got married at the farm. The day before, we'd rented a yacht. The vessel carried our immediate families around Lake Union and Lake Washington on a prenuptial cruise. Bill Gates's house was top-of-list to see for our out-of-town guests. But as we approached, men in dark glasses emerged from the bushes and shadows. Life re-creates the movies. We took the warning and kept our distance.

We dined aboard that evening. In our do-it-yourself fashion, I cooked rack of lamb, scallops with asparagus and mint and a few side dishes in the galley, while Carrie served our guests on the deck above.

We worked most of the next morning with nursery and garden visitors. In the afternoon we planted a "Closed for Wedding" sign in the main driveway and changed our clothes. Our wedding invitations had been the labels on jars of keepsake "Herbfarm Wedding Tea," neatly boxed and mailed to friends and family. Joe Tanner, who'd changed my life ten years before with his samples of Gore-Tex, and his wife Judy flew out from Delaware to attend.

Our staff garnished the white tents with garlands of herbs and fresh flowers. Dad freaked out upon seeing a caterer's food table decorated with *Conium maculatum*, better known as poison hemlock—that which Socrates had died upon drinking. We took it off the snack table before anyone else followed suit. "'Til death do us part" was reserved for the ceremony, not the celebration.

The ceremony began at five o'clock. Carrie was a beautiful bride. She wore her mother's wedding veil and ivory satin gown, recut in a flattering style. Sewn on to the gown was a hand-beaded lace bodice and sleeves donated by her brother, Ronnie, and his wife, who ran a wholesale wedding gown company in New York City. Draped around Carrie's neck was a double strand of Mikimoto pearls that I'd given her after a business trip to Japan. After we said I do and stomped a glass, the wedding party repaired to the lawn behind the restaurant where we grazed the raw oyster station, sampled the sushi bar, and loaded up on appetizers. We sat for a salmon and pit-roasted pig dinner prepared by our friend Chef Tom

Douglas. Carrie and her mom had bought and raised the pig. The Frederick & Nelson wedding cake was spectacular. We enjoyed live music and fine wines. I still don't remember much about the evening's end, which Carrie still reminds me of from time to time.

Our wedding coincided with the final weeks of the Expo 86 World's Fair in Vancouver. Carrie, her sister Judy, and mom, Eva, and I headed north to see it. The grounds for the World's Fair were built on False Creek, which until then had been a dingy railroad yard at the edge of town. This was Vancouver's coming-out party. As a result of the Expo, Chinese investors discovered Vancouver real estate. While foreign money drove up prices beyond the means of many locals, it also brought a new wave of Chinese businesses and restaurants. Richmond, just south of downtown Vancouver, is now one of North America's best areas for dining on Chinese fare.

Eva and Judy boarded a ship for a cruise of Alaskan waters. Carrie and I took the island-dotted ferry passage to Vancouver Island for our honeymoon at Sinclair and Frédérique's Sooke Harbour House. At Sinclair's request, chef Michael Stadtlander prepared a dinner for us, beginning with a garden vegetable broth with grilled rabbit loin and liver. Sinclair had scored a skate, a member of the ray family. Stadtlander grilled the "wings" with a blackberry vinegar glaze. The Gewürztraminer-lavender sorbet glided us toward a venison loin breaded in chicken mushroom with rosemary and juniper. We finished the culinary tour our friends had created with Stadtlander's loganberry yogurt mousse with caramelized hazelnut sauce and honey-glazed apples. As I stood and gazed from the dining room across the waters where Captain George Vancouver had first explored in 1792, I wondered what new adventures might lie ahead. But for then, we were content to linger by the ocean bathed in the fragrance and pops and stutters of a warming wood fire. After an intense summer, this was our first chance in a long time to truly relax.

■

In 1986, Seattleite Paul Brainerd and his Aldus Corporation released the first desktop publishing program, PageMaker. For those who have come of age after PageMaker magically appeared, it may be difficult to understand how monumental it was. Previously if you needed a brochure, catalog, ad, or menu, you'd write copy and drive or mail the manuscript to a company that would set the type according to your specs. Then you had to take the columns of outputted type and cut and paste them to your layout board. If you used line art, you could also paste that down. If you wanted a photo, you created a black box into which the print shop would "strip" a halftone-screened negative. Then the printshop assembled the pieces and used a special camera to create a complete negative of the page. The negative was "burned" to a printing plate and a pressman would print your finished piece using real ink from a can. With PageMaker, you could do all of that yourself. If you had an early expensive laser printer, you could even "print" black-and-white copies without a printing press.

"It could be said that The Herbfarm is the product of desktop publishing. The catalogs, newsletters, dinner menus—even the signs and labels on the plants and products—are all produced with PageMaker."

Lucy Mohl, "Herban Grown," *Eastsideweek*, August 1991

I got hooked and became a proselytizer. Now, instead of pasting and photocopying our daily menu, we could create a new take-home menu each morning with fonts of our own choosing. More importantly, I was now able to assemble our twice-annual thirty-two-page activity booklets and the pair of herbal product catalogs with greater speed and ease. Since Bill Kraut and I were the only ones cooking, the time PageMaker saved in the office made life a lot easier in the kitchen.

A couple of Aldus employees came to lunch that year. Seeing what we were doing with PageMaker, they asked me to be a beta tester of their software enhancements. "It'd be an immense help if the program could group objects together," I told them. The next release of PageMaker featured grouping. Soon thereafter, *Aldus Magazine* published a four-page story about how a small, innovative restaurant used its flagship composing and typesetting product. As someone enthralled by typography and printing since childhood, this delighted me.

In late September, we sent a flyer and press release informing people of the restaurant's upcoming reopening. We activated the reservation lines on a Tuesday. With multiple phone lines at our Seattle home office, we filled up in minutes. From then on, we elected to book reservations twice a year on a designated Tuesday starting at 9 a.m. At first, we split our service week between luncheons and dinners. With time we moved to the all-dinner format of nine courses with six included wines. We booked no more than six months in advance and reserved a quarter of seats to be released every Friday at 1 p.m.

Thus began ten years without an empty seat. And a business model where we paid our staff to answer phones and tell guests over and over that we were booked and would be happy to put them on our (rather lengthy) waiting list.

The *Seattle Post-Intelligencer* called The Herbfarm "The most elusive reservation in the Pacific Northwest." As Yogi Berra the great Yankee ballplayer said, "No one goes there nowadays, it's too crowded." So, too, I now found conversations all-too-often beginning with "The Herbfarm! I've never eaten there. Nobody can get in." Being full didn't keep the national magazines from discovering us, though. These ultimate influencers of culinary taste were all located on the East Coast. Though they loved the story of a little farm restaurant serving noteworthy food in a remodeled garage, they didn't understand our commitment to serving local foods in season. To their mind, plants and animals were "products" or "ingredients" available year-round, not natives of a specific place and time.

"Salmon," for instance, seemed to be an art director's generic concept: fish, nice and red. Never mind that nature supplies spring and autumn runs of Chinook, coho, sockeye, pink, and chums. Add winter Steelhead and farmed Atlantic Salmon, and you have a diverse range of flavors, colors, and textures. No matter that these fish returning from the sea to spawn seek out the very creek or lake where they were born. Or that salmon from long or very turbulent rivers (the Columbia, Yukon, or Copper) need more fat to reach the spawning headwaters than those born in short coastals river. Or that fat hoards flavor and makes the texture oily and sublime. These bits of knowledge informed our menus but found no place in national reviews.

Those national magazines did have hidden rules, though. "If they can't cook it in Iowa City," one writer told me, "we won't print it." "Keep it simple," explained another.

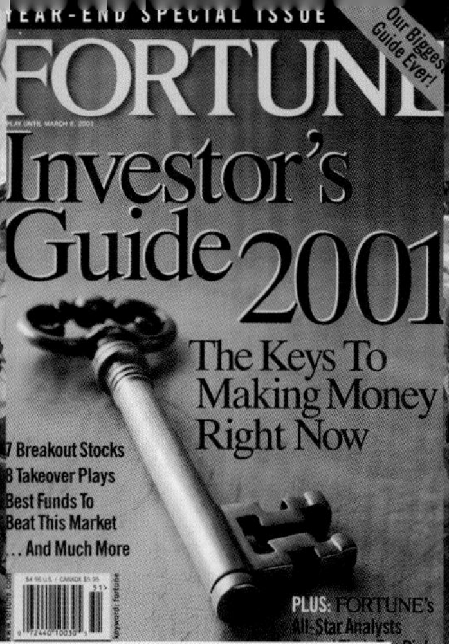

Herbfarm: A fabulous experience

FROM Previous Page

thoughtful details. Framed, personalized name cards and individual salt and pepper cellars enhance the beautiful table settings, which include a souvenir menu for each guest. Ice is doled into your goblets from a silver bucket. Candlelight makes everyone look good. And the service is smooth and smart and cordial, anticipating our needs but never hovering or fawning.

If anything detracts from this blissful scene, it is the graciously brief appearance of a furry puppet – "Herb," the restaurant's hyperactive ursine mascot – that comes to life courtesy of the hands of Van Dyck. The gimmick interrupts the engaging dialogue between Traunfeld and Zimmerman as chef and sommelier introduce the evening's meal just after the first course, holding up the wines to be drunk and showing off the more unusual ingredients. As Zimmerman gamely receives bottles of wine from the hands of the stuffed bear, Traunfeld looks slightly embarrassed to be sharing stage with the puppet.

But having to put up with five minutes of such silliness is a small irritation in an otherwise fabulous dining experience. The Herbfarm isn't just a meal. It's a milestone.

■ The P-I food critic arrives unannounced and pays for all meals and services.

STAR RATINGS

★★★★ Extraordinary
★★★ Excellent
★★ Good
★ Fair

The New York Times

SUNDAY, NOVEMBER 28, 1993

CHOICE TABLES

Seattle Chefs Showcase Northwest's Riches

By BRYAN MILLER

The Herbfarm

What began as a backyard herb garden selling at a roadside stand in this gloriously rustic area bout 30 minutes east of Seattle has evolved into a leafy wonderland and one of the best restaurants in the Pacific Northwest. It is also highly sought after, with an extremely restrictive reservations policy. The Herbfarm is open Fridays, Saturday and Sunday only.

A visit to The Herbfarm can be much more than an extraordinary meal. It also includes a tour of the magnificent, meticulously cultivated theme gardens — 17 in all, covering 6 acres — and kitchen garden. In addition, guests are given talks on the food's provenance and preparation by the owners and the chef during the nine-course tasting meal (there is only one menu, which changes weekly), and samplings of greenery that you never suspected were suitable for two-legged species.

Doug Wilson for The New York Times

Jerry Traunfeld, chef, and Colleen Herrick, assistant chef, of The Herbfarm, which serves a nine-course dinner.

A recent dinner in the enchanting cottage that houses the restaurant, which seats only 32, started with a glass of dry 1988 Argyle Oregon Brut topped with sprigs of lemon verbena.

"You will notice that the herb gives the sparkling wine a wonderful aroma, but it does not affect the flavor at all," explained Ron Zimmerman, who owns the restaurant along with his wife, Carrie Van Dyck. The table was set with name cards atop mini-pumpkins, elegant silver and stemware and an arrangement of wildflowers and herbs.

Each course is prepared in an open kitchen by the chef, Jerry Traunfeld, with detailed explanations of each ingredient. "During the evening you will be served many strange and different flowers," he said. "And all are edible unless we say otherwise."

The first course was an aromatic tart of wild boletus mushrooms from southern Alaska, onions and marjoram, along with nasturtiums stuffed with nasturtium capers, and tiny Olympia oysters. From there it got exotic: a briny combination of Dungeness crab-and-fennel dumplings, Whidbey Island mussels, Pacific spot prawns and wild cauliflower mushrooms; little pumpkins containing pumpkin gnocchi with chanterelles and sage under shavings of a local sheep's milk cheese, and herb-smoked wild king salmon ("Line caught," Mr. Traunfeld assured us) with beet and arugula sauces.

The show went on at a blissfully slow pace — more than three hours — as we reveled in herb-encrusted local lamb with a ginger and coriander sauce, a magnificent salad of wild greens and flowers, a splendid apple soufflé and apple-caramel ice cream. Five Pacific Northwest wines accompanied the meal, which concluded with a vibrant 1927 Madeira.

All of this luxury comes at a price: dinner came to $115 a person with wine; the six-course lunch is $50.

The Herbfarm, 32804 Issaquah-Fall City Road, Fall City, Wash., (206) 784-2222. Prix fixe dinner is $115 to $120 a person with five wines; lunch is $50, without wine. The restaurant, which closes in March, is open three days a week, usually serving lunch one weekend, dinner the next (the kitchen serves one meal a day). Lunch is served Friday, Saturday, Sunday; dinner, Friday and Saturday. Reservations can be made only on one of two call-in days a year — this year April 6 and a Wednesday in August, as yet undetermined; any remaining seats may be reserved Fridays at 1 P.M. for the following weekend. A 50 percent deposit — or your credit card number — is required.

"IT IS HARD TO IMAGINE A TASK MORE DIFFICULT for food lovers than choosing the best restaurants in the United States. We sifted through hundreds of reports, ate thousands of meals, and traveled millions of miles. Like an Ivy League admissions committee able to put together a class consisting solely of valedictorians, we agonized about overstocking the list with luxurious French restaurants, big-city restaurants, or those with famous chefs."
Gourmet—OCTOBER 2001

Restaurant founders Carrie Van Dyck & Ron Zimmerman accepting the AAA's 5 Diamonds, its highest honor

AMERICA'S BEST 50 RESTAURANTS

The Herbfarm
Woodinville, Washington

15 Northwesterners speak with awe of Ron Zimmerman and Carrie Van Dyck's legendary Herbfarm, as they well might. Although the restaurant moved into larger quarters in Woodinville, there are only four seatings a week, and the 60 coveted places are all fully booked several months ahead. It isn't for everyone. You commit yourself to a tour of the well-used and far-from-mundane herb beds and kitchen garden, a reverent discussion of the evening's dishes, and a nine-course dinner with Northwest wines that unfolds slowly over four and a half hours. Whatever the season (the October menu, "A Mycologist's Dream," showcases 16 different wild mushrooms; a summer one, "An Exaltation of Vegetables"), Jerry Traunfeld and his kitchen staff come as close as anyone in the Northwest to the Japanese ideal of *umami*—capturing the essence of ingredients at their peak of perfection. There is nothing flashy about the succulent slow-roasted Copper King salmon on dill, but you remember the wild taste of it for days. You savor a tempura of foraged salicornia (sea beans); yearling Quilcene oysters with lovage cream; a silky Copper River gravlax tart with fresh Oregon-grown wasabi; a gathered salad of microgreens with shavings of Sally Jackson's sheep's-milk cheese. For cooks, The Herbfarm's use of strange and familiar herbs can be inspiring—angelica in ice cream (you've seen the stout, celery-like herb before dinner), lavender in a lyrical shortcake with strawberries, a sorbet of strawberry and rose geranium. Around midnight, you'll be glad you booked a room at the luxurious Willows Lodge next door. But if you haven't, it's almost a straight shot back to Seattle.

What the Critics Say

DiRōNA

★★★★ *Mobil Travel Guide & Fodor's Best*
★★★★ *Best Places Seattle & Best Places N.W.*
★★★★ *The Seattle Times*, August 2001
★★★★ *Seattle Post-Intelligencer*, October 2001
★★★ *Frommer's Washington State* (HIGHEST RATING)
♦♦♦♦♦ *AAA 5-Diamond Award* (1 OF 52 IN AMERICA)
The James Beard Award—Best American Chef, N.W. 2000
2004 Award of Excellence—DiRōNA (Distinguished Restaurants of N. America)
Fine Dining Hall of Fame—*Nation's Restaurant News*, May 2003
"Top 50 Restaurants in America"—*Gourmet*, October 2001
"Best Washington Restaurant"—*Northwest Palate* 2002
America's Top Restaurants—*Zagat Survey 2004*
"Top 50 Restaurants in the World"—*Travel-Leisure*
"Best of Award of Excellence"—*Wine Spectator* 1997-2004
"Best Northwest Wine List"—*Wine Press Northwest, 2000-2004*
"America's Best Wine List"—*Monterey Wine Festival 2004*
"Best Overall Restaurant"—*Where: Seattle*, Editor's Choice
"Best Washington Dining"—*Northwest Palate Magazine*
"Futile search for synonyms for 'Bliss'"—*Seattle Weekly*
"An unparalleled dining event."—*The Seattle Times*
"A must-experience. The fastest five hours you'll ever experience."—*Best Places Seattle*
"The Northwest's most-celebrated restaurant; the ultimate expression of the Northwest's bounty."—*Frommer's*

SEATTLE TIMES REPRINTS • FRIDAY, AUGUST 3, 2001

The Seattle Times

TICKET

Nancy in wonderland

Our restaurant critic leads the way to an Herbfarm fantasy

By Nancy Leson
Seattle Times restaurant critic

Photos by Ron Wurzer
Seattle Times photographer

Dinner at the Herbfarm is not merely dinner: It is an unparalleled dining event. This five-hour, nine-course theatrical production stars an incomparable chef/genius aided by a crew of 20, features five splendid Northwest wines, a classical guitarist and an audience of culinary enthusiasts willing to spend a small fortune for a meal they won't soon forget.

Northwest ★★★★ $$$$

What price perfection? A jaw-dropping $436 for two, including tax, gratuity and the opportunity to leave spellbound and sated after sipping such vintage treasures as a 100-year-old Barbeito Malvazia Madeira.

You may not be able to imagine spending half so much on a meal, even if it's a once-in-a-lifetime experience such as this. All the more reason to read on, and let me lead you through the looking glass on an armchair journey to the Herbfarm.

Herbfarm co-owner Ron Zimmerman, far left, introduces the staff to diners before the meal.

The story of this flawless food fantasy – a genuflection to the Northwest's early-summer bounty dubbed "A Summer Sketchbook" – began at 6:45 p.m. on a Saturday when my husband and I entered an antiques-filled parlor. There co-owner Carrie Van Dyck greeted us, offered us herbal ice tea floating with edible flowers and led us, with fellow diners, on a narrated garden tour.

Newly landscaped, this pretty profusion of raised beds is a far cry from the lush acreage that inspired the Herbfarm's original Fall City restaurant. Destroyed by fire in 1997, the restaurant found temporary quarters at an Issaquah winery before reopening this spring in the heart of Woodinville.

With doubled capacity, a private dining room, a chef's library and a very visible 10,000-bottle wine cellar, the Herbfarm is – finally – ensconced in a rustic European-styled structure where it shares a view of Mount Rainier and a resemblance to a fairy-tale cottage.

Today, chef Jerry Traunfeld finds inspiration for his seasonal theme dinners at a 1-1/2-acre farm plot a mile away, leaving the show garden to curious diners and the Herbfarm's "recycling unit" – a Vietnamese potbellied pig whose stylish sty is adjacent to the Willows Lodge. The garden, and the restaurant, may be viewed from two luxury Herbfarm suites available for overnight guests wise (and wealthy) enough to spend the night.

Back indoors, patrons are led to tables dressed with chintz and charm and set with

three-tiered candelabrum, flowers tucked into linen napkins, heavy Christo ware and a flight of crystal wine glasses generously filled throughout the e

As Van Dyck's husband, co-owner Ron Zimmerman, and "Wine Godde tine Mayo poured a 1996 St. Innocent blanc de noirs – a bone-dry sparkle tableside with herbs snipped from a fragrant basketful – eyes turned to th piece of the dining room: the expansive kitchen.

In this red-velvet-draped stage set, Traunfeld and his white-coats are corps du ballet. Their well-rehearsed first act included a single morel plumped with goat cheese, chubby Mediterranean mussels skewered on and smoked over basilwood, and pearl-gray orbs of Montana paddlef gleaming on a wild ginger jelly. The clear, clean, mild-tasting jelly was flav the locally foraged rhizome – as we'd later learn when Traunfeld and Zimmerman acquainted us with the evening's offerings.

The crisp citrus notes of Chateau Ste. Michelle's 1999 Horse Heaven sauvignon blanc played off sorrel flan adrift in a froth of lemon-thyme sabayon and topped with Dungeness crab. Somehow Traunfeld magically coaxed the lemony flavor from the sorrel, leaving its noted sourness behind.

The brilliant pink of Chinook Winery's 2000 cabernet franc rosé was echoed in Yakatat sockeye salmon, slow-cooked at 140 degrees. Resting on a mix of delicate herbs, briny sea beans, pea-shoot tendrils and striated watermelon-radish, the salmon's gravlax-like texture was refreshed by the dry, fruity rosé.

Course after course, the pairings of food and wine proved uncanny and precise.

The Herbfarm

14590 N.E. 145th St., Woodinvi

Reservations: 206-784-2222.

Hours: Dinner served Th through Sunday (with additio day dates) by reservation on seating nightly; allow 4 1/2- (time flies!) for dinner.

Price: $149 per person (with a charge Friday and Sunday nigh $20 surcharge Saturday night), and 18 percent gratuity. A $50 son credit-card deposit is requ confirm your reservation; a full is given with 30 days advance With less than 30 days notice, charge may apply if the rese cannot be rebooked.

Parking: Private lot.

Sound: Patricio Contreras' guit

N APPETIT
AMERICA'S FOOD AND ENTERTAINING MAGAZINE

resh
ROM THE
arden

ers' Market Menus
or Outdoor Entertaining
ct Peach Desserts

northwest
Palate
FOOD, WINE, AND TRAVEL OF THE PACIFIC NORTHWEST
JANUARY/FEBRUARY 200

Best of the
Northwe

Sunset
THE MAGAZINE OF WESTERN LIVING
JUNE 1992

How You Can Add a
**Private
Patio**

Wildfire:
he West's
ver-Pres
hreat

pecial Section:
ummer Entertaining

our Family's Best
Day at Disneyland

Old-Fashioned Roses
or Today's Gardens

$2.50
$2.95 in Canada

• Spinnakers Vine

Victoria
November 1991
A Time for Family

A Harvest
Dinner at The
Herbfarm in
Fall City

BEAUTIFUL WAY
to
*Embrace the
Holida*

An Herb Lover's
Thanksgiving

Best Friends by
Letters Bound

HOME & GARDEN FASHION & BEAUTY
Cooking & Entertaining Crafts & Collectibles

Food & wine

t, drink and get back to those roots

ers' interest in fresh,
food grows, so does
Herbfarm's appeal

West
Woodinville

Outside Seattle

Where it comes from: Diners, told to allow about five hours for dinner, listen as co-owner Carrie Van Dyck gives a tour of The Herb

CRITICS AROUND
THE WORLD AGRE

GOLD IN FRANCE...
Challenge International du Vin
Bordeaux, France

"...may be the best

wh
dining out

The Herbfarm: A tasteful tale in nine acts

Quest for a 4-star experience finds
fabled food in a storybook setting

BY TOM SIETSEMA
P-I FOOD CRITIC

RESTAURANT REVIEW

■ **The Herbfarm.** 32804 Issaquah-
Fall City Road, Fall City. (206) 784-
2222.

Rating: ★ ★ ★ ★

The Herbfarm's executive chef, Jerry Traunfeld, says, "Planning a menu
for 32 that everyone will enjoy is a big challenge."

This is food that impresses more with its clean,
clear and true flavors and intriguing pairings
than with visual flights of fancy, though the
cooking is always attractively presented.

SEATTL
METROPOLIT
95
NEIGHBORHOO
PROFILES

REAL ESTATE 2008 | GREAT OUTDOOR RES

USA
TODAY

...and get back to those roots

The Seattle Times
WASHINGTON'S LARGEST NEWSPAPER

Grammys
Nominations in 3 recording artist
Kenneth 'Babyface' Edmonds gets 12,
Celine Dion receives four
SCENE, D 1

species
mans
t?
A 6

e destroys The Herbfarm,
ted area gourmet restaurant

THE NEW YORK TIMES THE LIVING ARTS WEDNESDAY, JULY 5, 1989

At the Herbfarm, a Sweet Smell of Success

By MARIAN BURROS

FALL CITY, Wash. — What started
with 300 herb plants as a hobby for
Lola Zimmerman in 1974 had already
outgrown the definition by the time
her son Ron and his wife, Carrie Van
Dyck, joined the Herbfarm in 1985.

Ron Zimmerman, left, and Carrie Van Dyck is one of the
greenhouses with Bob Lilly, their nursery manager.

FOOD ART
AT THE R...

FRESH I
EUR
EVERGRE

Familiar Dishes, Seasoned With the Unfamiliar

Salmon With Lemon Verbena
and Nasturtiums

Preparation time:
25 minutes
Cooking time:
15 minutes

Herbfarm Meadow's Edge
Salad Dressing

Preparation time:
10 minutes

Spring or Summer Salad
Of Herbs, Flowers

Television food guru Rachael Ray ruled that no recipe could have more than eight ingredients. I had to argue with one of Rachael's magazine editors before she granted me a special dispensation to include the forbidden ninth ingredient to a potato recipe: a pinch of cayenne pepper.

With six-month lead times, New York–based writers and art directors often called up in February, wanting to send a photographer right away to shoot our gardens for an article on their schedule for July. Of course, there was little in our gardens in February save cabbages, kale, and winter-sweetened root vegetables, much less the bursting abundance of crops and color that summer brings. Despite these misunderstandings, The Herbfarm got splendid multipage coverage from *Gourmet, Bon Appétit, Food & Wine, Travel+Leisure, Country Living, Sunset, Condé Nast Traveler, Food Arts, Every Day with Rachael Ray, Country Living*, and *Martha Stewart Living*.

For each menu theme, I created artwork for the souvenir menus and the theme's posters. Also, to help celebrate each guest, I created a small silver sign commemorating the occasion of their visit. We wanted diners to take them home and put them in a prominent place so they would remember to come back again.

Repeat guests would require more and more creativity as repeating artwork or poems was not "permitted" by my standards. One of our frequent diners and long-time supporters had collected so many of our silver frames, they used them to decorate their Christmas tree!

My own test of excellence was to imagine that I'd dined that day at the restaurant. As I stepped out the restaurant door, I'd think to myself, "Is there anywhere in the world where someone had a better experience today?" I hoped that our guests would think not when asking themselves the same question. I told myself and the staff our goal for our guests was "for a few short hours to make life as perfect as you had always hoped it would be."

That was the unwritten motto for all the years I tended to The Herbfarm.

Of course, there are detours even on the Road to Perfection. On a sunny day in our second season, the main course that day was "sablefish," now usually called black cod. I had tested a particular poaching method that seemed to ensure perfectly cooked pieces of that buttery fish. The test involved placing a portion in a hotel pan, then gently pouring in a boiling herb-infused fish stock. The trial was a great success.

When it came time to serve the black cod to a full house, Bill and I dutifully ladled in the boiling stock over the twenty-four perfectly trimmed pieces of fish. We covered the hotel pan with a cookie sheet to help hold the heat. As this sort of cooking would take a bit longer than normal, Bill set about answering questions from our guests and regaling them with herbal lore. I peeked under the sheet pan and poked a piece. It still needed time. I told Bill and took over the banter and "instruction," something we had to do in order to comply with our new zoning. When I looked back at the stove, I saw blue gas flames blazing below the hotel pan.

When I removed the sheet pan lid, there was no fish.

The hard-boiling stock had reduced every bite of our main course to gray liquid. It was an appalling sight. In our tiny restaurant, there was nothing else we could cook. I was beside myself. But I did my best to present a calm front. What should I say? What *could* I say? Our trusting guests gazed at us in smiling anticipation. Finally, after some hesitation, I realized I had no choice.

"I'm so, so sorry. We won't be able to serve you the black cod today," I told the group with a tremor in my voice. "There's been an accident. We'll finish your luncheon with the salad and dessert. The Herbfarm will refund all your money."

Our guests met my announcement with silence. Everyone was polite. But to the best of my knowledge, not one of them ever returned.

In 1988, we expanded The Herbfarm grounds. Between 80,000 and 100,000 people now visited us each year. Our initial five acres were stuffed with gardens, nursery plants, animal pastures, and space for events. Fred Koba was still farming strawberries across the road, but he was tired of growing corn on the twenty-acre parcel kitty-corner from us. The owner agreed to lease it to us for overflow parking. Right next door to The Herbfarm, Marie Nichols lived in the original white Victorian on what was once a portion of her family's dairy farm. Though Marie was only seventy-five at the time, she wanted to simplify her life by moving to a retirement center in North Bend. One day she dropped in and asked if we might want to buy her house and seven-acre property. "Yes, of course," my father said. We paid for the property in installments.

Marie lived to be 101 years old.

The Herbfarm grew.

Bernie Bevis helped Dad remodel my folks' new-to-them home. When he redid the kitchen, he discovered that the place had been insulated with old newspapers—dating from 1907. He added a big sunny deck. After my folks moved in, Bernie turned his attention to converting my parents' old house into a set of spacious on-farm offices.

Rustic though it was, the farm had to live up to what I believed were our visitors' expectations. "Every morning, the grounds crew would 'do the groom,'" office manager Cindy Sattler remembers. "First, they'd blow the leaves that had fallen across the driveway and parking area. Then they raked the gravel driveway, back and forth, in a way that reminded me of how my mom raked her shag carpet in the 1970s. The driveway was flawless each morning. If there was a day when the grounds crew was short-staffed, Ron would do the groom. To this day, I love blowing leaves, then raking the ground smooth. Ron would turn the blower into the trees to get the loose leaves to fall, too. I've also adopted this practice."

"I remember being on the porch one day while Ron walked back to his office across the driveway. He stopped midway, picked up a cigarette butt, and walked over to the trash can to throw it away. It was an example I never forgot."

■

In addition to the restaurant as the charming come-hither to our farm, we added elaborate weekend mini-festivals. Carrie oversaw these. One weekend would celebrate lavender while others showcased rosemary, thyme, and basil. The staff rigged beautiful handprinted banners across the drive announcing each theme. Mom and Dad set up large plant displays and encouraged everyone to sniff and taste. Chef Bill crafted a lemonade with the current herbal star as the flavoring. From a canvas-covered booth, "Small Bites," we did a brisk business with walk-around snacks and refreshing beverages.

For the 4th of July weekend, we put our two llamas, Paco and Poncho, to work, for a Llama Fest. Once a year when we worked at Early Winters, we'd offered an extravagant, one-of-a-kind holiday gift. These included the world's fastest human-powered vehicle, a one-person hot-air balloon I flew

for the catalog shot near Mount Shasta (thereby officially earning my aviator's solo wings), and the world's rarest Swiss Army Knife. Paco and Poncho were the ultimate-gift stars one year, and Carrie had become their skillful llama trainer. Since that holiday gift package didn't sell, the llamas moved to our farm.

Joining Paco and Poncho at Llama Fest was a troop of other Andean camelids provided by Rory Russell, outdoorsman and guide who led backcountry trips, where his llamas toted the bulk of the gear. Our Llama Fest featured llama rides for kids, llama wool weaving and spinning, llama care by a vet, and llama training and packing demonstrations.

For "Scarborough Faire," we closed the restaurant to regular service and created pseudo-medieval dishes for sit-down dinners both in the backyard and in the main dining room. We stationed costumed actors throughout our display gardens. Each had a persona such as "Sir Basil," a dignified gentleman with a neatly trimmed gray mustache, or "Miss Thyme," a sprightly, puckish young woman perched in a tree. These living herbs would tell stories and answer questions about their namesake plant.

A Harvest Pole—hung with ribbons—awaited the dancers. Musicians, minstrels, and mummers joined the puppeteers, jugglers, and actors for our two-day Medieval Faire.

During festivals, while Mom worked the nursery tables, Dad was typically in front of the restaurant with some sort of bird. His most-friendly chicken, Henny Penny, rode around on his left shoulder. To entertain kids, he'd say, "I'm going to show you how to hypnotize a chicken." He'd calm a bird with a few pets, before stretching it out on its belly on the ground. He'd move his finger back and forth above the chicken's eyes without touching the bird. When Dad removed his hand, the chicken lay still and silent until he'd gently nudge it, at which point it would arise and walk away.

Our weekend events grew even more elaborate, made possible by Carrie's organizational skills. The Labor Day "Harvest Festival" in 1989 was rife with activities. For $1, you could take a mile-long horse-drawn hay wagon ride. A blacksmith worked his forge. Jugglers and jesters made the rounds. Want to make your own cider? Step right up and feed some fresh apples to the press. Six different musical groups played. Of course, there was a face-painting clown who'd do up your kids at fifty cents per. Taste foods and wines?

Four booths. Hungry? Stop by Harvest Bites for sausages and other snacks. Or enjoy some of Chef Kraut's fare in the big sit-down dining tent. Twelve booths demonstrated everything from making corn husk dolls to spinning Angora rabbit fur. At the piggery, you could watch sheepshearing at 1 p.m and 4 p.m. The 4-H Club milked a cow several times a day. And of course, there were hosted tours of The Herbfarm grounds, gardens, and nursery every hour on the hour.

The deep crack-a-boom of muzzleloaders periodically punctuated Harvest Festival days from the Mountain Man Encampment next to our back woods. These reenactors' shelters, tools, and hand-stitched clothing were impressively authentic. Here you could watch flint on steel spark a fire, taste venison stew from an iron cauldron over the smoke-wisped wood fire, hear tall tales, and watch as men poured a measure of powder down the barrel of their long rifles and shot at targets for prizes. I still regret contributing my bearskin blanket as a grand prize.

For the unforgettable "Slug Fest," we paid local kids to round up resident gastropods. For the slug races, participants chose their slug and placed it in the bull's-eye of a target. The first slug to reach the outermost ring won. Another competition was Slug in a Bottle, where each contestant used a soda straw in their mouth to pick up as many slugs as possible and drop them into a jar before the clock ran out. This test of skill and bravado was entertaining enough that it won a spot on the TV news.

In our kitchen, just for fun, I'd purged and prepared slugs in the French escargot fashion. I filled each indentation of a snail plate with a cooked slug slathered in butter, garlic, and parsley. I placed this as a display piece, a tongue-in-cheek *pièce de montage*, in one of our festival booths. Accented with a colorful Provençal napkin, silverware, vase of flowers, and glass of wine, it made the maligned critters look *très beaux*.

As I walked by the booth that afternoon, I noted the "escargots" had vanished. "People keep eating them!" the attendant told me. "I couldn't stop them. They say they're delicious."

This episode became a minor legend in the local food community. From time to time, a brave (or attention-hungry) soul would ask that we prepare slugs as a supplemental Herbfarm course. I usually declined, but did create a slug special for Jon Rowley: beer-battered slugs with french fries and dipping sauces of carrot-tarragon and basil aioli, served in a paper-lined fish and chips basket. Jon eagerly shared the gustatorial rarities with his table. Though initially hesitant, everyone seemed game, enjoyed their bite, and survived to tell the tale.

My first college roommate was Frank Richard Aloysius Jude Maloney. We met at the University of Washington. Maloney was studying for his master's in poetry with the revered poet and professor Nelson Bentley. I'd sit in at Bentley's evening workshops, where Frank was a regular. Frank taught me a lot about dining and wining, including foisting on me his favored stinger cocktail, a drink I now righteously condemn. Good Cognac should *not* be mixed with crème de menthe.

We often joked about the culinary possibilities of slugs. Frank wrote a slug-in-cheek poem. Since he also introduced me to a civilized sipper, Pouilly-Fuissé, I recommend that charming white Burgundy as the wine pairing for "Slug Escargots."

HOW TO EAT A SLUG
by Frank Maloney

The hardest part is holding it.
A joy to drop,
The curl into steam.
Parboil it quickly, vengefully,
Drain away the melted snot,
Far from creek or brake.
You run your knife along its belly,
Peel off the jaundice, the liver,
Spots, the curving leprosy.
Shut your eye and thrust,
A thumb into the half-congealed guts.
What's left is firm,
White & altogether
Mild. Garlic, butter,
And you've escargot.
You've earned your appetite.

Slugs Escargots recipe on the following page.

Slugs Escargots

Serves 4–6

24 to 32 live slugs, ideally fed on lettuce or apples or bran for several days to purge (Note: Don't use yellowish banana slugs. This Pacific Northwest native gastropod is endangered.)

½ cup	Water
½ cup	Vinegar
1	Clove garlic
⅜ tsp	Salt
1	Stick (½ cup) butter, unsalted, softened
1½ tsp	Minced shallot
2 Tbsp	Chopped parsley
	Black pepper
1 Tbsp	Dry white wine
24–32	Escargot shells to stuff with slugs or cook slugs in small ramekins

Mix vinegar and water. Add slugs to their "vinegar spa." Let sit 10 minutes. The slugs will release almost all of their slime and any residual waste. Remove and rinse the deceased slugs in two or three clean water changes. Using a sharp knife or X-Acto, slit slugs on their ventral side and remove the gut. Turn slugs over and make a small slit on top. Remove the slug's vestigial shell, which is about the size of a contact lens. This may not be necessary, but I do it anyway.

Preheat oven to 450°F.

Mince garlic and mash on a cutting board with ⅛ teaspoon salt using the flat side of a knife. With a hand mixer, blend this salted garlic paste with the butter, shallot, garlic, and parsley and the remaining salt and pepper. Whip in the white wine. If using empty snail shells (available online), put half with the seasoned butter in each shell. Stuff in a slug and top with the remaining butter. Set shells upright with the opening at the top so that the butter doesn't run out. You can nest the shells in coarse salt to hold them upright in the oven and for serving. Bake in the preheated oven until the butter sizzles, 6 to 12 minutes. Serve hot. Use tongs if picking up. Eat with cocktail forks or skewers. Serve with a sliced toasted baguette brushed with melted butter to sop up all the goodness.

■

In 1988, after the success of the Harvest Fest, we dabbled with Halloween. The first year we called the event "The Great Pumpkin Celebration." Beside the requisite pumpkin patch, where you'd meet the Great Pumpkin (costume by Carrie), choose your own pumpkin, and then work on pumpkin carving, Bernie built sturdy wood bleachers in the Old Grey Barn. You entered the half-darkness of this weathered edifice through creaking doors to listen to scary stories.

Tuesdays and Wednesdays were days when buses brought low-income kids from schools with limited finances to The Herbfarm. They'd spend a half-day with us. Many of these kids had never been out of Seattle nor had they seen a live chicken. My dad delighted them by walking around with Gertie the Goose in his arms, letting the kids pet her. I didn't find out until years later that an anonymous benefactor paid for the buses that brought the kids.

The following year, Halloween morphed into the Halloween Adventure. The scary stories and pumpkin patch entertained weekday school groups. On the weekends, we added a horse-drawn wagon that traveled a one-mile circuit to a secret pumpkin patch. Our apple press stirred from hibernation to make fresh cider to take home. Kids rode ponies or painted Halloween masks. Using straw, 2x2 wood crosses, and burlap for shaping a stuffed head, families created scarecrows dressed in their clothes or ours.

The highlight of Halloween Adventure was the Hay Maze. Semitrucks laden with bales of hay brought the "building blocks" for the maze. This outdoor puzzler was built from three and four bales stacked high, lorded over by tall, darkling evergreens. Even grownups couldn't see out. Over the entrance to the vast maze, we hung a painted sign: "Abandon Hope All Ye Who Enter Here"—the same warning posted at the entrance to hell in Dante's *Divine Comedy*.

Strangely, children could run through the maze—despite the many dead ends and confusing turns. Grown-ups often became lost. More than once, cries summoned us to rescue an adult who had abandoned all hope.

I loved it.

Ninety-Nine Bottles of Beer

The granddaddy of all of our festivals started as a fluke. We announced a Strawberry Festival on Father's Day during our second summer at the farm. Though it was already the third week of June, few local berries were ripe. We somehow managed to bake some strawberry shortcakes. As festivals went, this was not a winner. Strawberries weren't high on most dads' life lists. Crafting Hacky Sacks with goat scrotums probably would have had more appeal.

But there was a new trend emerging.

Beer. But not just any beer. Craft beer.

A century of local breweries being gobbled up by big nationals (here's looking at you, Anheuser-Busch) left most Americans believing that only low-hopped, low-flavored pilsners were beer. Easy to drink, they offended no one. But other beer styles, honed by centuries of brewing, were headed for extinction. Only the most dedicated ale enthusiasts knew of smoked beers, wheat beers, pale ales, bitters, dunkels, bocks, porters, oatmeal stouts, and fruit-flavored brews—let alone outlier ales flavored with the likes of heather, aged with bacteria in wooden casks, or mashed with red-hot stones. Most all of these were brewed in Europe.

The year after the Strawberry Fest Disaster, Carrie and I invited five microbreweries to showcase their brews on Father's Day. These five brewers represented almost all of what was happening at the time in the Pacific Northwest. Even so, we were able to write with truth, "In all the world, only Belgium and England offer a wider variety of local beers than are brewed here."

The Liquor Board required that we secure a designated area for alcohol service. We chose the grassy backyard behind the restaurant. It seemed big enough, and the old wisteria arbors lent it charm. We put up extra fencing and the requisite signs.

Festival admittance was $4.50. That bought you a souvenir engraved 5-ounce tasting glass, a tasting fact sheet, and scrip good for six glasses of beer of your choosing. On his accordion, winemaker Lou Facelli kicked up the festivities with polkas and oompah-pah music. Bill Kraut was in charge of the pretzels and bratwurst.

Those first five festival breweries were Hale's Ales, Hart Brewing, Kemper Brewing, Widmer Brewing, and Yakima Brewing & Malting Company. Between them, they served twenty different beers on tap.

Yakima Brewing & Malting was better known as "Grant's." Before founding his brewery, Bert Grant had already had a notable career in mainstream brewing. His influence on the craft beer scene can't be overestimated. Though ther're everywhere now, Grant's opened the first brewpub in America since Prohibition. Bert controlled every aspect of brewing, from malting and roasting the raw grains to final bottling. He brewed America's first true IPA and the first high-octane Russian Imperial Stout. A bigger-than-life

personality, he appeared at our festival fitted out in his trademark tartan tam-o'-shanter atop his thinning crown. He sported Scottish Highland stockings, bare knees, and a full-on belted kilt in the Grant tartan of striking scarlet, forest green, and navy blue accent lines. His spouse and partner, Sherry, wore the same outfit. On Father's Day, I was out early under clear skies, setting orange traffic cones along the road with the hope of keeping cars from parking on the shoulders. We'd learned that a single errant parked car announced that parking was okay. Or that at least you could get away with it. A rent-a-cop was supposed to keep the streets clear. Fred Koba's old cornfield became our festival parking lot, with plenty of paid volunteers to admit and guide the vehicles.

The first festgoers arrived before the official gate time of high noon. They milled about. As the crowd swelled, Carrie sensed potential chaos. She grabbed a stick, got everyone's attention, and started walking, using the branch to scratch a serpentine line in our gravel driveway. "Follow me—line up. And stay in line!" she commanded with authority. For the next five hours all arriving festivalgoers stayed on that gravel serpentine line.

What happened after that is a blur. Over 500 people arrived thirsty for beer—we had expected 150! Our backyard venue was stretched to its limits. I could hear Lou Facelli playing his music, but couldn't see him. It was so crowded that at one point, I couldn't raise my arms to take a picture. Even if I had, the shot would have only shown the backs of people's heads. We had to close the entrance gate. New festivalgoers were allowed entrance only when someone else left still standing in that gravel marked line.

At day's end, the backyard lawn—green and lush in the morning—was reduced to an unrecognizable black smear. Our pioneering brewers, tired as they were, hailed the event as a success. They sampled each other's products from what stocks remained. All of them would come back the following summer.

For the Second Annual Microbrewery Festival, we opened up our whole five-acre farm. Each brewer had a

wood-framed shelter with a white canvas roof and a sturdy green and white placard engraved with their name. The larger space made for a less frenetic experience for our two thousand guests. Charles Finkel, who had recently opened his Pike Place Brewery, was the festival host. Ten breweries took part. There were educational talks given throughout the day on styles of beer, beer making technique, hops. One of the hallmarks of our Brewery Festival and subsequent Wine Festival was that we only invited companies whose brewer or owner would attend to personally represent the brand. This meant that the festivalgoers really did get to meet the brewmasters. And so did I.

More importantly, it forged camaraderie among brewing and winemaking professionals. They came to look forward to the events as sorts of "mini conventions," the one time during the year when they were all in the same place at the same time.

The brewers, as Carrie and the staff came to learn, were cats that needed constant herding. The winemakers, once the Northwest Wine Festival started up, seemed more cerebral. A few rare brewers, however, were true students of their craft. Charles Finkel, who'd been VP of marketing at Chateau Ste. Michelle in Washington, was the first to introduce Belgian beers to the American market. Charles also convinced Samuel Smith to bring back Oatmeal Stout, which he imported along with esteemable European beers before opening his Pike Place Brewing Company in 1989.

Some of the brewers had big thirsts and lax habits. The Liquor Board required us to pay in advance for the kegs of beer, but the brewers, who were charged with collecting guest drink tickets, always fell short on the number of tickets they collected to verify their pours. Despite our cajoling, pretty girls and brewers' buddies drank liberally on our dime.

Cindy Sattler, our office manager at the time, had her own take on the subject. "Before working at The Herbfarm," she said, "I would have guessed that brewers were down-to-earth regular folk, and winemakers were snobby, uppity people. What I found was that brewers were bullies and frat boys who never grew up. Winemakers attending the Winefest were farmers at heart and down-to-earth, kind-hearted, hardworking people. To this day," she went on, "I'm particular as to what microbrews I'll drink based on their staff's behavior. I learned to love wine and the winemaking industry due to the winemakers' kindness and generosity in sharing their knowledge."

■

By 1994, the seventh Microbrewery Festival spread over all thirteen acres and we hosted thirty-three participants, plus vendors of homebrewing gear and expanded food offerings from The Herbfarm's kitchen. Ten thousand people now converged for the two-day Father's Day affair. Carrie was in charge of procuring original art for posters and T-shirt uniforms, ordering T-shirts, preparing signage, printing name tags, organizing the educational talks throughout the festival, and signing up hundreds of volunteers. She ran a crew of 250 to handle every detail, from bringing fresh beer kegs from the refrigerated semitrucks to accounting for redeemed scrip to picking up garbage at precise intervals. The parking lot now had a twenty-foot-tall steel-scaffolded tower that spotters would use to find open parking spaces. They reported these to the crew of twenty on the ground via walkie-talkies. We hired a professional dog sitter to watch over attendees' pets that weren't allowed on the festival grounds. Top guns in the American craft brewing scene—many now legends—gave informative talks throughout the day. Kids were welcome. We provided safe places to play, craft-brewed root beer to drink, and farm animals to pet.

The twelfth annual festival in 1999 brought fifty craft brewers and 145 different beers to the Farm. A new "Brew Debut Competition" invited home brewers to have their creations judged. The winner's beer recipe was to be brewed and served at the following year's festival. This was the last Microbrewery Festival that we'd host. The Washington Beer Commission picked up the event, renaming it the Washington Brewers' Festival. Large regional parks became the new venues, and the festival continues to draw thousands each Father's Day weekend.

■

On a trip down the Oregon coast in 2019, Carrie and I stopped at Rogue Brewing on the harbor in Newport. Gulls whirled and screeched behind cruising trawlers returning from the sea. After lunch in the Rogue brewpub, brewmaster John Maier gave us a tour of his beer-making premises. John had been one of the original guests at our Microbrewery Festival. Now he was about to retire from Rogue after thirty years and 22,582 batches of beer.

His dark brown beard had gone gray. Always on the lookout for something different, John had once plucked nine hairs from that beard. From the yeast on those hairs, he brewed "Beard Beer," a controversial wild-yeasted brew that some people dismissed as an April Fools joke. The beer got national PR.

As we walked through the brewery, John pointed out the mash tuns, boiling kettles, and fermenters while sharing facts and stories about Rogue and his time as a brewer.

"You know," John said, "we 'old-timers' still reminisce about your beer festivals. It was an era of goodwill and learning. Thank you for a special event in a beautiful place at a special time."

Microbreweries are called "craft" or "artisanal" breweries now. As I write this, Oregon has over 250 and Washington nearly 400. I'm so pleased we were there to usher in the beginning.

The Northwest Wine Festival

After the success of the beer fest, we founded the Northwest Wine Festival.

Both festivals had "Northwest" in their names and in their genes. This is the region we inhabit and celebrate at The Herbfarm. No political boundaries divide the plants, animals, and climate of a region. Oregon and Washington were both known as the Oregon Territories until 1859, the Northwest thereafter. Every brewer or vintner from the "original Oregon" was welcome at our festivals.

During the years the wine festival ran, I was privileged to meet Washington and Oregon's wine pioneers. This list is now an estimable Who's Who: the Adelsheim brothers, Brian Carter (Apex and Brian Carter Cellars), Rollin Soles (Argyle and later ROCO), the iconoclastic Gerard Bentryn of Bainbridge Island Winery (years ahead in his fight for the *recognition terroir* of cool-climate grapes), David Lett of the Eyrie Vineyards, Ken Wright (Panther Creek and Ken Wright Cellars), Veronique Drouhin and Bill Hatcher (Domaine Drouhin), Rick Small (Woodward Canyon), Alex Golitzin (Quilceda Creek), Greg Lill and Chris Upchurch (DeLille Cellars), Kay Simon (Chinook), Rob Griffin (Barnard Griffin), Dick Erath (Erath), Steve Doener (Cristom), Patty Green

and Jim Anderson (then of Torii Mor before founding Patricia Green Cellars)—and so many others. Many of these friendships have lasted over thirty years.

In 1987, with our initial problems with permits and zoning cleared up, the Washington State Liquor Control Board granted The Herbfarm a beer and wine license. To my mind, that made us a full-fledged restaurant. I began building The Herbfarm's cellar, donating much of my private collection to kick-start the restaurant's stores. Our focus was on Oregon and Washington wines, a then-nascent, fast-growing category measurable in both winery openings and product quality. I also started investing in world wine classics.

Our six-course luncheon now included in the price a pair of wines with the meal for those who wished. The nine-course dinners included five wines in the bundled price, plus a venerable Madeira to cap off the evening. Because fortified wines were vastly underappreciated, I was able to find and buy Madeiras from the eighteenth, nineteenth, and early twentieth centuries. It didn't take long before we had compiled what was perhaps the best Madeira cellar in the country. In time, it became an Herbfarm tradition to serve a bottle of 1863 Malvazia Madeira for Thanksgiving—1863 being the year Lincoln declared Thanksgiving a national holiday. Regrettably, this historic vintage now goes for over $1,000 per bottle, and we lost ours in the fire.

■

During the winter break before our third season at the restaurant, I got a call from a woman in Seattle's well-connected food inner circles.

"Marian Burros is on a book tour for her *20-Minute Menus*. Seattle is one of her stops. And she wants to dine with you," my caller explained. The woman seemed impressed or maybe baffled that a high-powered *New York Times* food columnist might want to dine at our farm.

"I'm flattered," was all I could say at first. "But . . . but, we're closed for three months to give all of us a winter break. We're going to catch up and plan for the coming season. Some of the staff has left town on vacation. The gardens are nearly dormant. Our cupboards are bare."

"Look, this is your big chance. It's the *New York Times*! Do whatever's necessary. Don't blow this opportunity," my foodie friend said.

But I did turn them down.

The mere thought of a winter restart for a one-off dinner exhausted me. I *was* exhausted. During that year, I'd sometimes prepped food until 2 or 3 a.m. Every six months, I wrote, designed and printed activity schedules and Herbfarm product catalogs. Rather than drive the fifty-mile round trip home and back, I often plopped down on the farm office floor to grab a few hours of sleep. I'd grossly underestimated what a taskmistress a restaurant like ours could be. And I'd foolishly committed to twice-a-year versions of the Farm's lengthy activity schedules and the catalogs.

More than once, Carrie canceled dinners for me when printing deadlines loomed. But she got impatient—rightfully so—with this ad hoc "scheduling." So, to give me a bit more breathing space, we convinced Karl Beckley of the Greenlake Grill to become a "Guest Chef" for two weeks. Likewise, Tom Douglas, in between jobs, served a short stint, It was time to raise prices. Bill and my dad had expressed doubts when the luncheons went from $12.50 to $16.50 to $21.50. But fast as the price went up, the tables stayed full. And the restaurant's portion of our farm income—even with me taking no salary—wasn't yet paying its fair share of the bills. We needed more kitchen help, too.

But how?

We soldiered on, striving to improve each day. The little end-of-meal rating sheets were working. We kept refining our food and service. My foraging skills were now at their peak. I knew the best spots to find the wild plants we harvested to use in our meals. I'd spend long days crossing the Cascades to collect the fragrant, ineffable blossoms of blue elder or gather morel mushrooms and "porcini" in the Wenatchee National Forest.

And our work was paying dividends. The Herbfarm received the highest rating, "Extraordinary to Perfection," from the national *Zagat Guide of "America's Top Restaurants."*

Listen to the Music

One evening, Carrie and I were dining in Seattle at Serafina, a charming candlelit restaurant on Lake Union. A young man with dark hair and chiseled features sat on an elevated platform to one side of the small dining room. He played Spanish guitar. "That's Patricio Contreras," the waiter told us. After dinner, we told him how much we'd enjoyed his music. Patricio was born in Chile. He had already lived, studied, and taught for ten years at the Royal Conservatory of Music in Madrid. I liked him immediately. He handed me his card.

With our 1990 dinner service season, Patricio began years of augmenting The Herbfarm dining experience with romantic live music. He had an uncanny way

of sensing the collective mood of our diners and matching that with his choice of music, its cadence and volume throughout the night. He had an uncanny awareness of everything going on in the restaurant as he performed. Even while he was entertaining the room, he was reading the diners' needs. Without missing a beat, a flick of his gaze would tell us that a patron needed a new napkin or a water top off.

During our spring break one year, Carrie and I caught up with Patricio in Zihuatanejo, Mexico. At a sunny table overlooking the tranquil bay, we savored the first pitcher of margaritas, then ordered another. As sunlight softened into night, Patricio ordered a third. A local rabbit kept us company under our table. Was there ever a sunset so pink? From time to time, still, we remind ourselves about that "day of the margaritas."

Patricio became a staple of the dining experience at The Herbfarm, playing for over six thousand Herbfarm dinner services, with only a few nights off. Since he eats the menu's main course on his break, I reckon he holds the world record for dining here.

■

After Bernie remodeled my parents' original home into a new office suite, Carrie and I finally had our own offices. It was a relief to have operations all in one place. Not only could the farm office greet and work with guests in person, I was now able to engage some on-site help in copywriting and editing our constant stream of catalogs, newsletters, and class schedules.

With only nascent email and crude internet, paper still ruled the word. Even the arrival of Prodigy, CompuServe, and AOL ("You've got mail!") didn't initiate e-commerce. Still, the innovations were exciting. Chicago's Craig Goldwyn, now famous in barbeque circles as "Meathead," joined me as cohost in the Wine & Dine chat room on America Online. Since Goldwyn was the publisher of the *International Wine Review*, I let him carry most of the vinous weight. After a long stretch of being sight-unseen colleagues, we finally met up in Chicago where we dined with our spouses at the chef's table in the kitchen at Charlie Trotter's. My old friend Larry Stone graduated from a doctoral candidate working at Pete's Red Cabbage on the Seattle waterfront to master sommelier, heading up the wine side of Trotter's restaurant.

On business trips to Chicago, I'd sometimes dine alone at Trotter's. Twice, Charlie picked up the tab. The first time, confused, I asked the waitperson when my bill failed to appear. "Oh, yes, she responded, "it's Charlie's thing. He almost always comps one dining party every night."

Laura Flaherty, my chief copywriter at Early Winters, worked with me on a catch-as-catch-can copy basis. When she moved permanently to Chicago to be closer to her mother, Laura recommended her friend, Karin Snelson, for writing and editing. Karin's fast wit—honed by her four years of copywriting for Seattle's goofy Archie McPhee catalog of things no one needed—was refreshing. She became the best editor I ever worked with.

"Ron," she asked one day in my new farm office. "I've been offered a position at a company called Amazon. What do you know about them?"

"Well, I've bought some books. 'Earth's Biggest Bookstore' is their motto. Their selection is vast," I said. "Though they've yet to make a nickel, I think you should consider this opportunity."

So she did. Then she invited me to come and visit Amazon. The company occupied a couple of floors in a nondescript four-story brick building two blocks from Seattle's Pike Place Market. The carpets were stained. Everyone, including Karin, had desks fashioned from hollow-core doors. The floor of Karen's small office was piled high with books. I heard a distinctive laugh around the corner down the hall. Jeff Bezos? Was the name pronounced as "bees-zohs" or "bay-zos"? Hardly anyone knew back then.

His little dog dozed in the hallway outside Mr. Bay-Zos's office.

Visitors

Early in the summer of our third season, I had noticed a reservation for a "Waters" party of four. I'm usually only not overly impressed when celebrities dine with us. But these weren't television food entertainers—those would swarm the airwaves later. No, coming to lunch were Alice Waters, Paul Bertolli, Angelo Pellegrini, and Angelo's wife, Virginia. These four were the foundation of the Cook Local, Support Local trend that would eventually inspire half the restaurants in America to claim to be "farm to table." They would become icons for the American Slow Food movement.

Keep in mind that the term "farm to table" wasn't invented yet. But Alice lived the talk and walked the walk. With her frequent trips to France, she'd become friends with a host of French gastronomes, including the brilliant eater, author, and serious wine-imbiber Richard Olney. Olney's hand-built hillside stone house and casual lifestyle in Provence were an inspiration, as was his uncommon ease in creating French classics over glowing coals with little fuss. Alice brought these skills and sensibilities to her restaurant. Paul Bertolli, traveling with her, would spend ten years in Berkeley as executive chef at Chez Panisse. Later, Bertolli became the father of American "Cal-Italian" cooking at Oliveto, which many considered the best Italian restaurant in America.

Angelo Pellegrini, eighty-nine when he joined Alice and Paul for lunch that day, had lived his life growing his food and making his wine. A cherished English teacher at the University of Washington, Pellegrini had written ten books on the good-food life and how to live it. Years later, his son, Brent, bequeathed us a dozen "Little Nuns"—the Monachine, a family heirloom bean that the California vintner Robert Mondavi had given Pelligrini in the early 1950s. Grown at Pellegrini's Seattle home for over forty years, the bean had adapted to the Northwest climate and was now a modified offshoot, or "landrace." We planted the precious beans. After several "growing out" seasons, we had sufficient harvests to start serving the "Pellegrini Bean." The Pellegrini is a superior bean during any stage of its life cycle. But it was the mature and dried autumn seed that packed the legendary flavor and texture. Angelo so loved his bean that he'd eat them with only a thin blessing of olive oil and savor just one bean at a time.

As Alice and her party embarked from their car, a gaggle of chattering guinea hens sped single-file across the drive. Gertie, my dad's favorite goose, honked a welcome, and our llamas, Paco and Poncho, came to the fence to check them out. After Carrie's garden tour in glorious sunshine, the foursome dined on our six-course afternoon meal.

I was understandably nervous about hosting these legends. Everyone was genial, though Angelo seemed gently gruff. I do remember that it was an excellent progression of dishes. We prepared Copper River sockeye salmon, probably with a sauce flavored with the aromatic leaves of Mom's pet lemon verbena bush.

At a break toward the end of the meal, Paul Bertolli asked how we had prepared the salmon. I explained that Bill and I had wound and packed slices of the sockeye inside inch-deep steel rings as an experiment. This technique allowed the fish to cook evenly.

When the luncheon was over, I mustered my courage and asked Pellegrini how he liked it.

"It was pretty good. Pretty good," he said. I took it for a compliment.

Years later, I asked Alice what she remembered of that day.

"I remember it as a perfect day," she said. "There was nothing else like it at the time. And maybe there still isn't."

■

In 1990, Jon Rowley called.

"I have a friend coming in from New York. He's heard about your place. Can you find us a table for two?" he asked in his thoughtful and laconic way.

"I'll do my best, Jon," I said, wondering who the guest might be.

Back then, our nine-course, six-wine dinners started at 8 p.m. We started late because—well—it seemed sophisticated. But it was also necessary when the western sun beat down on the dining room. With no air-conditioning yet on site, we'd open all the doors to try to blow out the hot air. So 8 p.m. it was, even though the dinner would last nearly four hours, leaving guests to drive home after midnight. Once we installed air-conditioning, dinner started at 7:00.

An eight o'clock start in late October meant that Jon and his guest would arrive at the farm in deep darkness. Only soft pooled lights marked the way between the parking lot and the restaurant.

It was almost Halloween. A modest wind scratched and rustled about in the needles and branches of the cedars outside. Hens roosted deep in the branches clucked and squawked in the darkness. Inside, Jon and his guest handed over their jackets, which Jodell Campbell, our dining room manager, tucked away. Before they could be seated, Jon said, "Ron, let me introduce Bryan Miller, the restaurant critic for the *New York Times.* Bryan's a longtime friend."

Jon was always full of surprises.

As it was late October our massive hay maze slumbered in the depths of rural darkness. It had become the custom near Halloween to spice up dinner with a trip to the hay maze. Carrie would gather small groups of four to six in between courses and lead them to the labyrinth. With a dim flashlight, she'd fan her light across the entrance sign: "Abandon Hope All Ye Who Enter." Then some of the guests were handed candles; some got flashlights. In they went two by two. The thick hay bales muffled the good-natured barks and shrieks. Guests returned invigorated by the autumn air, ready to tell their tales and refreshed for the next course.

Whether by chance or plan, the last to go mazing that night were Jon and Bryan. Carrie escorted them to the mountain of hay and handed them two lit candles. It was the buddy system. If one candle went out, the other could relight it.

Back in the dining room, we were serving the main course. I noticed that Bryan and Jon were taking longer than expected to return. Then Jon walked in.

"Where's Bryan?" he whispered to me. "I thought he'd beaten me back here."

We checked the restroom. Not there. Carrie went for the maze and called out. A faint unsteady voice returned, "I can't find my way out. I'm lost in the dark," came Bryan's muted plea.

Carrie found Bryan fairly shaken and walked with him back to the restaurant. "My candle blew out," he told Jon. He'd tried to find his way back but became muddled and confused. They both had a good laugh as they tucked into their food.

Jon called the next day.

"Did the hay maze ruin the dinner for Bryan?" I blurted out.

"Not at all. He had a great time," Jon said. "By the way, I asked him what he thought of The Herbfarm as we drove home. He just said, "Four Stars.""

■

Over the years, many people have asked me if Julia Child ever dined at The Herbfarm. Child's masterpiece, of course, was her massive cookbook, *Mastering the Art of French Cooking*. Its 1961 publication coincided with the Kennedy Camelot years, when French-trained chef René Verdon was chosen to man the stoves at the White House. Americans with culinary aspirations and/or adventurous appetites began to look to France for its newly visible refined cuisine.

But it was Child's *The French Chef* series on PBS—recorded live and full of engaging goofs and mishaps—that solidified her legacy as the *mère* of French fare in American homes and restaurants. People loved this ever-enthusiastic six-foot-two-inch woman whose high-pitched voice, seasoned with smatterings of French, both instructed and entertained. Child wasn't a one-trick pony. She and her colleague Simone Beck (too little praised) wrote and published a second volume. Over the next forty years. Julia invented and inhabited the job of TV chef.

Child had planned to dine at The Herbfarm, but her Seattle handler made the last-minute decision to keep all her dining in the city. Through a comedy of errors and because we were with Sinclair Philip, Carrie and I found ourselves in the Public Market at François Kissel's restaurant, Maximilien, which had opened specially for Julia Child and entourage, where we were welcomed.

We said "bon soir" and joined the table camaraderie. Child had no tolerance for fad diets or abstemious eaters.

"When her husband died, I sent Mrs. Pritikin a note of condolence," we heard her say. "had your husband had a decent meal now and again, perhaps he would be alive today to read this letter."

Julia went on to predict, correctly, that a "fear of food" would impact the country's eating habits.

She was right. When we first opened our restaurant, few guests made special dietary requests. Over time, though, food bugaboos whittled away at dining pleasure.

■

Entering my fifth year in The Herbfarm kitchen, I knew I couldn't keep carrying the workload that launched the restaurant. Long hours cooking in the kitchen, long hours commuting from Seattle, long hours spent creating advertising and PR materials and activity schedules added up to many more hats than I had heads. I was worn out.

Then a miracle walked through the door. It came in the form of a man with a neatly trimmed mustache and spine-straight posture. If you put him in a long horseman's duster with a Clint Eastwood cowboy hat, you could plausibly cast him as the nineteenth-century sheriff whose fast draw never lost a gunfight.

This unexpected visitor was David Kellaway. He hailed from a Texas family of overachievers. While his siblings became heart surgeons and the like, Kellaway took on the culinary world. Much later, he confided that he needed to prove to his family that he was among the elite in *his* chosen field.

As David gradually shared his story, I learned he was one of only sixty-seven Certified Master Chefs in the world. Kellaway had won three gold medals and the World Champion title at the International Culinary Olympics in Frankfurt, Germany. He held the Medal of the French Government. He'd been the youngest executive sous-chef at the Plaza Hotel in New York as well as the department chair at the Culinary Institute of America.

"My God," I thought. "I must be dreaming."

David said he was searching for a break, for permission to experiment. At a place like The Herbfarm, he could return to cooking for guests, not judges or hotel conventioneers.

We offered him the position of chef. He accepted.

Word immediately got around that he'd be joining The Herbfarm. Before meeting us, David had previously interviewed with Rob Pounding, his friend from the Culinary Institute of America. Chef Pounding was now in charge of overseeing food service at a trio of upscale Washington lodges: The Salish (right upriver from us), the Salishan on the Oregon coast, and Skamania Lodge overlooking the Columbia River. Pounding offered Kellaway the Salish executive chef position, free menu control, and considerably more than we could pay. David accepted.

"But," David told us, a bit sheepishly, "I'm keeping my word. I'll cook at The Herbfarm through the end of the summer before I start at the Salish."

■

David Kellaway's skills expanded our expertise. He showed Bill and me how to rapidly truss a loin of lamb into an even-cooking work of art. Bill and I made translucent potato crisps and fashioned "hippenmasse" almond leaves using templates we hand cut ourselves. Food-grade PVC pipe became molds for fragrant, quiveringly soft Bavarian desserts.

Precision and perfection were Kellaway's standards. "Okay" wasn't in his vocabulary. As I had always insisted, we had to scrape rack of lamb bones until they shone like ivory. Bill could be satisfied with close-to-perfect, but to David every little detail mattered.

Kellaway's coming was only a reprieve. Soon enough, we'd need another chef to lead the kitchen. The search was on again.

Since Carrie and I still lived in Seattle, we'd dine out on non-service days and got to know many regional chefs. One whose potential attracted our attention was the thirty-one-year-old executive chef of the Alexis Hotel in Seattle, Jerry Traunfeld. As a kid, his favorite TV show had been Julia Child's *The French Chef*. After high school, Traunfeld moved from Maryland to California and took a novice chef position at the red-velvet-draped Ernie's in San Francisco. Bill Edwards and I had dined there and marveled at the basket of puffed-up potatoes, a house specialty. These air-filled spuds, a signature dish at Ernie's, were Traunfeld's domain. Moving to Jeremiah Tower's see-and-be-seen Stars as a pastry chef, he mastered desserts.

Jerry was one of several candidates we interviewed. He did not have Kellaway's quiet intensity. But he was at ease in the kitchen and a good and willing teacher. Mom and Dad loved him. So did Bette Stuart, our local assistant in most cooking classes.

Additionally, it seemed as if Jerry could identify any flower, was interested in working with fresh local foods, and wanted to master more herbs. And what better place to do that than at The Herbfarm? We'd found our next chef.

Schuyler Ingle, then the restaurant critic for the *Seattle Weekly*, had reviewed the Alexis Hotel dining room eighteen months earlier. "I would say I had a pleasant meal at the Alexis," Ingle wrote. "Several days later, I am still thinking about that meal, retasting the sauces, surprised that it is all still with me and facing off into a haze of one more night on the town."

Real estate developers and hotel management know the money is in the rooms. Hotel dining plays the second fiddle to rentals. But on-site dining helps fill the hotel. The restaurant may not be fiscally sound nor even strive for better-than-average American fare. Ingles's meal, though, had begun with rosemary-cured beef.

"The meat alone had authority, a dark, muscle flavor that quickly grew," he wrote. "The cabernet underpinning kept everything floating in air. The sauce acted as a complement to soften it up, giving the potency of the beef a splash of laughter."

As I mulled over our applicants, I assumed that the beef dish in the *Seattle Weekly* review had been Jerry's creation. But Bruce Naftaly had been the Alexis chef the year before Jerry. When I had worked in Naftaly's Le Gourmand kitchen, Bruce was making a similar dish with rosemary and a double-veal reduction stock underpinning a red wine sauce. Who could say? The combo seemed classic. Such preparations require excellent ingredients and a chef's palate that can precisely balance the pieces. And Jerry had done that.

I offered him the position. "I want to take a few weeks off to vacation before starting," Jerry announced. He went to Greece. His first day on the job was July 20, 1990.

Now there were four of us in our little kitchen. We all worked together for the next five weeks before David left for the Salish. David would later become the director of food operations at Mandalay Bay and the Mirage in Las Vegas and the managing director of the Culinary Institute of America in San Antonio.

Jerry's career at The Herbfarm would span the next seventeen years.

After the fire, Jerry had time to write *The Herbfarm Cookbook*. It was an outstanding work that would win a cookbook award from the International Association of Culinary Professionals in 2001. That previous year we had all traveled to New York for the James Beard Foundation awards where Jerry took home the prize for "Best American Chef: Northwest and Hawaii." He had been nominated previously in both 1996 and 1997.

After Jerry came on board, Bill and I continued in the kitchen for a few more years. To his skill and credit, Jerry took our vision of the restaurant to heart. Menus from that era still invoke spectacular meals, menus we'd be proud to serve today. The tuberous nasturtiums gathered from Sinclair Philip at the Sooke Harbour House appear on a "Holly and Ivy" holiday menu with tiny Olympia oysters. We did sea urchin soufflés with saffron sauce, Fraser Valley duck foie gras on herb-smoked salmon with Oregon black truffles, wild mushrooms in myriad forms, our signature Douglas fir sorbet, and meats like herb-crusted local venison with a green walnut wine sauce. The signature rosemary biscuits vanished, replaced by sourdough and yeasted loaves of bread baked daily in our only oven. And the desserts soared under Jerry's deft hand and vision. He delivered.

That fall, with the dining room expansion complete, we announced the second of the "Call-In Days" for the year. From nine to five, we'd open phone lines and book reservations for the upcoming six months. The phone company had installed eight telephone lines in our Seattle home to handle the traffic.

"I've never put in so many phone lines to a house before," the installer said. "I can't imagine you'll get that many calls at once."

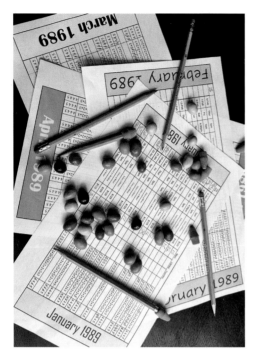

By 8 a.m. on Call-In Day, all eight buttons on each phone glowed orange. Our staff (many borrowed from our farm) sat around a large table with headsets, many pre-sharpened pencils, and bowls of M&M's—both plain and peanut. At 9 a.m., we turned on the phone lines and started to answer. The eight lines' breeing and warbling became an instant raucous concert. Reservations were taken with paper and pencil. Everyone hunched around a central table to share the same paper calendar recording the bookings and avoiding double-bookings.

> *Good morning!*
> *Thank you for calling The Herbfarm.*
> *How may I direct your call? (Pause).*
> *One moment may I put you on hold?*
> *How may I direct your call?*
> *One moment may I put you on hold?*
> *One moment may I put you on hold?*
> *Our human voices added lyrics to the song of the phones.*

And then, about twenty minutes into the morning, all the orange lit buttons went dark.

Half an hour passed without an incoming call. We couldn't call out either, and cell phones weren't a thing. But just as I was starting to panic, the lines lit up again. As the telephone company later explained, a breaker in a local substation was set to trip when volume exceeded 100,000 calls in thirty minutes. With everyone on redial, guests seeking reservations had taken down telephone service to most of the north end of Seattle. The story made the local news and became apocryphal.

And all of our tables were booked by noon.

∎

Bill Kraut decided to move on from The Herbfarm in 1992. He had been my conversational companion, helping to while away the long kitchen hours. I was grateful for the endless hours and energy he had put into the restaurant, and I was sorry to see Bill go.

As Bill Kraut went out the door, Jerry hired Colleen Herrick as the new assistant chef. She was young and seemed unseasoned. Having added The Herbfarm to her résumé, she was gone within the year, recruited by the Inn at Ludlow Bay as executive chef for their new thirty-seven-room hotel.

At The Herbfarm, the kitchen cycled through two more sous-chefs, who would later open their own restaurants. A young man, Matthew Dillon, had been coming to The Herbfarm to volunteer in the kitchen. When he saw our help wanted ad for a dishwasher in the *Seattle Times*, he rushed to apply. He'd graduated from culinary school three years earlier and yearned to be a part of The Herbfarm. Jerry quickly moved him out of "the dish pit" and elevated him to sous-chef.

In 1995, Bernie Bevis expanded the dining room for us. He enclosed the back patio (where my folks used to sit with a beer after the nursery closed at 5 p.m.) into a dining area to seat eight more guests. One end of the new dining space showcased my silver-plated duck press that had been presented to me by Orvis early in our "courtship."

At the opposite end, we added a service bar to enhance our wine service.

■

With the new addition, we could now serve thirty-four guests. The extra income was welcome, as the restaurant was getting by on thin margins. Carrie and I had never taken any pay for our work in the kitchen or dining room. Though considered pricey, dinner at The Herbfarm was actually a bargain. With only one sitting each evening, your table was yours for the night. That let us care for our diners as we would a guest in our home. Nobody pushed you to finish to make room for the next reservation. And the one-price-gets-it-all included not only the 3 ½ hour, nine-course tasting menu but six wines with ample top-ups as needed. No other fixed-price restaurant did that. And where else did you get a farm and garden tour and live Spanish guitar music every evening?

The answer, of course, is nowhere.

■

Before the internet, diners and travelers relied on guidebooks for trusted advice. We had been fortunate, earning the highest praise in *Northwest Best Places* and *Seattle Best Places*. These accolades attracted the attention of Fred and Mardi Nystrom, who were launching *Special Places for the Discerning Traveler*. More than just a full-color guide of inns, B&Bs,

lodges, restaurants, and retreats, *Special Places* showcased people committed to being the best at what they did from central California to British Columbia. Once or twice a year, Fred would invite us "Special People" to convene at a member's establishment. We discovered new friends at these meetings, where we all shared our insights freely.

Because of these get-togethers, my desire that The Herbfarm be a total wraparound experience gained momentum. We would include overnight stays on our farm. A countryside farm retreat is called "agriturismo" (agriculture+tourisn) in Italy, where guests come to stay on working farms. When, after World War II, Italians began leaving their farms for better opportunities in cities, Italian lawmakers rewrote land-use rules to let farmers offer rooms and meals provided that a certain amount of what they served originated on their farm. Many farms that could not sustain themselves with olives, sunflowers, livestock, or small vineyards were saved. Sadly such enlightened zoning that would save smallholder farms had not been entertained, let alone passed, in King County.

Just as I had picked brains to learn fine dining, I relied on our new friends to learn everything I could about operating an inn. Carrie and I hoped to build a whole new Herbfarm Restaurant inside an inn toward the back of our property. Friends Mark Carter of the Carter House and Hotel Carter on the northern California coast as well as Sinclair Philip at Sooke told us that the ideal capacity for a manageable independent inn was roughly twenty to twenty-two rooms. I knew that getting zoned for such a retreat outside Seattle would be hard if not impossible. But the project might be approved if we could operate under the existing B&B rules, with a half dozen suites. We would increase the size and quality of our dining room, a necessary move to sustain the restaurant moving forward. And we would significantly improve the facilities. At the time, the secret AAA inspectors had already awarded us with a Four Diamond Award, a high honor for a converted garage. But as much as we might try to put makeup on a pig, our beautiful little garage could never achieve five diamonds.

We explored the idea of buying the twenty acres kitty-corner across the street, where we dreamed of building a bespoke inn and restaurant with a view of the Cascade Mountains and an elegant, expanded restaurant where you didn't have to exit the "garage" to access the restrooms. We wanted to go for the fifth diamond. To achieve it would put us with a mere fifty other restaurants in all of America. The step up to Five Diamonds is steep. It includes "leading-edge cuisine, ingredients, and preparations with extraordinary service, facilities, atmosphere, and ample and gracious surroundings." It was a ballsy goal. Could a restaurant that started in a garage pull it off?

We decided to try.

Carrie and I started the process early in 1996. Land-use attorneys Alison Moss and Keith Dearborn drafted proposed language allowing rural expansion of food service and limited lodging on properties like ours. Our King County Council representatives, Brian Derdowski, Cynthia Sullivan, and Louise Miller, spearheaded zoning changes to be taken up by the whole King County Council that would allow a country inn in our zoining by special permitting. The matter was scheduled to be voted on that December but at the last minute was tabled until after the holidays.

■

Not know how the zoning vote would turn out and knowing any construction would take years, we continued to improve the existing garage restaurant. We hired general contractor Dow Construction to add a prep kitchen, a chef's table for four in that kitchen, wine cellar dining, and an office for Jerry. We were able to start using that expanded kitchen midsummer and had many guests dine at our "chef's table" in the kitchen overlooking our kitchen gardens. The wide-open space of the kitchen made it possible to have more than two people working at a time and the small paned windows created a most pleasant kitchen to work in.

In anticipation of our new facilities and the expanded service of the proposed inn, a local coffee roaster loaned us a fancy espresso machine. We parked the device in the service bar. The staff loved it. They made liberal use of the new toy, practicing their barista skills while drinking their handiwork. The machine would blow a circuit on occasion, but the electrical subpanel was just steps away, so restoring power only required the flip of a switch.

■

To make way for the construction of wine cellar and private cellar dining in the fall of 1996, we moved all of our wine, save the ancient Madeira collection (which was tucked securely in my office on-site), from the basement to a twenty-foot rental trailer with temperature control.

■

December 1996 was unusually wet. A county culvert that should have diverted water from a hillside instead sent a small river through our farm. As the groundwater rose,

the basement flooded. We installed a sump pump. The ceaseless river flowed through our property to roads and houses beyond.

Then we lost power.

The biggest snowstorm in years dropped two to three feet of snow. Ice-laden trees crashed into homes and power lines. Our greenhouses sagged. Despite continually sweeping snow from their tops, they collapsed under the weight. We suspended dinners. The most painful part was canceling the New Year's Eve festivities, which had been months in the planning.

The electricity died for eight long days and nights.

As the groundwater rose in the basement, we bought the last gas-powered generator in the area to run the basement-and-wine-cellar's sump pump and the heater in the wine storage trailer. Carrie called the insurance company, filing a claim for the greenhouse damages. We started sleeping on the office floor so we could refuel the little generator every five hours.

It was a glorious moment when the lights finally flickered, then came alive. Worn out by the ordeal, we checked on the animals and cleaned up the farm as best we could. Now we could leave for a short sortie to town. Carrie and I headed to a Chinese restaurant for our unwinding.

Just as we'd settled in and were pouring hot tea, a muted ringing came from the phone lodged deep in Carrie's purse. "Carrie, Carrie, come quick!" Mom cried. "The Herbfarm's on fire!" I didn't wait for the bill but threw a handful of money on the table. A few loose coins jingled and hopped on the floor behind us as we sprinted to the car.

Our Famous Little Restaurant Ablaze

When the chaotic night gave way to the dawning gray, the details of the damage emerged. The fire had gutted the restaurant. Only charred walls held up what remained of the ceiling. The main section of the attached office was rubble under the open sky. A jumble of soaked and charred cookbooks lay helter-skelter in deep piles. I peeled waterlogged volumes open and found signatures from Julia Child, Rick Bayless, and my friend Darina Allen, the most-influential chef in Ireland. In the kitchen I was amazed that a heavy aluminum pot was a silver pool of molten metal on the right side. The left side was untouched, completely untouched. The intense heat had been bewilderingly capricious.

The local TV news crews returned and set up. They interviewed my folks, Carrie, me, and some of the retail store and farm help. The news coverage exceeded anything I had expected. Somehow it was a big, easy-to-tell story that appealed to many people. If anything, the coverage was excessive. Even the *Los Angeles Times* ran an article about the fire. The notion that the *entire* Herbfarm had been destroyed began to take hold. We would discover what this would mean for our retail sales in the coming months.

Late in the morning after the fire, our insurance inspector drove in. He was perplexed. He'd been sent out for the claim on the snow-smashed greenhouses. Instead, and without warning, he had just walked into our disaster, a significant loss with a swarm of TV reporters. As we surveyed the wreckage together, I could barely answer his questions. I was hoarse and had to whisper. I'd lost my voice from the yelling over the noise of pumper trucks in the night.

Though he didn't say so, I knew his first thought was that we might have set the fire. In the restaurant trade, such things were not unheard of. Both the fire and insurance folks called in their own forensic investigators. They combed the ashes for days.

At the end, neither could say precisely what had started the fire. Both did agree the fire began in the bar of the dining room addition. And, since this had been home to that espresso machine that constantly tripped the electrical breaker, the blame settled on an overtaxed wire or electrical short.

Jerry drove out that morning. He offered condolences to family and staff and drove off, concerned about his and The Herbfarm's future. The day of the fire was also my nephew Paul Zimmerman's first day on the job with us. He'd been shocked to see the flashing lights and flames shown live that night on the TV news. My brother's kids, Anne and Thomas, also worked for us. We all wondered what lay ahead.

I must tip my hat to our insurance company. After a few days of investigating, they were cutting checks. Using these emergency funds, we leased a job-site office trailer and installed a large restroom trailer with excellent accommodations for men and women. The health department required restrooms before anything else. Good-natured Bernie Bevis built steps, handicap ramps, and a porch with an awning for the new facilities. Architect friend Barry Hoyne quickly drafted plans for an addition to our retail store, which the night flames had not touched. Dow Construction started building our new half-timbered, stuccoed office space. We fixed the greenhouses as best we could, tearing down some and rebuilding as the case might be.

Though it was winter, we kept our retail and mail-order business operating. We'd already mailed our holiday catalog, and the order forms kept coming. With no office, we moved much of our in-house product packaging from the back of our retail store to a warehouse in Preston, Washington, a fifteen-minute winding drive along the Raging River. Here our fulfillment team packed up the famous herbal-filled Sleep Bunnies, teas, salves, and beer bread kits for shipment.

Every week, Carrie would gather the entire staff in the evening darkness. In front of the store, we built an ample bonfire and gathered around, cupping hot drinks. Someone came up with the idea of penning our wishes on scraps of paper. Taking turns, we'd read our wish and then toss the text into the flames. As it curled on the coals, smoke and ash carried our thoughts skyward. We wondered if the gods were listening. Wearing freshly printed purple T-shirts sporting golden "From the Ashes, We Will Rise," those who remained with us through that first winter bonded as a team.

A Memory of
The Herbfarm Restaurant
This jar contains the ashes of the dining room of the original Herbfarm restaurant which opened on May 25, 1986 and was destroyed by fire, January 6, 1997. Proceeds from this jar will help build the new restaurant

TV and newspaper coverage in the week after the fire was so thorough and unrelenting, most of the world was left thinking all aspects of The Herbfarm were destroyed and that we were planning to rebuild.

A few of our neighbors decided to ride our coattails to the King County Council and prevent the rebuilding of The Herbfarm until their drainage problems were addressed. The Council tabled the vote that should have happened in December until the community came together. Many a meeting was held under a tent at The Herbfarm as we tried to hammer everything out.

■

In the end, limitations of both time and money quashed the idea of the inn on the hill across the street, and we focused instead on rebuilding on our own thirteen acres and got started on a design for the new Inn at The Herbfarm and Restaurant. The rebuild envisioned an elegant dining room with a curve of banquettes facing a beautiful open kitchen, a central table with a display of flora and fauna of the night's menu, and six large one-of-a-kind thematic overnight suites. The grandest suite would dominate the southwest corner of the inn. It was to be wine-themed, with a living room and stone fireplace on the ground floor and the bedroom above enjoying a vista of our fields and gardens. A spiral staircase would descend to an underground, fully stocked stone-walled wine cellar for guests to use and enjoy. And we submitted permits to the county.

■

But, to build anew we would need external funding. Sweat equity had created our restaurant in the garage. We had made do and we had created a thing of charm and rustic country beauty. But a project of this scope would require more resources than we had.

At that time there was no crowdsourcing allowed. Raising funds for a project like this was seen akin to issuing stocks, whose transactions were controlled by the Securities and Exchange Commission. We needed a law firm (which came with good-sized billings) to draft essentially the constitution for a new Herbfarm in a private placement memorandum. The thick PPM prospectus took weeks to hammer out. It was a lengthy contract with investors. It highlighted virtually everything that could go wrong. For a restaurant, this is an immense list. Investors (actually called "members") needed to be high-net-worth people who would attest in writing their wealth status. Each would need to make a minimum contribution as outlined in the prospectus. The funds for this new Herbfarm went directly to an escrow account. We wouldn't be allowed to spend any of it until the project was fully funded.

You'd think that after a decade of success with myriad kudos from the press and our guests, raising funds would have been easy. But, if anything, securing members for the new Herbfarm became the most difficult part of the rebuild process. I mailed PPMs with nondisclosures to many people. Many demurred. But we did start to build a coterie of members. Many were from Microsoft, riding their stock options to new heights.

■

Meanwhile, we had to keep going. In the winter of 1997, I approached Sam Benowitz of Raintree Nursery in Morton, Washington. Raintree offered a substantial collection of fruit trees, berries, vines, nuts, and unusual edibles. All of them with rare and exciting stories were better suited to the Northwest climate than standard fruits and berries. While growing hot-weather fruit like peaches is iffy here, Sam offered the Nanaimo peach and Orcas pear. Both could take our damp winters, and the Nanaimo, particularly, was resistant to leaf curl. Their Chehalis apple was found wild north of the town of the same name in 1937. The apple resembles the Golden Delicious but is larger and crisper. As a kid, I had feasted on the wild native strawberry. These tiny red berries—no bigger than a thimble—can attain a flavor unmatched by other strawberries. Sam offered these too.

What I had in mind was another way to increase nursery sales. Sam's location was a long ninety-minute drive south from the Seattle area. "What if we set up a satellite outlet at The Herbfarm with a curated selection of your best edibles for the Pacific Northwest?" I suggested to Sam. Raintree had heritage and rare fruit trees as well as berries bred in Russia and Siberia that were available nowhere else. Sam was skeptical, but we cut a deal to buy his plants at wholesale. We would split the cost of running the new offshoot fifty-fifty. One of Sam's trusted horticulturist friends, Neil, came with the deal. He handled the plants as well as advising customers. We provided the venue, foot traffic, and mail marketing to pump the word out.

"Edible Eden," as we named this cooperative subset of our plant business, was a charming place. With great imagination and skill, Bob Hise painted beautifully illustrated signs for the prominent entry arcade we created. Unfortunately, we ended Edible Eden after two summers. Sam was disappointed with the sales.

By the winter of 1998 we were broke. No, not broke. Far worse. We were utterly upside down with our eighteen maxed-out high-interest credit cards. When the loss-of-business insurance ran out, we used the cards to make payroll and keep the lights on.

We could no longer afford to keep Jerry on the payroll. At that time, he had started writing *The Herbfarm Cookbook*.

That October, we decided to offer a dinner-without-a-restaurant in a back field. Calculating that we'd have to serve one hundred guests a night, we sketched up a tented arrangement for kitchen and dining. A carpenter friend built a 2x4 framework to which we screwed sheets of plywood for the rigid and stable floor. All the lumber for this project, including a wood façade that became the entry to the dining tent, was loaned to us by Eric Fritch, who owned Chinook Lumber. You can use the lumber," Eric graciously admonished. "But you can paint only one side!" Carrie and I, hunched over in fatigue, finished painting the dark brown plywood floor one evening just as the rain began.

Carrie's previous career as stagehand paid dividends as she was able to borrow scenery to build out our "set." The entrance to our "Witch's Brew" Boo-Ha-Ha dinner was a fabulous conceit. The door was a two-inch-thick medieval affair with iron straps and a curved top. It was painted black and was the yawning mouth of a giant gargoyle through which one had to enter. Bob Hise had pulled off another of his wonderful art projects. Outside the tent we placed an open fire over which a huge iron kettle bubbled and steamed. A stunning witch with a regal crescent cap stirred the great cauldron with a long-handled paddle. She recited the witches' incantation from Shakespeare's *Macbeth*: "Double, double toil and trouble, Fire burn, and cauldron bubble."

At the back of the dining room, we put up a faux brick wall and rigged stage lighting graciously loaned by the Seattle Opera. We covered the dining room floor with old Oriental rugs.

For a kitchen, we rented a pair of six-burner propane commercial ranges with ovens. Plywood and stainless-steel tables allowed for food prep and a place to plate the large number of dishes. Except for hand and prep sinks, there was no scullery. Every night we would take a pickup-load of dirty plates up to the catering kitchen at the Salish Lodge and return them, clean, near dawn, for the next meal.

Jerry did not want to work from an imperfect kitchen to create a perfect meal, so we hired talented chef Eric Leonard to embrace the quixotic challenge of running a kitchen of high standards from a tent. Though our cooking facilities were basic, I was proud that the five-course dinner was a showpiece. The menu was creative and satisfying. We served a rich crayfish bisque with crayfish tails in a roasted baby pumpkin with a Madeira sabayon; herbed loin of fallow venison scallops with shaved matsutake; chanterelles and foie gras with caramelized quince; a witch's sorbet; and molten chocolate-pumpkin cake with sage crème Anglaise (see recipe on page 250).

We lined the path from the parking to the tent with candles glowing in brown paper bags. As our female guests wobbled in heels while walking the graveled road to the tent, we were delighted to see their enthusiasm supporting us. Each night, Patricio played his Spanish guitar by candlelight. A colorful troubadour in medieval garb wowed guests with tableside magic between his jokes, juggles, and japes.

The three weeks of Boo-Ha-Ha dinners were wonderful. The whole team bonded. Once again, we improvised and created something special. Importantly, too, it put a little change in our pocket.

■

One morning the phone rang. It was Anne-Marie Hedges. "Is this Carrie? *Bonjour*!" she said with a fetching French accent. "This is Anne-Marie at the Hedges wine cellar in Issaquah. I've heard you might be looking for a temporary home for your restaurant."

It was true, we were looking at a *lot* of places but had not yet found anything appropriate. The bank had pulled our loan. Creditors from before the fire were calling daily. The county was taking their time processing our permit requests. The remaining insurance was reserved for rebuilding. We couldn't touch any of the privately pledged money until we'd funded the entire PPM. We had to act fast to do something to stay in business and avoid bankruptcy.

■

So. "Yes, of course," we replied without hesitation. "What do you have in mind?"

Anne-Marie was looking for someone to partially cover costs in their tasting facility and barrel room. The facilities came with a full special event kitchen which had a large, open "pass" from kitchen to barrel room so guests could watch the cooking and plating. The opportunity looked propitious.

So, she outlined her plan. She envisioned us temporarily sharing the tasting room and their barrel cellar. By day the building would be the Hedges Wine Cellar. At night

Mallard Duck & Duck Foie Gras
With Cherry, Wild Rice and Walnut Stuffing,
Madeira-Black Truffle Sauce
1989 DOMAINE DROUHIN OREGON PINOT NOIR

Watercress and Orange Salad

Dessert: *Tastes of Madeira*
Hazelnut and Vanilla Soufflé with Maple-Madeira Sauce
Poached Sekel Pear with Madeira Sabayon
Toffee and Lemon Peel Ice Cream
1900 BARBEITO MALVAZIA

Coffees & Teas in the French Manner

A Selection of Small Treats
Victorian Crescent Rolls

it would transform into The Herbfarm restaurant. How we'd pull this off was unclear. But there was a large storage room where, by turning tables upside down on top of each other, we could store the tabletops. Shelves would hold china. We could keep a modest cache of service wine.

Oh. The other problem to overcome was that, per law, one couldn't have two liquor licenses on the same premise. We scheduled a meeting with the Washington State Liquor Control Board. The three men—wheat farmers and political appointees—sat at a long table before us. They heard our story. Instead of "premises," we would use time to separate the licenses. It was unorthodox and had never been allowed. But after some debate, they voted yes. We'd reconfigure into our restaurant in time for dinner service.

So, we cut a deal and set to work getting everything we needed.

To fund the move to Hedges my old friend, Jim Willenborg, from the River of No Return raft trip, gave us a bridge loan that would be converted into his member shares. I don't remember how but within a few months we had new tables, chairs, china, glassware, silverware, linens, and staff opening on Memorial Day weekend 1999.

When we opened our interim restaurant in the Hedges wine cellar, we served fifty guests a night. Besides nightly service, from time to time we hosted special events such as a dinner with Mario Andretti, race car driver extraordinaire, and an authentic re-creation of a Madeira dinner from the nineteenth century. We celebrated the turn of the century at The Herbfarm Hedges Cellars, which was located right next door to Boehm's Chocolates and Chapel.

New Year's Eve 1999 was a grand event. We brought in a barrel of Hedges Reserve Cabernet and guests recorded their thoughts on a scroll that was inserted in a tube. Each guest was given a deeply engraved magnum bottle which they filled from the barrel. The last wines bottled in the twentieth century! Then they dropped their missives into their bottles and sealed them to be opened years in the future.

At midnight we sang "Auld Lang Syne." Just then, the bell in the bell-tower of Julius Boehm's chocolate shop rang out. It was a still and perfect night. We all thronged outdoors and toasted each other—staff and guests alike. A good sign for the future, we hoped.

Jerry was at the helm with an all-star team as we transitioned to our temporary home at Hedges Winery. Many of the young chefs who worked at The Herbfarm around this time such as Matt Dillon and Jeremy Faber (who later would start an amazing foraging business called Foraged and Found Edibles), and many others, went on to make a name for themselves. The Herbfarm would be the incubator for future successful chefs, writers, and teachers. I watched the magic unfold each night. The space at Hedges was the perfect transition while we built a new restaurant.

■

Since The Herbfarm Restaurant was open for one seating per day, we would prep each day for that evening using the freshest ingredients and counting out enough for each course we were making to make sure we had a few extra servings as backup and, of course, for the staff to taste.

The prep time that went into each dish was a testament to the final gastronomic experience. For example, to make the perfect round hole in the top of a farm-fresh egg requires a special tool that cuts the shell with the pull and release of the spring-loaded device placed at the conical top of the egg. As you let go both the pressure and vibration create a perfect circle. After emptying the egg, you remove the membrane from inside each eggshell, dry them upside down, swirl each one with butter, then add a small amount of lightly toasted bread crumbs, turning to coat the entire inside of the egg.

This would set the stage for either our creamy soufflé with herbs, soft scrambled egg with Dungeness crab and paddlefish caviar, or salmon mousse with salmon caviar. (See page 250 for soufflé recipe.)

We are always seeking out the freshest local ingredients, perfectly prepared with herbs and spices to complement the course without repeating that flavor in other courses. It's a science and a passion, and that shows with each bite.

As much as I have always loved foraging for the wild edibles we used, eventually, I had to call upon others such as Jeremy Faber to bring in wild foods. Year-round we looked forward to what was to come. In spring, the combination of morel mushrooms (see page 120), stinging nettles (see page 122 for Nettle Soup recipe), and fresh shelled peas would call for fresh Alaskan halibut or freshly made pasta. Our "A Mycologist's Dream" menu (see page 260) highlighted the most beautifully executed courses that gave these myriad wild fungi center stage. Cauliflower mushroom, hedgehog, lion's mane, chanterelle, king bolete, morels, and many more. All would be transformed.

One of my many fond food memories was the smell of chanterelle, hedgehog, and lobster mushrooms sautéing in butter with shallot and herbs. This ragout would then be cooled while preparing strudel dough stretched to the size of a large rectangular table. This amazing combination of flavors would be added to the length of the dough. It took two people to firmly, but gently, roll the strudel dough into one long, cylindrical tube. The strudel would then be brushed with an egg wash and baked to crisp perfection.

These were artists in action; this was something I wanted everyone to witness, which was one of the reasons I always wanted an open kitchen. At Hedges Winery we were lucky that it worked out that way. Guests could come up and see their dinners being plated and watch what is normally "behind the scenes."

Meanwhile, permitting the project for the rebuild was always "next week." It was taking too much time. For starters, the county now wanted us to move telephone poles, take a slight "kink" from the roadway to straighten it, and move all the parking away from the planned new site. The project would now be too expensive. Maybe a million more.

Forget the Stadium. Rebuild The Herbfarm.

Some wag printed bumper stickers: "Forget the Stadium. Rebuild The Herbfarm." This was while the funding for the baseball stadium to replace the Kingdome, which had recently been demolished, was on the ballot—a somewhat contentious project at that time. It was nice to see ongoing support for The Herbfarm. But, due to cost and community resistance to any new development, we needed to abandon our Fall City farm to rebuild elsewhere.

**FORGET THE STADIUM
REBUILD THE HERBFARM**

We turned our attention to developing an all-new stand-alone building on the grounds of the new Willows Lodge in Woodinville. This change of location meant that we had to essentially cancel the original fundraising efforts, offer all members their money back, rewrite the PPM, and start all over raising funds for the Woodinville Herbfarm. Most stuck with us. The continuation of the fundraising efforts was always like an albatross around our necks.

∎

Being the optimists we were, we moved forward as if we knew we'd succeed. For our new digs, we needed a designer.

One day, Seattle designer Gary Dethlefs stopped by to show us some of his past restaurant projects. He turned out to be a genius. In our weekly meetings from that point forward, we covered every detail from the space division to the 1910 fireplace I purchased on eBay, the huge stained glass window I found at the Restore in Ballard, to paint and wallpaper decisions.

Having recently returned from a trip to Ireland and France, Gary designed a building with European flair. The main spaces of the interior were supported by heavy timbers and cross supports. The main dining room's ceiling soared to twenty-one feet.

Our lease was for the restaurant, large kitchen gardens, and two overnight suites. Both large and beautiful, the suites were to be furnished with antiques, custom wood-work, and original art. It was the suites that made The Herbfarm an inn and thus viable for the Five Diamond honor. *And* access to the restrooms was indoors!

With building permits in Woodville secured, the new PPM funds were released. Now we could move ahead building out the restaurant and creating our overnight rooms. We established our new farm just down the road.

■

So, we sold our farm.

Before we sold the Fall City property, my folks had decided to move into a retirement apart-ment in North Bend. When the shell of the new restaurant building was up, I took Dad to see it. He had cancer and was weak. I offered to carry him upstairs to see the office, the private rooms, the great view of Mount Rainier. But he declined. He died shortly afterward.

A few years later, while Mom was getting her annual physical, she suffered a heart attack. The doctor and his staff tried to revive her, but she died in the doctor's office.

Mom and Dad had always been quiet and behind-the-scenes. In Fall City they would be out early watering the herbs in the greenhouses, feeding the animals, or cleaning the dove cage. As much as Carrie and I did, they were the key to running The Herbfarm in the early days and teaching us how to run a nursery. I will always be grateful.

■

More than four years after the fire, we moved to our permanent location in Woodinville.

Our dinner service schedule was Friday through Sunday, and we packed up Hedges on a Sunday night after service and had our first "guinea pig" service the following Thursday in Woodinville. We had our dream inn, restaurant, and gardens.

The New Restaurant in Woodinville

We served our first dinner in the new restaurant on May 25, 2001, The date was ten years to the day since we first opened the doors on our little restaurant on our farm. We'd done so many things there. The Northwest Microbrewery Festival and Wine Festival. And three hundred classes yearly organized by Carrie. We served 150 different themed chef-selected menus with all of the ingredients from Washington, Oregon, and southern British Columbia.

We had created the first true "farm-to-table" restaurant with courses sequenced by the chef.

The term "farm-to-table" hadn't been coined yet. With time there were lots of places claiming farm-to-table, or serving "local food "whenever possible." Between our own farm and local sourcing, we were creating orchestrated dinners where (truly) everything was sourced from our region. This philosophy revealed the true flavors of the Northwest, the terroir.

We filled every seat each night.

■

Ironically, September 11 was our first biannual "call in day" in our new home. Carrie was listening to the news as she drove to Woodinville from Fall City wondering if anyone would call. At nine o'clock, the phones began to ring. People apologized for calling on such a horrific day. After 10 a.m, the calls dwindled as everyone absorbed the horrendous news. That was the final Herbfarm call-in day as we now served more guests more often with a manageable waiting list (except for Valentine's Day!).

We managed to fund our PPM and were awaiting a check from just one more investor to be complete. He had an appointment with Carrie on Sept 11th to drop off that check. "I wasn't going to come," he said. But I thought about it hard. "They're not going to intimidate me! I'm in. Here's my check." It was a fine and moving moment for us.

Awards

"I am still young aren't I?" I said turning to Carrie. The plane noisily crossed the Cascades and started its descent. At this point in 2007 we had built one of the best wine cellars in America. Our temperature and humidity controlled wine "cellar" housed a total of 4,384 different wines and 17,000 bottles. The Herbfarm's collection of Northwest wines went back to the 1970s. We also had an impressive collection of world classics. We'd won *Wine Spectator*'s "Best of Award of Excellence" several times as well as *Wine Enthusiast*'s highest award. *Santé* magazine named us the "Best Wine List in America."

We were just arriving in Richland, Washington. The next night the Washington Wine Commission presented me with their Walter Clore "Lifetime Achievement Award." This was an important recognition of our years supporting the explosion of winemaking in Washington. And I still thought I was too young for a lifetime award. But I accepted it, "young" as I was.

■

That same year Jerry ventured to India, where he was taken by the cuisine. But even more, he came back impressed with the "thali." Instead of serving nine sequenced courses, the thali that Jerry envisioned would be a plate with nine compartments. Each would have a small bite of food.

Jerry announced that after seventeen years, he would be opening his own restaurant in Seattle, Poppy.

We needed a new chef. We hired Keith Luce. Luce had worked at high-end restaurants on both coasts. He had been the sous-chef in the Clinton White House. Years before, he had stopped in Fall City to introduce himself and gave me an Air Force One cap and handsome shoulder patch.

While Luce was here, we raised Mangalitsa pigs, also known as the woolly pig. The woolly pig hails originally from Austria and Hungary. It was a favorite of smallholders, self-sufficient farmhouses who raised these pigs not only for meat but also their valuable lard. In 1997 we reared seven Mangalitsas.

Continuing our efforts to provide educational opportunities for staff and guests, we invited Isabel and Christophe Wiesner from Austria and Kate Hill and Dominique Chapoulard from France to give hands-on seminars on field slaughter, seam butchery, and nose-to-tail use of the pig. Seam butchery follows the lines of the muscles, which is different from most American butchery. The large muscles are cured in their large pieces. Smaller muscles are dealt with whole or cured in smaller groups. There is *no* waste; every part of the pig is used.

Keith worked in our kitchen for close to two years until he had to move back home on the North Shore of Long Island to care for his family's land.

A Child Is Born

Ironically, within a few days of The Herbfarm Restaurant's first opening in Fall City, a baby was born. His name was Christopher Weber. Chris was not quite twenty-one when he joined our team as line cook. He worked under both Jerry and Keith. Chris had great kitchen instincts but was still very young. We asked him to be co-sous-chef while we searched for Keith's replacement.

During our nationwide search, Carrie and I were also subtly working with Chris to help him develop his leadership skills. When we took him out to dinner in 2010 and asked him to step into the chef position he seemed quite surprised to be asked, but he accepted graciously. He became the youngest AAA Five Diamond chef ever—he was twenty-four years old even though he didn't look it!

Chris did an admirable job heading up our farm, foraging, searching out new artisan sources. He was kind and smart and had a team approach in the kitchen. And, importantly, he was and is a wonderful and creative cook.

All Restaurants Are Closed around the World: The Herbfarm Becomes a Community-Sponsored Restaurant

In 2019 a virus appeared in a nursing home in Kirkland, Washington. COVID-19. A few months later, The Herbfarm and all other restaurants were shut down by the state for indoor dining.

We wanted to keep our staff employed and our local purveyors in business so we didn't have to start all over when we were allowed to reopen. Who could even imagine that it would be two whole years before that was to happen!

We decided to support Seattle's first responders. Each day, we cooked 150–200 three-course hot, individually packed meals. We delivered these meals with a small army of volunteers to local hospitals for those on the front lines. Funded with a GoFundMe page created by one of our longtime guests, we became a community-funded restaurant serving over 20,000 total meals before the hospitals, who were short-staffed, became unable to handle the meal deliveries.

Willows Lodge had just reopened, so we began then serving meals to guests in The Herbfarm suites located across the driveway inside Willows Lodge. Carrie and Chris got quite the workout running up and down those antique stairs fifteen to twenty trips each day for breakfast and dinner. Serving and clearing and resetting.

A couple months later, the state closed everyone down once again. In the fall of 2020, we commissioned wooden crates with The Herbfarm logo burned on the sides. This time, we offered multicourse meals for folks to take home—including two bottles of appropriate wine and detailed instructions on how to prepare. We offered these through Valentine's Day 2021, when we were once again allowed to reopen and serve in our dining room.

Chef Chris again helmed the stoves. Patricio Contreras once more played his moving Spanish guitar. And we were once again able to make life as perfect as it could be for our guests for just a few hours each night.

In 2021, Carrie and I retired and passed The Herbfarm on to our talented chef Chris Weber and his best friend, Jack Gingrich. It is gratifying to see that they continue to take our basic ethos to heart as they continue to provide great service for their multicourse chef-selected menus featuring local, seasonal cuisine.

Afterword

So, why go to the trouble of sourcing foods from the Northwest? To help keep the food supply close to home rather than factory produced nationally and overseas. Amazingly, most grocery store food has traveled 1,500 miles before hitting the shelves.

Local cheeses, foraged foods, fresh farm crops, nearby fish, fowl, and meats keep artisan craftspeople in business. More importantly such treasure allows the true taste and terroir of this region to shine. Over the years we teased out obscure off-grid cheesemakers, hunted down exotic fowl breeders, found lamb from clovered pastures, and featured a host of foods that had never hit—at least in those days—the local plate, palate, or grocers' shelves. These quests were to form the thread that ran so true for decades at the restaurant.

As Americans have left the farms of the early twentieth century, foods have been molded for convenience. Most any food can be found in a can, box, or the freezer section. Few butchers now cut your meat to order for you. Chickens are reduced to tightly plastic wrapped pieces. The complex flavors of real cheese from local creameries is forgotten and then eventually lost. The flavor of heritage lamb, goat, and beef raised on pasture is no longer even a memory.

So, each year we set about adding more special and forgotten crops to our farm. Among these was Abenaki Calais flint corn. Not the sweet corn of the grocery, but a corn for milling to flour or cracking for polenta. Native tribes had grown the corn for over two thousand years. It was the corn that Squanto gave to the Pilgrims.

The Ozette Potato is a small fingerling. The tuber was left in a garden on the Olympic Peninsula by Spanish explorers in 1792. It had been tended continuously by the Makah tribe and had been gifted to us in 1994. The local tribes boiled the potatoes and ate them dipped in seal oil. The little tuber has a nutty flavor and a smooth, creamy interior. Geneticists have established that this is the only potato that came straight from the Andes with the Spanish.

The Pellegrini Bean is a favorite. The mottled bean was first passed on to Dr. Angelo Pellegrini from his friend the winemaker Robert Mondavi. When Angelo died, a few vines remained in his Seattle garden. Pele's son, Brent, gave us eleven of the beans, from which we've bred up to a full crop each year. The flavor is perhaps the best we've ever had.

Now as I think back on my mountain peak–bagging days, of the balding man who visited our little shop with a new, unnamed fabric, Gore-Tex. How, starting with Gore-Tex, Early Winters developed a host of innovative outdoor gear and was named the best catalog in America.

Then joining my folks on their farm. How my parents believed in me and Carrie and let us expand the nursery, start offering classes and weekend events, and convert their garage into a small restaurant serving multicourse meals chosen by the chef alone. That hope-of-a-restaurant won nearly every award, and ultimately our goal of being awarded a place among the fifty top restaurants in the country. The Five Diamond plaque hangs proudly at the entrance to the restaurant.

Now many are gone. Mom. Dad. Bernie. Bette. Poncho and Paco the llamas. Gertie the Goose. Dad's hypnotizing chicken, Henny Penny, our first farm and a host of others. I know my parents would be proud of how we persevered and were able to pivot during difficult times. Carrie and I never gave up and we were grateful that they believed in us and our determination to make The Herbfarm what we wanted it to be.

But the restaurant evolves and learns as we go. It puts us closer to walking with Chief Seattle. All knew that all was linked. We are not just voyagers through the landscape. We are woven into the fabric of nature and participants in the great cycle.

All know that the drop flows into the ocean. Few know that the ocean drains into the drop.

Meanwhile, we strive nightly. For a few short hours, we hope to make sure your life is as perfect as you'd always hoped it would be.

From our table to yours.

and friends, dined at your
Spanish virtuoso "conversed with
and played some of our favorite
works. As for me, I enjoyed my
short interaction with Carrie a
she told me that she had no
only enjoyed her work, li
she had actually "found her
in your work at the HerbFa
And it wasn't until our dinn
was over that I realized you had
graced us with complimentary f
of port and iced wines. How very
generous and kind. My husba
and I thank you deeply f

appreciation for classical guitar.

that I have never had such a
dining experience. Your personal
we met Ron in the wine cellar
ie on the herb tour, made our
much more than a worldclass
enjoyed all of your gifted
able staff. I personally
the detailed description
acies of each culinary
so I could better savor

re so many details of
and the evening

My heart still smiles when remembering
my 60th birthday celebrated with you on
December 20th, 2009. The word "perfect" comes
to mind. The warmth of the staff and exacting
attention to detail brought sensory delights from the
moment we were greeted. There was a connection ma
with earth's bounty, human artistry, friendship an
love that was a true celebration of life.
So sublime!   Best regards
                                    Heather Tay

120 Second Street, Juneau, Alaska 99801
SILVERBOW
info@silverbo
www.silverbo
86-4242   restaurant • catering

th drowning in accolades, I just wanted to take a
inary dining experience that I had at your restaurant

val, to the informative, witty displays in the wine
1885 Madeira, your taste and your attention to every
so many restaurateurs are busy duplicating their
far, it is a rare pleasure to come upon a grand
by its owners and chef, and so firmly grounded in

nk you for making our
big day so special and memorable from
have received numerous comments from
our guests praising the food, atmosphere, and
service. We cannot express how much it
all the work and thought that went into
evening. We very much ha
we enjoyed experie
next dining experie
to disturb

Dear Carrie, Ron, Joey and the
"Herbfarm Family",
    We would like to thank
you for making our 30th
Wedding Anniversary even more
special and marvelous. We were
very happily surprised by the
opportunity to stay in the special
Herb Farm room at Willow Lodge.
We really appreciated your
generosity.
    As usual, the meal was

meal was bursting with fl
and beautifully presented
    You have done a terri
job for some adoring fa
of the Herb Farm.
         Thank You Again
         Best Wishes,

    Dr Carrie Anderson & Virgin

Ron,
    I dreamed of treating my
Herb Farm for years and

Borage and Basil, and app
beautiful landscaping on t
Even Mt. Rainier was s
    Thank you so much
our anniversary were spe
also, thank you for supp
Woodinville Montessori
Our two grandsons are s
there, and we know the
receiving an excellent ed
         Sincerely,
         Marge Skeen

& CARRIE & the OUTSTANDING
of the HERBFARM:
e for a simply wonderful
ing... Let's get some of
ford onto the Space Station!
aot C Anderson

Dear Ron
    We know o
the amazing
now as you
want to once

For us The He
memories. W
Herbfarm and
Herbfarm was
and anniversari

It remains a mys
earlier visits. Our
1994 but we certa
then. We believe
and recall several o
the tent, and at He

gai
Dear Carrie & Ron
    Gregg, Martey a
enough for the gloria
last Sunday. It w
experience. The pa
every member of y
every bite and even
who requested non-alc
particularly blown a
me. WOW. I will
and I will eagerly

iah loved the
kept appearing
you really
for entertaining
a memorable
re of the
of our lives.
much.
ee you both
spiring to
so well
as well

Dear Carrie and Ron,
    Although you have heard
before what a fabulous
dining experience, you provide
I have
added compliments. You
were so kind and
welcoming to Sarah. It is
a risky proposition to have
a four year old in for
dinner. You were both so
accepting it really eased
the tensions for us both

magical
e of energy
We are
sincere hop
e peace

TO RON, CARRIE, & THE HERBFARM STAFF —
    JUST A NOTE TO SAY 'THANKS'
WONDERFUL

Dear Herb Farm,
I would like to express my appr
12, 2002. I think all the staff ne
French restaurant in Kirkland a
India restaurant. I was thorough
of another special place to have
always wanted to go there for s

Ray and I wanted to thank you for your wonderful New Year's Eve dinner. You made the once in a lifetime chance a memorable experience. It is one we will never forget, and have yet to stop talking about! Your enthusiasm, joy, dedication and service have furbished that evening into our memories. We could not have asked to be part of

---

...t & Carrie,

...you so much for the opportunity ...nce The Herbfarm. Your restaurant ...an exalted reputation, I have ...I was concerned nothing could ...live up to it - I was wrong. The ...e and presentation created an ...ly memorable evening. I have ...en able to introduce some of ...to your concept and hope to ...om backings soon.

Regards, Sandra

Dear Mr. Zimmerman and Mrs. Van Dyck,

Thank you ever so much for your splendid hospitality on February 11th when we were able to join the Herbfarm adventure. Looking back on the meal, we both agreed that the food was tremendous, the service flawless, and the wine fit seamlessly into the meal. Most importantly, the warmth and generosity of everyone at the Herbfarm was spectacular. We were made to feel at home. The whole room, while busy and bubbling with the drone of dozens of conversations, was a serene place to enjoy one of the finest meals of our lives. The spectacular rendition of Moonlight Sonata by the excellent guitarist was spiritual.

...just wanted to thank you again for the ...nderful experience I had @ the Herb Farm ...cant say whether the food, the atmosphere ...the service was the best part of the eveni... ...thing seemed so effortless and came tog... ...tly. I have been raving about my ...er to everyone that will listen and ...be back again very soon. Thanks aga...

Charles...

Thank You

...Thanks for a delightful ...at Herbfarm. It is ...way to be with my ...but this was an ...cial event. Usually ...ters around who ...ing and want attention. ...who sat at the table ...e perfect. You must ...me guidance when ...the table lists.

Carrie & Ron -   6/17/02

Thank you for a spectacular evening at the Herbfarm Friday night!

I hosted a $CO_2$60 client and referral source who very much enjoyed a memorable evening.

The attorney from Florida says he definitely will bring his wife out next spring for a visit and wants to take her to the Herbfarm. He also has several northwest clients who I'm sure will be hearing about your spectacular restaurant from him.

Our client is a company that works with Japanese businesses and rarely has an evening away from "Japanese hours"! They so enjoyed the food, your hospitali...

---

and a normal late they having night

So much success for me

K...

Carrie and crew -
...just wanted to say thank you ...truly memorable experience ...ll made our wedding a wonderful ...from the wonderful courses to ...edding cakes and all the extra ...ouches for the kiddos...

...your attentions and efforts. We are ...served a lifetime gratitude
...We wish you great success ...in all your endeavors, and may ...your entire staff benefit from a ...year of glad tidings and ...prosperity.

With sincere affection,
Ray Fabricius &
Joyce Fujinobu

Dear Ron and Carrie,

We would like to thank you so royally entertaining the Anelson... We had a magical evening and w... effort that Ron made to be there to make the evening so special... of a Anelson Family Crest and per... favorite song, not to mention the...

Carrie Van Dyck & Ron Zimmerman
The Herbfarm Restaurant
32804 Issaquah-Fall City Road
Fall City, WA 98024

Thanks to all of you!!

On behalf of Julie and Frank VanDeventer, Li... Zorn, and Judy and I, I want to thank you for t... we all enjoyed last week. When I purchased th... year, I knew it would be a treat, but it exceede... opportunity to enjoy a dozen years (plus the [5... up with such a fabulous dinner was a wonderf... time.

We enjoyed our visit to your lovely home, and... enjoy dinner at the Herbfarm Restaurant when...

Thanks again for a fun evening.

Lloyd D. Wiebe
Executive Vice President/CFO

...nan

...annot thank you ...you prepared for us ...ofoundly moving ...d thoughtfulness of ...n is reflected in ...nt. As a vegan diner ...irings, I was ...what you crafted for ...rget this evening, ...e the next visit.

...nks, Gail

Thank you so much for the opportunity to dine with you as the FB contest Winner! The experience is something I have always wanted to do, will never forget, and hope to enjoy again!

As someone who works in customer service (and has 2 small children) your

---

...is ...on ...ort...

Th...

July 10, 2003

Dear Ron Zimmerman & Carrie...

Recently I was swept away to a culinary dream world, thanks to both of you. Last Thursday my mother (Susan Payne) treated me to an evening at your wonderful restaurant. It was a birthday gift that will linger in my memory and taste buds for years to come.

The charming atmosphere of the restaurant and gardens enhanced the magic of the divine meal. The quality of each course quickly surpassed that of past experience with "good" restaurants, in which I often feel exhausted by the masking flavors of too much salt and butter. Instead, the courses embraced the delicacy of live fresh flavors so that I found myself deeply appreciative of the careful and complete design of flavor and texture that was presented on each plate.

As a recently turned 21-year-old I am unschooled in the subtleties of wine. However, Christine Mayo's perfectly picked wines were revelations to my mouth. Each course that was accompanied with the chosen wine seemed to make a marriage of complementary flavors and aromas. The complexity of the wines appeared to me more clearly, thanks to your (Ron) delightful descriptions at the beginning of the evening.

The Herbfarm surpassed my expectations, (the expectation being high already, considering the glowing reputation that the Herbfarm continues to hold). Another aspect of the evening transcended the functional and luxurious purpose of a quality restaurant. The entire staff appeared to maintain the highest of standards in order to create an experience of beauty and harmony. This sets it apart and, to me, creates a truly artistic experience. So when, near the end of the evening, Christine Mayo said to me, " you sound like the kind of person who should work here at the Herbfarm," I was more than excited at the possibility. She must have heard me jabbering enthusiastically about the evening's culinary delights.

...eleven years of professional dance training and active painting, I have ...standard for creating beauty to share with others. I have also worked as a ...ver and job captain with Baci Catering and Cafe. I believe that I could have ...e high standards that the Herbfarm maintains with enthusiasm...

Thursday January 18, 2001
Dear Ron, Carrie and Jerry,
This comes to you all with a huge and heartfelt thankyou for our exceptional and unforgetable dining experience we had with you at the Herbfarm on Sunday Jan. 7th. Our friends are very envious and will make sure they book in time for their next trip to the area, and we are looking forward to sharing your wonderful concept with...

Subj: Fwd: rest praise
Date: 7/7/2000 9:42:14 AM Pacific Daylight Time
From: Herborder
To: Herbs WA, HerbsCVD, Jerryherbs@home.com

just thought I'd pass this on
Carol

Date: 7/6/2000 3:28:27 PM Pacific Daylight Time
From: anita@heiling.com (Anita Heiling)
To: Herborder@aol.com

We had dinner at your wonderful restaurant on June 17 and we are... talking about it. We really enjoy fine wine and good food and have... a lot of great restaurants around the world but, I must say, your's to... the list! Just wanted to let you know.

Anita Heiling

Ron Zimmerman

From: Brian Riseland [brianr@fidesic.c...
Sent: Friday, August 31, 2001 1:32 P...
To: CustomerService@TheHerbfarr...
Subject: thanks!

Just wanted to say thanks for a wonderful ev... parents of a 10-month old, and are always on... time - but it was amazing how quickly we bot... had a truly fabulous evening to celebrate ou...

Thanks for the memento and for the extra spi...

Brian Riseland and Janett Garcia-Riseland

...day of my birthday dinner, January ...we had made reservations at the ...ce. When we got there it was an ...and distraught. We tried to think ...of the Herb Farm. I had ...you had the fire in the original

---

To the Herbfarm family -
We had the pleasure of expe... dinner with you on Sunday... I can not tell you h...

A Memoir . . . and a Cookbook
A Few Words from the Wife

IN OUR HOME kitchen, after teaching Ron how to make the vegetables, potatoes, and meat all ready to serve at the same time, I was essentially disbarred for thirty-plus years.

During the last year of his life, I suddenly became the one cooking. Of course, my first move was to organize the kitchen and the pantry! After a lot of whining, he was pleasantly surprised that when he got into the kitchen to cook for the photos for this book that it was, indeed, easier to find whatever he needed!

Even though we didn't share a kitchen well, Ron and I shared a business and a life. Now that he's not here, I find that even though I was not allowed to cook, I did, somehow, learn a lot about the thought process around cooking and food from this man. I hope, as you use this book, that you too take away some of the concepts and techniques if not the actual recipes.

> At The Herbfarm, the best recipes are strong suggestions; informing cooks on how to use their intuition. We work with unique ingredients that require cooks to assess ingredients daily, as nature changes them constantly. Each day a cook must assess their ingredients for their quality and flavor before making decisions on what to do next. Recipes are secondary to flavor.
>
> —Chris Weber, Chef

Having spent the better part of my life with Ron, I understand the power of this credo, the permission it gives you to create the life you most want to live, in the company of the people who help you be and do your best.

This book contains some of Ron's recipes, tips, and techniques that he felt were unique enough not to be found elsewhere. If we didn't invent them, maybe The Herbfarm was first to incorporate these ingredients and methods into a fine-dining experience. Most of the following recipes were never served at the restaurant exactly as they are printed.

Ron wrote this entire book (aside from the memoir section) using his favorite program, Adobe InDesign. I think he felt most comfortable writing to fit the pre-defined limited spaces he created for himself as he laid out each spread. Being both artistic and scientific, he enjoyed the combination of artistry and technical mastery in finding, editing, and positioning the photos or drawings.

All of the recipe spreads were created by Ron from researching and writing the recipes to designing the graphical layouts and choosing the fonts. From sourcing the proper china and props to cooking the dishes and directing the photo shoots, all of which were shot in our home.

During the last two weeks of his life, knowing he needed to finish this book, he desperately documented the special events and details that he felt were the most unique and identifiable aspects of The Herbfarm.

At the end of the book, where Ron wanted them to be, you will find the final pages he created in his favorite visual medium detailing the menu theme The 100-Mile Dinner. This theme began in 2008 and has evolved over the years into as local a meal as you could hope to find anywhere in this world. Ron believed it to be the best expression of what we strove for every day, in every meal we served.

Over the years of developing this theme and experimenting with the making of local baking powder, salt, and cheeses, many of the items in this 100-Mile meal have evolved into 10-Mile ingredients—as close as we would ever get to what Ron envisioned when he read *The Auberge of the Flowering Hearth* so many years ago.

He always wanted to create an experience for our guests where life could be as perfect as possible for just a few hours.

I hope you enjoy his creation!

Carrie

—Carrie Van Dyck

Ron in 1986 as the first Herbfarm chef

Food Guidelines at The Herbfarm

Regional Foods

    The Herbfarm will reflect the best of the foods of our region. We will not use foods which can be only grown or raised an another climate.

Seasonal Foods

    Menus should feature foods at the height of their quality. Therefore, major food items should be served in season. Any ingredients used out of season should be dried, fermented, or otherwise preserved by our farm and kitchen itself.

Highlight Herbs

    The Herbfarm is an herbal resource. The restaurant should experiment with these diverse flavors.

No Ingredients Repeated

    Menu must not repeat herbs or major ingredients / flavors from one course to the next.

Diners Challenged But Not Intimidated

    Herbfarm menus must offer something new for adventuresome diners while assuring that each preparation is so successful that even the hesitant will delight in the experience.

I wrote these guidelines before we opened on my parents' farm in 1986. They have served well, allowing us to truly discover the essence of the Northwest, and its terroir.

In the kitchen at The Herbfarm in Woodinville

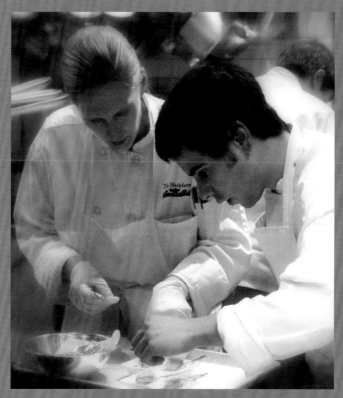

Spring bloom of the pie cherry at the entrance to The Herbfarm

SPRING

When the Robin Sings Again

WHEN THE LEAVES CLIMB up the mountains, we pull the curtain on spring. Plants and animals alike begin shaking off their winter dolor, quickening from their dark-days' slumber. Robins sing from barren branches. The wiry skeletons of alder and maple, woven all winter with fog and damp lichens, begin a yellow-green transformation. The trembling color

begins first along Puget Sound and in western valleys; then moves day by day as it creeps up the Cascade mountainsides, ultimately ending at timberline.

Now is a time of culinary transition. In the kitchen, we are still working with winter's deep flavors. From the fields, we're enjoying over-wintered beets, chards, and kales. Onions planted last fall divide sending up multiple green stalks. These are calçots, a welcome spring crop we introduced after a trip to Catalonia. If we like, bright red tulips become edible salad cups or a springtime sorbet.

But it's the wild plants and new farm greens that beckon. After thousands of years, these green-leaved plants have evolved to be the early risers of the season.

Now's the time for nettles in sauces, soups, and pasta stuffing. Tangy wild watercress awaits in clear shallow streams. The bigleaf maples fool the eye with edible flower clusters, which momently pass as leaves. Dip these in a light batter, quickly deep-fry, and dust with powdered sugar for an unusual delight. The first morels push through the forest duff. Time to get outdoors again.

Some Wild Spring Plants to Know

Wild Nodding Onion

This native onion looks like grass in the early season. Break a stem and smell it. If it smells like an onion, it is an onion. By May it begins to flower, with the head "nodding" down. Bulb and stem make a fine vinaigrette: Mix 6–8 onion bulbs with 1″-cut green stem, ½ cup neutral oil, ⅓ cup lemon juice, 3 Tbsp honey, salt, and pepper. Process in a blender until homogeneous.

Dandelion Flower Wine

Gather a pound of flower heads. Remove the green bases. Pour 1 gallon of boiling water over flowers. Steep 2 days. Bring mixture to a boil, add 6 cups of sugar and the juice of 4 oranges. Strain mixture. Cool to room temperature; add 1 tsp of yeast. Ferment in a clean gallon jug for 2 months. Siphon into sanitized bottles and age at least 6 months.

Licorice Fern

The rhizomes of licorice fern are at their culinary peak in March. The plant is most often found on the mossy bigleaf maples. To harvest, peel back the moss and tease off the rhizomes from their rootlet bases. Simmer a piece of licorice fern in a stock or sauce to add a hint of Pernod-like flavor.

Wild Ginger

Though not related to tropical ginger, our native is aromatic in the same way. The rhizome roots are more subtle and more peppery. The plant has flavored indigenous foods for centuries. Simmer the roots in water for a tea. Or use it to flavor custard-based ice creams.

Sweet Woodruff May Wine

This beautiful ground cover loves shady spots. Its distinctive aroma and flavor dosen't appear until the plant is dried. Traditional May Wine: Add 12 dried stems to 1 bottle of light white wine. Recork bottle and let sit overnight. Refrigerate. Strain out woodruff and serve.

Spruce Tip Lemonade

Rich in vitamin C, the spring growth of the spruce tree is a delightful flavoring for sorbets and drinks. Add 6 sprigs of spruce to 2 cups of boiling water. Steep over low heat 45 minutes. Strain and add juice of 3 lemons, ½ cup sugar, and 1 quart of water. Chill and serve.

WHY BOTHER FORAGING in a country with a surplus of so many domestic food products? Because, in part, foraging for food helps balance the feeling that we are living a secondhand sort of existence, and that we are in danger of losing all contact with the origins of life and the nature which nourishes it. —EUELL GIBBONS

Morels

The flower pictured is a trillium. Trilliums often indicate morel mushrooms in the area. Clean by quickly agitating in several changes of cold water. Pat dry on a towel. Sweat with butter and shallots. After 10 minutes increase heat, add a splash of Madeira, reduce, add more butter and season with salt and pepper. Heavenly!

Miner's Lettuce

This choice edible is a native of the Pacific coast. Though prized by Native Americans, the plant is named for the gold miners who ate it in the wilds as a salad or vegetable. It is rich in vitamin C. The flavor is slightly earthy. The so-called "Siberian" version has narrow leaves; the more common have round leaves with the stem in the center.

Wood Sorrel

What looks like a giant shamrock or a species of clover but tastes like a lemon tastes like a lemon masquerading as a leaf? Wood Sorrel. This shade-loving plant sports white blossoms starting in May. Other US wood sorrels have yellow flowers.

When cooking, you can substitute this wild sorrel for French sorrel. A few leaves in a salad add zest.

Salmonberry

About the time of the first spring salmon run, salmonberries push up their first shoots, which can be steamed and eaten. The flowers make a pretty garnish. When fully ripe (dark orange to dark red), the berries await as a trailside snack or an ingredient in Native American pemmican.

Oxeye Daisy

One of my favorite spring greens are the leaves of oxeye daisy. Though unassuming, the flavor is sensuous and sweet. Besides being a great base in a wild salad, the leaves make tasty fritters.

Before flowering like a daisy, you can pick the buds to pickle like a caper.

Stinging Nettle

Here in the Pacific Northwest, the stinging nettle is the granddaddy of green spring edibles. The earliest leaves are choicest, but you can harvest the tops of nettles well into summer. Nettles should be picked with gloves. The stings come from the underside of the leaves. Soups and sauces are its natural partners.

Two Little Eggs

Serves 6

FOR THE FIRST YEARS of The Herbfarm Restaurant, we served a myriad things in eggshells. Nature's natural packaging begs to be stuffed with layered flavors. You can pretty much make up your own egg delights. To remove an egg top, carefully use a sharp knife or an egg topper. After you've emptied each egg, be sure to remove the translucent membrane inside. Pastry bags are great for filling the eggs and for piping fancy rims or caps.

CREAMY SCRAMBLED EGGS & CAVIAR

6	Eggs, large, topped and cleaned
3 Tbsp	Heavy cream

Coarse salt, pepper, to taste

3 Tbsp	Butter, unsalted
2 Tbsp	Crème fraîche or sour cream
2 oz	Caviar, paddlefish or sturgeon

Whisk eggs with cream. Season with salt and pepper. Melt the butter over medium heat in a nonstick skillet. Add egg mixture. Stir gently with a rubber spatula to create curds, sliding eggs from the edges toward the center of the pan. Cook until just set.

Fill eggshells about ¾ full with the scrambled eggs. Then fill almost to the brim with the crème fraîche. If you want a little collar at the top of the egg, pipe a line of crème fraîche around the rim. Top with caviar.

SALMON MOUSSE WITH SALMON CAVIAR

4 oz	Cream cheese
2 oz	Smoked salmon, mousse or shredded
1 Tbsp	Lemon juice
½ tsp	Lemon zest

Salt, pepper, cayenne, to taste

6	Eggshells, empty, cleaned (reserve eggs for another use)
2 oz	Salmon roe (Ikura)

Mix the first 4 ingredients. Add salt, pepper, and cayenne to taste. Pipe or spoon into eggshells. Top with salmon roe.

Tea Smoked Morel & Caraway Broth with Mushroom-Stuffed Morels

Serves 4

ALMOST SINCE OPENING day at The Herbfarm restaurant, we've used the "secret" affinity between wild morels and caraway. With this dish, we imbued our broth with morels. If you have the time, lightly smoking the mushrooms with black tea or fruit wood chips will add another subtle layer of forest flavor to the caraway imbued broth.

STUFFED MORELS

12–16 oz	Mushrooms, fresh, quartered, assorted, such as well-cleaned morels, white button, porcini, crimini, or shiitakes
16	Morels, large, cleaned, for stuffing
1	Shallot, large, minced
1	Garlic clove, minced
4 Tbsp	Butter, unsalted, more as needed
12 sprigs	Parsley, Italian, fresh, chopped
¼ cup	Cream
	Salt, pepper, to taste
⅛ tsp	Nutmeg, grated

Melt 1 tablespoon butter in a large skillet. Add shallots and garlic. Cook over medium heat until soft. Transfer to a food processor with assorted mushrooms and pulse until finely chopped.

Melt 3 tablespoons butter in the skillet. Add the chopped mixture and cook, stirring frequently until all juices are released and the mixture is dry. Deglaze with cream. Season with salt, pepper, and nutmeg. Stir in the parsley.

Cool, and transfer to a pastry bag. Pipe into large morels. Sauté the stuffed morels in a little butter, turning to cook all sides until heated through. Place in bowl and ladle on the warm broth. Garnish with picked parsley leaves.

MOREL & CARAWAY BROTH

1 oz	Morels (about ½ cup), dried, whole, brushed to remove grit. Optional: Smoke lightly over black tea or fruit wood chips (see directions below)
5 cups	Beef stock, low sodium, preferably rich homemade. Or use chicken stock for a lighter yet flavorful broth.
3 Tbsp	Butter, unsalted
⅓ cup	Yellow onion, diced
2	Garlic cloves, peeled, cut in half
1½ tsp	Caraway seeds
	Salt, to taste

Rehydrate the dried morels in hot stock for 20 minutes. Agitate to remove remaining grit, strain the liquid through a fine sieve. Reserve both separately.

Melt butter in a medium saucepan. Add onions, garlic, and caraway seeds. Sweat for 5 minutes. Add the stock and simmer 30 minutes. Strain out the onions and caraway, reserving the liquid.

Slice hydrated morels into rounds. Add to pan along with the broth. Simmer 20 minutes. Keep warm.

The Beekeeper's Smoker

We've put the stovetop smoking method to work for many years. It's great for fish and vegetables. But, about 5 years ago I tried our beehive smoker with the same foil tenting. It worked like a champ. It was so easy to drop in wood chips, hit them with a torch, and pump smoke under the foil. Bee smokers are available online for $20 or less.

How to Smoke on Your Stovetop

If you have a smoker, by all means use it. To smoke on the stove, place a tablespoon of wood chips in the middle of a pan. Set a similar-sized rack on top.

Place food on rack and tent everything with aluminun foil, leaving space above to circulate smoke around the food.

Place tented pan over a stove burner. Heat until smoke leaks out of foil. Turn off heat. Let set 10 minutes then Repeat. Remove food after 30 minutes total.

Bruce's Naftaly's Nettle Soup

Serves 4

EVEN BEFORE WE opened our restaurant, chef Bruce Naftaly advised us on our kitchen-to-be as we converted my folks' garage into a countryside restaurant. He also let me work and learn alongside him in his Seattle restaurant, Le Gourmand.

I first met Bruce when he cheffed in Seattle at Robert Rosellini's The Other Place. His saucing of dishes was extraordinary. Created in the best French tradition, they mesmerized with flavor and balance. You could have made a whole meal just eating his sauces, which Naftaly insists are integral to a dish.

Chef Bruce Naftaly

1 Tbsp	Butter, unsalted
1	Leek, medium, white and light green cut into ½" slices
½	Onion, cut into 6 wedges
2	Shallots, peeled, quartered
1	Potato, yellow, quartered (6 oz)
4 cups	Stock, chicken or vegetable
¼ cup	Lovage (or celery) leaves
6–8 oz	Nettles, leaves picked, stems discarded
Salt, pepper, to taste	
2 Tbsp	Chives, thinly sliced

A few dots of sauce on a plate isn't a companion to a dish. If you're saucing a preparation, you should be able to eat the goodness with a spoon or mop it up with bread. Naftaly's Nettle Soup invites mopping to the last drop. For a cream of nettle soup, add a few tablespoons of half-and-half or cream. Use this soup as well to sauce fish, oysters, and similar dishes.

Melt butter in a medium saucepan. Sauté shallots, leek, and onions until soft (don't brown). Add potato quarters and stock. Simmer covered on medium until the potatoes are cooked, 30–40 minutes. Separately, blanch the nettles in salted water for 2 minutes and shock in ice water to retain the color. Squeeze water out of nettles.

To finish, add nettles and lovage leaves to soup, then purée with blender. Season to taste. If too thick, thin with a bit more water or stock. Serve hot, garnished with chives or chive flowers.

Dandelion Crowns with Shiitake and Pancetta

Serves 4

SO COMMON THEY'RE considered a pest, the dandelion presents lots of culinary options. Roots, leaves, and flowers are all edible. For this dish, dig the plant before it flowers, otherwise, it is certainly too bitter. Leave a quarter-inch of root and trim the leaves to create these "crowns." Wash well and agitate in several changes of water in a bowl. Soak in cold water to keep them refreshed and plump.

To set the color, blanch for a minute in salted water, then chill in ice water.

The flavor of the crowns is somewhere between young artichokes and celery.

Dandelion crowns cleaned, trimmed, and ready to cook.

24	Dandelion crowns, blanched
1	Shallot, minced
2 oz	Pancetta, diced or sliced
2 oz	Shiitake mushrooms (about 1 cup)
1	Garlic clove, minced
2 Tbsp	Neutral oil
Pinch	Red pepper flakes
1 Tbsp	Red wine vinegar
½ tsp	Sugar
2 tsp	Soy or fish sauce
	Salt, pepper to taste (remember, the pancetta is already salty!)

Preheat a large skillet on medium. Add oil and shallots. Sweat until translucent. Add mushrooms and sauté until they begin to brown. Add pancetta, garlic, pepper flakes, sugar, vinegar, and soy sauce. Cook 3 minutes.

Add dandelions, reduce heat, and cook, stirring often, for 2 minutes to coat the dandelion crowns well. Taste and season with salt and black pepper, to taste.

Asparagus Soup with Crayfish & Nodding Onion Sauce

Serves 4

THE NORTHWEST'S NATIVE "Signal" crayfish are abundant in lakes and streams. But they can be hard to find in the market. In the early years of the restaurant, I trapped these wild natives from nearby streams. If you can't find these little "lobsters," use precooked Louisiana crawdads.

CRAYFISH

32–48	Live crayfish, depending on size
2 tsp	Celery salt
1 tsp	Chili flakes
1	Bay leaf, preferably fresh

Bring a large pot of water with celery salt, chili flakes, and a crushed bay leaf to a hard boil. Add live crayfish. When the water returns to a rolling boil, cook 60 seconds and drain. Shell the tails. If the crayfish haven't been purged, remove the dark intestinal tube. Cover tails so they don't dry out.

ASPARAGUS SOUP

36 oz	Asparagus, thick stalks preferred
3–4	Nodding onion bulbs, minced finely, or a large shallot, minced finely
4 Tbsp	Butter, unsalted
¾ cup	Chicken stock, rich
1 cup	Whipping cream

Salt, pepper, cayenne, to taste

Bring a pot of salted water to boil. Cut 8–12 three-inch asparagus tips. Cook them 2–3 minutes, then plunge into ice water to set the color.

Snap off the woody ends of the uncooked stalks and discard. Cut the remaining uncooked stalks into ½-inch pieces. Simmer these cut pieces in the salted boiling water until tender. Drain, but reserve a little of the cooking water for thinning the soup if needed.

In a medium saucepan, melt 2 tablespoons butter. Sauté the minced shallot until translucent. Add the chicken stock and bring to a simmer. Then add the cream and cooked ½-inch pieces of asparagus. Simmer 30 seconds. Remove from heat and purée in a blender. Season with salt (if necessary), pepper, and cayenne to taste.

NODDING ONION SAUCE

Makes 1 cup

1	Egg
3–4	Nodding onion bulbs (or 3 cloves grated garlic)
4 tsp	Mustard, prepared yellow
¾ cup	Neutral oil
4 Tbsp	Lemon juice

Salt, to taste

Pulse the egg in a blender until frothy. Add wild onion (or garlic) and mustard. Blend. Gradually add the oil until the mixture emulsifies. Stir in lemon juice and salt.

FINISHING AND SERVING

Reheat soup and whisk in 2 tablespoons butter. Reheat the asparagus tips in remaining butter. Add crayfish tails with salt, pepper, and a pinch of cayenne. Remove from heat as soon as tails are hot. Divide soup between 4 bowls. Arrange tails and asparagus tips on top. Add a drizzle of the onion sauce.

Forest Tea

Makes 1 quart

FOR A WILD-FOOD dinner, we wanted to combine flavors gathered from the forest floor and treetops. Herbfarm chef Chris Weber devised this wild and welcoming tea to greet our nightly guests.

2 qt	Water
¼ cup	Sugar
1 cup	Wild mushrooms, dried
2	6″ sprigs (tips) Douglas fir needles
3	6″ sprigs of red cedar needles
4	Fresh bay leaves

In a large pot, dissolve the sugar in the water. Add mushrooms and bring to a boil. Turn off heat and add other ingredients. Stir. Steep 10 minutes. Strain. Enjoy it warm or cold.

Sea Bean Sea Salt

Makes ½ cup

A **SALT MARSH PLANT** with many aliases—salicornia, marsh samphire, sea asparagus, glasswort, pickle weed, saltwort—"sea beans" have become the name of choice here in the Pacific Northwest. Raw or blanched briefly, it is a great garnish or accompaniment to many seafoods. Don't salt the plant, though, as it is naturally full of its own briny seasoning.

As I learned, you can also make a wonderful green marine salt from the plant. The process is simple. Gather your own "beans," or check local Asian markets in May and June. Later in the season, a tough thread forms inside. At this stage, they can't be eaten whole. But you can still turn your fresh beans into this real "sea salt."

1½ lb	Fresh sea beans
	Oven or dehydrator
	Mortar & Pestle

Bring a large pot of water to a boil. Blanch the sea beans for 60 seconds. Drain and immediately chill in ice water.

Dry the sea beans in a rolled-up towel. Place in a 140°F oven with the door slightly cracked open. Or spread them out in a food dehydrator and run it overnight. They are done when they're slightly crunchy.

Grind the lot with a spice grinder and finish, as needed, in a mortar and pestle. Sift to remove any large pieces. Use as a finishing salt for seafood and vegetables.

Crispy Skin Salmon with Lemon Verbena and Tuberous Begonia

Serves 4

TO THE BEST of my knowledge, The Herbfarm may have been the first to cultivate and cook with lemon verbena and tuberous begonia here in America. Lemon Verbena sports a citrusy perfume that spellbinds, while the colorful edible flowers of the Tuberous Begonia have scarcely any aroma at all. But the begonia petals are imbued with a bracing citric tang. Added to the sauce just before serving, the blossoms melt into an unctuous dressing with streaks of their Crayola color. The Herbfarm served a similar dish to acclaim for several years.

SALMON

1⅔ lb	Salmon fillet, skin on

Salt, pepper, Chinese 5 spice, to taste

3 Tbsp	Neutral oil, grapeseed or canola (not olive or butter)

Heat oven to 350°F.

Remove pin bones (if any) from salmon with pliers. Trim into four 6 oz portions. Season with salt and pepper on all sides. Sprinkle the Chinese 5 spice liberally on the skin side only.

Heat an ovenproof skillet until medium-hot. Add the oil.

Lay the salmon skin-side down in the the skillet. Press with a spatula or cooking weight to ensure even contact. Cook for 2–3 minutes then transfer to the oven. Bake 4 to 5 minutes. Salmon is done when firm to the touch; don't overcook.

SAUCE AND FINISHING

2	Shallots, minced
2½ Tbsp	White wine vinegar (or lime juice)
1½ Tbsp	Dry white wine
1½ Tbsp	White Port
4	Lemon verbena leaves
3 Tbsp	Cream
6 Tbsp	Unsalted butter
1–2	Tuberous begonia flowers

Ikura, as much as you like

2 tsp	Parsley, Italian, chopped

SAUCE

Melt a tablespoon of butter in a small saucepan. Add minced shallots and sweat on medium heat. Add vinegar (or lime juice), white wine, white Port, and Lemon Verbena leaves.

Simmer slowly until most of the liquid has evaporated.

Remove the leaves.

Add cream. Bring to a boil and remove from heat.

FINISHING

Bring sauce back to a boil. Remove from heat. Whisk in the remaining butter a little at a time. Salt to taste. With scissors, snip begonia blossom into fine shreds, letting the pieces fall into the sauce.

Plate salmon—skin-side up—and surround with the sauce. Garnish with tuberous begonia petals. Add a dollop of ikura. Sprinkle with chopped parsley.

Variation with Lemon Verbena Oil

Sauté a half dozen lemon verbena leaves in ¼ cup of a neutral oil such as grapeseed. Add a pinch of salt and grind with a mortar and pestle. Pass through a fine sieve.

Cook the salmon as per the recipe above.

Plate salmon and spoon the flavored oil over and around the fish. Garnish with snipped tuberous begonias, if you wish.

Trout Sheridan Anderson
with Brown Butter, Green Olives & Hazelnuts

Serves 4

Sheridan Anderson by Bob Hise

THIS HOMAGE TO Sheridan Anderson—artist, flyfisher, author, and raconteur—is a re-creation of a trout preparation improvised in the Sierra Nevada on the night I first met him. The brown butter sauce is made right in the pan. Chopped green olives add a salty-acid punch while hazelnuts give a nice sweet crunch and enhance the nutty flavor of the sauce. Have all of the ingredients ready. The cooking and finishing doesn't take much time.

2	Trout, whole, filleted, deboned, skin on
¼ cup	Flour with salt pepper added
4 Tbsp	Butter
3 Tbsp	Northwest hazelnuts or peanuts, chopped, sautéd in a Tbsp of oil, salted
4 Tbsp	Castlevetrano olives, pitted, coarsely chopped
¼ cup	Lemon juice or 3 Tbsp white wine vinegar
1 Tbsp	Parsley, Italian, chopped, optional

Pat the fresh trout sides dry. Season with salt and pepper. Dredge in flour. Shake off excess.

Heat half of the butter in a large frying pan over high heat. Add the halves of trout and brown on both sides. Lower heat and cook until the fish flakes, 4–8 minutes depending on the size of the fish. Remove trout and keep warm on a plate.

Meanwhile, wipe the pan clean. Add remaining 2 tablespoons butter. Cook over medium heat until butter just begins to brown. Add half of the lemon juice. Add the olives and chopped nuts to warm through. Plate the fish and divide the sauce among the fillets. Season with salt, pepper, and remaining lemon juice to taste. Garnish with the optional parsley.

THE PACIFIC NORTHWEST is ideal for raising lamb.

With its mild marine climate, the valleys of western Washington and Oregon grow some of the lushest grasses in the world. Sheep thrive on the rich pastures with winters not too cold and halcyon summers of little stress.

The Herbfarm sources its lamb from as close as the Snoqualmie Valley, a few minutes east of the restaurant. There you'll find shepherd Jeff Rogers. He breeds his Clun Forest ewes with UK Suffolk rams for April's lambing season. His lambs graze only on pasture grasses and are certified 100 percent USDA organic.

Photo credit Chris Weber

Rack of Lamb with Thyme and Grainy Mustard

Serves 4

WE'VE SERVED THIS EASY LAMB DISH in the restaurant and at my home many times over the years. By trimming off all of the fat, the "gamey" quality is removed. Salting the meat first draws out moisture, firms the flesh, and makes it easy for the herbs to adhere to the outside. Improvise by adding a little freshly chopped sage, chives, savory, marjoram, and/or rosemary. This recipe adapts well to the addition of these herbs. But thyme and parsley are the essentials. The grainy mustard adds just the right zesty counterpoint.

RACK OF LAMB

4	Lamb loin chops or rack, bone in, 1¼–1½ lb total, 1½" to 2" thick

Salt, pepper, to taste

2 tsp	Dried thyme
1 Tbsp	Parsley, Italian, chopped fine
1 Tbsp	Fresh thyme leaves, chopped fine
4	Garlic cloves, in their skins
2 Tbsp	Neutral oil such as grapeseed
1 Tbsp	Butter, diced

Preheat oven to 400°F. Trim off the fat and scrape the bones clean. Salt and pepper each chop and set aside a few minutes while you chop the herbs. Mix 2 tablespoons parsley with remaining fresh and dried herbs, then press the mixture all over the outsides of the lamb.

Heat a skillet to medium heat, add the oil and the cloves of garlic. Cook garlic cloves for 3 or 4 minutes. Push the cloves to the edge of the pan.

Raise the heat until the oil is smoking. Sear the chops in the hot skillet 2 minutes each on the large sides and 1 minute on the edges. Dot the chops with half of the butter then transfer the skillet to the preheated oven. After 5 minutes, remove from oven and place the skillet on medium heat. Flip the chops over, baste with the pan juices and cook until the internal temperature reaches 125°F on an instant-reading thermometer, about 3 more minutes.

Transfer the chops to a warmed plate, loosely covering them with foil. The lamb will continue to cook from the residual heat as it rests. Reserve pan for sauce.

SAUCE

½ cup	Water
½ cup	Whole-grain mustard
1 Tbsp	Extra-virgin olive oil
1 Tbsp	Butter
1 Tbsp	Parsley, Italian, chopped

With the skillet on medium heat, add water and scrape up the brown bits with a wooden spoon. Crush the garlic to release the cooked cloves from the papery skin. Remove and discard garlic skins. Add the mustard, olive oil, and butter. Bring to a simmer and stir to combine sauce. Remove from heat. Stir in parsley and any juices from the resting lamb chops. Add more water if the mustard sauce is too thick.

SERVE

To serve, spoon the sauce on warmed dinner plates and place the chops or sliced rack on top.

Easy Sides and Garnishes

NEW POTATOES: Steam or boil until tender. Toss with butter, parsley and salt.

SPRING PEAS: Boil or steam 5–6 minutes. Shock in ice water. Rewarm with butter and salt.

CURRANT-HORSERADISH: Mix ⅔ parts red currant jam with ⅓ part prepared horseradish.

Salad from the Meadow's Edge

Serves as many as you have ingredients for

A SALAD STRAIGHT FROM field, herb bed, and garden is a world in microcosm. Our Meadow's Edge Salad can be either tossed in three parts or more elaborately composed. It should be a combination of leafy greens as the base or foundation; herbs for accents; wild edibles, and culinary flowers for color and flavor. Chose ingredients from the three columns below. If you can find tender oxeye daisy leaves, use a lot of them for a wild, sweet base.

BASE GREENS
The foundation
Arugula
Chickweed
Chicory
Cress
Edible Chrysanthemum Leaves
Dandelion Greens, Young
Endive
Kale
Lamb's Quarter
Lettuce: Leafy & Iceberg
Miner's Lettuce
Mustard Greens
Orach
Oxeye Daisy Leaves
Purslane
Shepherd's Purse
Spinach
Violet Leaves
Watercress

HERBS
Taste and use sparingly
Basil
Chervil
Chives
Cilantro
Dill or Fennel
Lemon Balm
Lovage or Celery Leaves
Marjoram
Spearmint
Parsley
Sorrel
Sweet Cicely & Tarragon

EDIBLE FLOWERS
Do not toss fragile flowers with dressing
Borage Flowers
Tuberous Begonia Petals
Calendula Petals
Day Lily, Flower or Young Root
Daisy, Oxeye or English
Honeysuckles
Lilac Petals
Nasturtium Flowers & Leaves
Pansies
Pea Blossoms (but Not Sweet Peas)
Carnation Petals
Roses, Tulips, Violas

Meadow's Edge Salad Dressing

Makes 1½ cups

THIS IS THE SALAD DRESSING we developed during the first year at The Herbfarm Restaurant. It proved a keeper, and is wonderful with any green salad. Nut oils tend to oxidize or turn rancid in a matter of weeks. So if you're keeping this around for extended periods, put it in the fridge. Be sure dressing is at room temperature before dressing the greens—but not any edible flowers if you elect to use them.

8 Tbsp	Walnut oil
8 Tbsp	Extra-virgin olive oil
5 Tbsp	Sherry vinegar, aged
4 Tbsp	Balsamic vinegar
2 tsp	Dijon-style prepared mustard
1	Garlic clove, minced

Salt and pepper, to taste

Be sure all salad ingredients are reasonably dry so the dressing sticks. Combine all dressing ingredients. Whisk or shake well. Pour a little in the bottom of a generous bowl. Add salad greens and mix with your hands to completely coat all pieces.

Tip

In colder months, reverse the amounts of sherry and balsamic vinegars to complement the deeper tones of winter greens.

Bigleaf Maple Blossom Ice Cream

Servers 6

Maple blossom and sap-tapping "spile" for syrup.

MANY SECRETS RESIDE with the bigleaf maple (*Acer macrophyllum*), the world's largest in the genus.

We flavored one of our first spring ice creams at The Herbfarm with the April–May flower clusters. Their subtle honey-maple flavor hides in the long blooms.

We also experimented with tapping the trunks of these maples, then reducing the sap for a maple syrup. There's now a commercial supply. Adding a touch of the syrup will amp up the mapleness of this wild dessert.

ICE CREAM BASE

1⅓ cup	Half-and-half
2⅔ cup	Heavy cream
¾ cup	Sugar
5	Egg yolks
4–6	Maple blossom clusters
Pinch	salt

Tip

Use maple blossoms right up to the point where a few winged maple seeds have begun to form at the base of the flower cluster.

INFUSE THE ICE CREAM BASE

In a medium saucepan, combine the first 3 ingredients. Bring to a simmer. Add the flowers and the pinch of salt. Turn off the heat.Steep for 45 minutes. Strain out blossoms.

THICKEN THE BASE

In a bowl, gently whisk the yolks. Add the warm base a bit at a time, whisking constantly. Transfer mixture back into the saucepan and reheat over medium heat until it thickens and will coat the back of a spoon. Strain through a fine-mesh strainer. Set over an ice-water bath to chill. Refrigerate at least one hour before spinning.

FREEZE AND SERVE

Spin in an ice cream machine until stiff, then transfer to the freezer for at lease one hour to set up. Scoop and serve. Garnish with a sugared piece of blossom or drizzle with bigleaf maple syrup.

Spring Tulip Sorbet

Makes 4 cups

IN SPRING, when there is little color in the garden, the brave beauty of the tulip is a hopeful and uplifting sign.

Tulip petals are not only edible, but they're surprisingly good, tasting much like fresh green peas with a touch of pepper. The Herbfarm's 5-acre farm has grown tulips for many years. The kitchen transforms the petals into this sorbet.

For our luncheons in the 1990s, we presented the sorbet as an intermezzo before the entrée. It also makes a refreshing light dessert.

SORBET

10–20	Tulip petals
1 cup	White sugar, divided
3 cups	Water
1 cup	Riesling wine
3 Tbsp	Lemon juice (or to taste)

GARNISHING

Tulip petals (and mint leaves, optional)

Note: We have found that Red Emperor tulips provide the deepest flavor and an intense hue.

MAKE THE SORBET BASE

Combine tulip petals and half of the sugar in a food processor or blender. Liquify.

Add the remaining sugar, water, and the wine. Stir.

Let stand 30 minutes, then strain through a very fine strainer or layers of cheese cloth. Add lemon juice to taste. Sorbet base can be made in advance.

FREEZING

Spin sorbet base in an ice cream machine until stiff, then transfer to the freezer for at least one hour to set up. Or pour in a metal bowl in the freezer and stir and scrape with a fork every hour until set for an icy granita.

SERVING

Set a tulip petal or two in a chilled wineglass. Add a scoop of sorbet. Garnish with optional mint leaves.

Deep red, juicy, sweet Skagit Valley Shuksan
Strawberries are best eaten the day of picking.
Makes the world's best strawberry shortcake.

Summer

In the Realm of Sol

AS ANYONE LIVING HERE will tell you, "Summer begins the day after July 4th!" And what glorious summers. Weeks of clear skies. Just the right kiss of heat. And no apparent humidity.

You know it's summertime when the tender greens of spring toughen and fade, being replaced week by week with an abundance of flowers, soft fruits, berries, and vegetables. The big "keeper crops" of hard squashes, corn, wheat, apples, quince, potatoes, nuts, and their lot arrive come Autumn, what we call at The Herbfarm, "The Feasting Season."

When summer finally arrives, our kitchen relishes the cornucopia of pleasures, more choices than we can manage on any given menu.

Produce pours in from our farm down the valley. We forage for wild berries—salal, huckleberries, blueberries, and blackberries. From the fields, we're bringing in marionberries, currants, gooseberries, boysenberries, raspberries, strawberries, cherries, and the first grapes. And, of course, the first golden chanterelles mushrooms and long-awaited tomatoes and peppers.

The warming days of summer stir too the local waters as we serve the little-known but abundant native crayfish, firm ocean-caught salmon from Neah Bay, halibut from Alaska, and, when we're lucky, the occasional jar of fresh sturgeon caviar from the Columbia River.

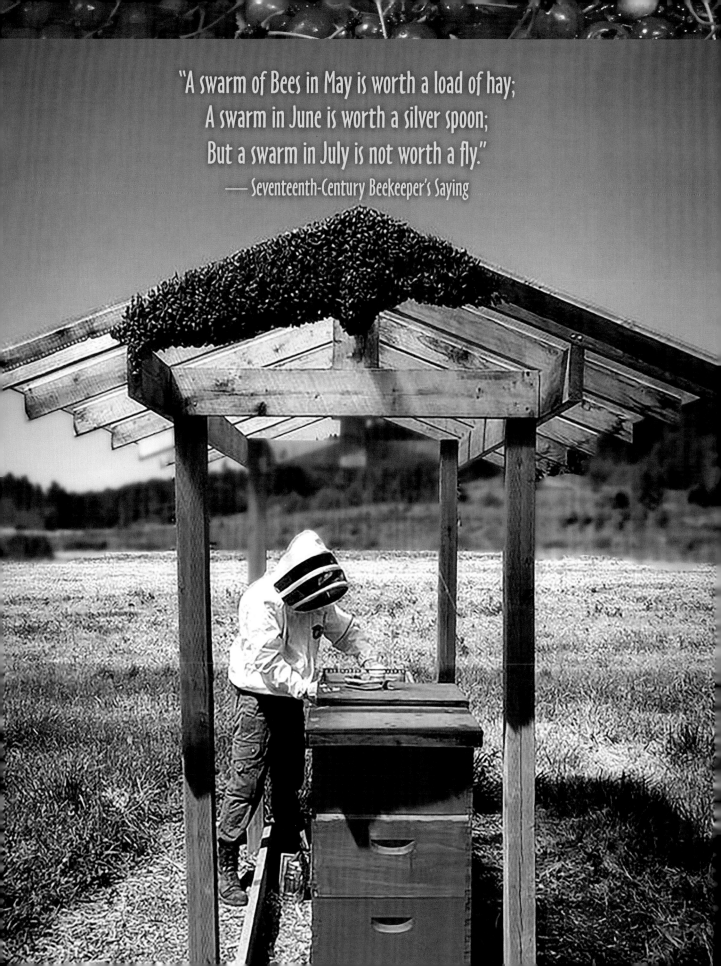

"A swarm of Bees in May is worth a load of hay;
A swarm in June is worth a silver spoon;
But a swarm in July is not worth a fly."
— Seventeenth-Century Beekeeper's Saying

Herbal Tips to Up Your Cooking Game

THOUGH EACH HERB has its own distinctive flavor, you can usually substitute one for another within their flavor families. Adaptability is an important kitchen skill. Stretch your creativity—or choose a substitute—if you don't have a recipe's specific herb.

Herbal Flavor Categories & Substitution Suggestions

Pungent	Rosemary, thymes, oregano, marjoram (mid-to-late season), sage, some basils
Minty	Mints, balms, some basils, catnip, monarda, perilla, costmary, hyssop, wintergreen
Lemony	Lemon balm, lemon thyme, lemon verbena, lemon basil, lemongrass, some scented geraniums, sorrel
Floral	Roses, lavender, violets, jasmine, honeysuckle, saffron, some scented geraniums
Fruity	Sage, fruit-scented sage, pineapple sage, sweet woodruff, bergamot, some scented geraniums
Spicy	Pinks, ginger, some basil
Anise	Anise, tarragon, chervil, fennel, anise hyssop, Mexican marigold mint, sweet cicely, licorice, Irish lace marigold le
Menthol	California bay laurel, horehound, some thymes
Bitter	Rue, costmary, horehound, hops, feverfew, tansy

Rules of Thumb

- **Don't overpower a dish** with an herb. Strive for subtlety and harmony of flavors. An herb should complement—not dominate—the main ingredient.

- **Dried herbs are typically stronger** than freshly cut herbs. They usually contribute a somewhat different flavor.

- **The dried herb rule of thumb**: A dried herb is typically three times stronger than when fresh. If a recipe calls for a tablespoon of a fresh herb, substitute a teaspoon of the dried produce. Or vice versa, except for bay and rosemary, which are similar dry or fresh.

Proven Herbal & Food Affinities

Beef	Bay, chives, cumin, garlic, hot peppers, marjoram, oregano, rosemary, savory, thyme, ginger root
Breads	Anise, caraway, coriander, dill, marjoram, oregano, rosemary, thyme
Cheese	Basil, chives, curry, dill, fennel, garlic, marjoram, oregano, sage, thyme
Eggs	Basil, dill, garlic, oregano, parsley
Fish	Chervil, dill, fennel, French tarragon, garlic, parsley, rosemary, thyme
Fruit	Candied angelica, anise, cinnamon, ground coriander, candied ginger, lemon verbena, mints, nutmeg, rose geranium
Lamb	Garlic, marjoram, oregano, rosemary, chervil
Pork	Coriander, cumin, garlic, ginger, hot pepper, sage, thyme
Poultry	Chives, oregano, rosemary, savory, sage
Salads	Basil, borage, salad burnet, chives, cilantro, dill, French tarragon, garlic chives, sweet marjoram, parsley
Soups	Bay, French tarragon, lovage, marjoram, parsley, savory, rosemary, thyme
Vegetables	Basil, chervil, chives, dill, French tarragon, marjoram, mint, oregano, parsley, thyme

- **Don't overcook fresh herbs**. Add fresh herbs during the last few minutes of a dish's preparation.

- **Store your dried herbs** in glass or pottery jars. Keep herbs and spices away from light and heat.

- **If you're not familiar** with an herb, mix it with softened butter or cottage cheese. Let set for an hour, then eat it on a plain cracker to experience its flavor.

Summer Rosemary Lemonade

Serves 4

AT OUR **FALL CITY** location, we served this rosemary lemonade every summer. The recipe is simple. The flavor, rewarding.

6 cups	Water, divided use
6	Rosemary sprigs, 4–5″ long
½ cup	Simple sugar syrup (¼ cup sugar + ¼ cup water)
3	Lemons juiced (about ½ cup)

MAKE THE ROSEMARY TEA

Boil 2 cups of water in a small saucepan. Add the sprigs of rosemary, cover the pan and let them steep over very low heat for 45 minutes. Strain and reserve the liquid. This will make enough tea concentrate for 2–3 batches.

SQUEEZE THE LEMONS

Roll the lemons on a hard surface to help release the juices. Cut and squeeze the lemons. Strain out the seeds.

BLEND THE ROSEMARY LEMONADE

Begin with remaining 4 cups of cold water. Add ½ cup of the rosemary tea concentrate, ½ cup of the syrup (or to taste), and ½ cup of lemon juice (again to taste).

Chill and serve over ice.

Herbfarm Haymakers Switchel

Serves 4

WHEN WE FIRST OPENED the restaurant, we needed a nonalcoholic beverage. This blend of herbs proved so popular that we offered it for years. The idea is based on one of the many kinds of nineteenth-century drinks that hardworking men would drink to quench thirst in the fields.

¼ cup	Mint leaves, fresh, chopped
¼ cup	Lemon balm leaves, fresh, chopped
2 tbsp	Lemon juice, squeezed from a lemon
¼ cup	Orange juice, squeezed from an orange
¼ cup	Simple sugar syrup (1½ tbsp sugar + ¼ cup water)
2 qt	Ginger ale

In a medium pot, bring a quarter cup of water with 1½ tablespoons of sugar to a boil. Turn off the heat and stir to be sure sugar has dissolved.

Add the chopped mint and lemon balm. Let stand 10 minutes.

Add the lemon juice. Let the mixture steep for 45 minutes, then add the juice squeezed from an orange.

Strain liquid through a fine strainer. Press firmly to extract all of the herbal flavors.

When ready to serve, add the sparkling ginger ale and serve with ice and a fresh mint leaf.

Summer Quenchers

Aromatics &
Fun Sippers

Marriage of Mints Tea

Fino Sherry with Rosemary Magic

Per Serving: 1 rosemary sprig with ice cube

ONCE IN A WHILE, serendipity strikes. Such was the case as I sipped a cold dry sherry before dinner one evening. I twirled and played with a rosemary sprig and dropped it in the sherry. When I brought the glass to my nose, the combination of herb and wine was revelatory. While you can place a sprig in a glass, I like to anchor the bottom in an ice cube. To make ahead, bring a small pot of water to boil. Blanch the rosemary 10 seconds and plunge in cold water. Place the stem base in an ice cube tray with water and freeze. Use one sprig and cube per glass. Rosemary goes best with chilled fino, manzanilla, or palomino sherry. Sherry likes almonds, green olives, and smoked fish.

Bloody Mary Lovage Straw

Per Serving: 1 lovage straw

LOVAGE'S LEAVES AND upper stalks look like celery. But lovage's savoriness is more robust. The taste is stronger, deeper, and darker. An endearing quality of the plant is the hollow stems. Cut and trim stems like soda straws. Anything sipped through your homegrown straws will take on a celery flavor: bloody Marys and tomato juice are obvious candidates. These "straws" will be the delight of your party.

Marriage of Mints Tea

Serves 4–6

HOT OR ICED, this mint infusion is welcome at any time. What sets this infusion apart is its aromatics originate from two different mints. If you make the base tea with peppermint, use a spearmint leaf in the cup. Or vice versa. Brew with either dried or fresh mint for the base flavor. If using dried mint, pour rapidly boiling water over a couple of tablespoons of the mint in a teapot with 16 ounces of water. If using fresh mint, start with a half dozen good-sized sprigs—a teaspoon of sugar in the pot pops the flavor without drawing attention. Let steep 5 minutes.

To serve, place a single fresh mint leaf in a cup and pour the hot tea over. If serving as an iced tea, crush the leaf first. Feel free to experiment with other mints, too.

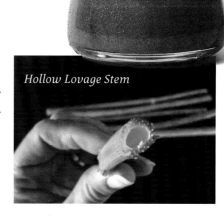

Hollow Lovage Stem

Caramelized Onion Tart with Lemon Thyme (as an Appetizer or First Course)

Serves 8 | 9-inch tart

THIS IS AN HERBFARM take on an enduring classic—the onion tart. Straightforward and uncomplicated, this hors d'oeuvre is also sophisticated and rustic at the same time. The satisfying sweet savoriness comes from the caramelization of the onions. Don't rush the caramelization and you'll have created something irresistible.

TART SHELL

1½ cups	Flour
8 Tbsp	Butter, cold
Pinch	Salt
1	Egg, lightly beaten
2 Tbsp	Cold water, or more as needed

FILLING

3–4	Onions, yellow, large, peeled, ¼" sliced
1	Bacon slice, julienned crosswise (bacon is optional, but adds umami)
4 Tbsp	Butter, unsalted (or bacon fat)
1 Tbsp	Balsamic vinegar
3 Tbsp	Lemon thyme, fresh, finely chopped, divided use
½ cup	Heavy cream
1	Egg yolk

Salt, pepper, nutmeg, to taste
Red pepper flakes, for garnish

Place flour, butter, and salt in food processor. Pulse until the mixture is the size of peas. Transfer to a bowl. Add beaten egg and cold water, tossing with your fingers, until the dough holds together. If dry, add additional cold water, a tablespoon at a time until dough forms.

Place dough on a lightly floured board. Roll it into a rectangle; fold in thirds, and roll again. Fold the piece in thirds once more, then wrap in plastic wrap. Refrigerate for at least 30 minutes.

Butter a 9″ tart pan. Roll dough on a floured surface until it is large enough to fit the pan. Line the pan with the pastry and press to fill edges. Prick the bottom all over with a fork. Roll a rolling pin over the top of the pan to trim the pastry edges. Cut a disc of aluminum foil to fit the bottom of the tart pan. Lay foil circle on top of the dough. Chill the pan for 30 minutes before baking.

BAKE THE TART SHELL

Heat oven to 325°F.

Bake the tart shell for 30–35 minutes. When the edges are lightly browned, remove foil and bake 5 minutes more. Remove fully baked tart shell from oven.

MAKE THE FILLING

While the shell is baking, heat butter and bacon (if using) in a heavy saucepan. Add onions and cook slowly, stirring until they turn very soft and light brown, about 30–40 minutes. Remove from heat.

In a separate small bowl, beat the egg yolk into the cream. Stir the mixture into the onions along with vinegar and 2 tablespoons of the lemon thyme. Season with salt, pepper, and a few good grates of nutmeg, to taste.

BAKING & FINISHING

Add the filling into the tart shell while still warm. Sprinkle remaining thyme and pepper flakes on top.

Return tart to oven. Turn off oven and let tart bake 1 hour in the residual heat. Remove from oven and let cool at least 10 minutes before unmolding.

Zucchini Blossoms with Zucchini Stuffing and Marinated Tomatoes

Serves 4–8

HERE'S A SUMMER PREPARATION begging for summer to never end. Serve it as part of a light alfresco lunch or an opening dish for dinner. If you raise your own zucchini, harvest the blooms early every day or two to keep the gold beauties coming. If the small zucchinis are allowed to grow and mature, the plant will stop sprouting new blossoms.

Check your local farmer's market and Asian groceries for blossoms in season. Likewise, the success of the dish also depends on having ripe tomatoes. If the tomatoes are lacking the wonderful ripe flavor, add a subtle pinch of sugar to the marinade.

FOR THE ZUCCHINI

8	Zucchini blossoms, females, with their baby zucchini attached, pistil inside the flower removed

FOR THE ZUCCHINI STUFFING

2	Zucchinis, medium, sliced (2 cups)
3	Garlic cloves, minced
1	Shallot, large, minced
¾ cup	Extra-virgin olive oil, divided
3 Tbsp	Thyme, fresh, leaves off of stem
5 Tbsp	Basil leaves, chopped
¾ cup	Bread crumbs
Salt, pepper, to taste	

FOR THE MARINATED TOMATOES

2 cups	Tomatoes, peeled, seeded, and diced
3 cloves	Garlic, minced
2	Shallots, minced
½ cup	Balsamic vinegar
½ cup	Olive oil
¼ cup	Basil leaves, finely chopped
Salt, pepper, to taste	

Serving Variation

Trim zucchini ends into a point. Make ¼ inch cuts down to the blossom. Fill blossom ¾ full and twist to seal well. Bake and stand these packets upright on the tomatoes.

MAKE ZUCCHINI STUFFING

Slice the zucchinis into rounds. Heat pan, add a tablespoon of olive oil, and sweat the zucchini until it softenes. Add shallots and garlic. Cook 2 minutes. Add thyme leaves. Cook until the zucchini is soft. Place in a food processor along with basil, bread crumbs, and remaining olive oil. Process until smooth. Add more oil or bread crumbs as needed until the mixture will almost hold together. Season with salt and pepper to taste.

MAKE THE MARINATED TOMATOES

In a medium skillet, cook tomatoes, garlic and shallots until most of the liquid has evaporated. Remove from heat.

In a medium bowl, combine vinegar, olive oil, and basil. Add the cooked tomato mixture. Season with salt and pepper to taste. Mix well. Let stand at least 1 hour before serving.

STUFF BLOSSOMS AND BAKE

Spoon the zucchini stufing into a pastry bag. Pipe the stuffing into the blossoms. Twist the blossom tips shut. Brush blossoms lightly with oilve oil and place on an oiled baking sheet. Bake 3 minutes at 450°F.

FINISHING

Serve blossoms warm atop a pool of the marinated tomatoes.

Gather blossoms before the heat of the day. Put stems in water and refrigerate to keep them fresh.

The "stems" of the female zucchini flowers are baby squash as they start to grow.

Northwest Mussel & Carrot Soup with Lovage

Serves 6

HARD AS IT MAY BE TO BELIEVE, when I was in my twenties virtually no one here in the north Pacific coast ate mussels. All mussels were wild. They were large and tough. Then in 1975, the first mussel farm in North America began in sheltered Penn Cove on Whidbey Island. These raft-raised mussels were gloriously fat, sweet, sassy and delivered fabulous flavor.

With this preparation, the sea sweetness is nicely set off by the carrots. A benefit of the recipe is that you need no stock. The mussels make their own! Serve the soup in shallow bowls garnished with your choice of dill or cilantro.

Cook the mussels until they *just begin* to open. No more or they will start to toughen.

1½ lb	Carrots, peeled and sliced
2	Shallots, large, sliced
4 oz	Butter, unsalted, divided use
4½ cups	Mussels, live (about 1 ¾ lb)
1½ cups	White wine, dry, not oaky
12	Lovage leaves

Salt, pepper, pinch of cayenne, to taste

Paprika, smoked, for garnish

Lovage leaves, cilantro leaves, or dill sprigs (optional)

Slice carrots and place in a saucepan with just enough water to cover. Bring to a boil, then simmer until soft.

Melt 4 tablespoons butter in a medium skillet on medium heat, add shallots and cook until translucent. Raise temperature, add mussels, wine, and lovage. Shake pan to evenly coat the mussels. Cook until the shells just begin to open. Immediately pull from the heat.

Remove mussels from shells and set aside. Strain the cooking liquid through a fine filter to remove any grit. Reserve the mussel cooking liquid. Discard shells, shallots, and lovage leaves.

Add the mussel cooking liquid to the saucepan with the carrots. Bring to a boil. Reduce heat and simmer 5 minutes.

Transfer the soup base along with half the mussel meat into a blender and pulse until smooth. Pass through a medium strainer. If too thick, thin with a little hot water until the soup is medium bodied. Season to taste with salt and pepper.

FINISHING

Place remaining mussels in the bottom of each heated shallow bowl. Ladle in soup around the mussel meat. Garnish with a dab of smoked paprika on top of each mussel. Finish with lovage, cilantro, or dill.

Multi-colored carrots

Wild King Salmon in Zucchini Blossom with Basil

Serves 6

THE FLAVOR OF zucchini pairs beautifully with salmon. Back in the early days of The Herbfarm restaurant, I grew a huge patch of zucchini just for the flowers. One of our first dishes was baking the blossoms with a nicely trimmed piece of king or sockeye salmon.

FOR THE SALMON

2¼ lb	Salmon fillet
Coarse salt, cayenne pepper, to taste	
12	Zucchini blossoms, with or without attached baby squash

FOR THE SAUCE

2	Shallots, large, minced
4 Tbsp	Lime juice or white wine vinegar
5 Tbsp	Dry white wine
½ cup	Basil leaves, divided use
4 Tbsp	Heavy cream
9 Tbsp	Butter, unsalted
Salt, cayenne, to taste	
2 Tbsp	Zucchini, small dice or minced
1 Tbsp	Salmon roe (optional)

PREP THE SALMON

Remove any pin bones. Trim off all skin. Cut salmon into twelve 2-ounce pieces of about 1 × 2 inches. Season salmon lightly with salt and a touch of cayenne pepper.

PREPARE AND STUFF ZUCCHINI BLOSSOMS

Pick the blossoms in the morning before the heat of the day. The flowers can be stored upright with their bases in water in the fridge until needed.

With a small knife, remove stamens or pistils from inside the flowers. Carefully insert a piece of salmon into each flower, closing the petals around it.

START SAUCE

Melt 2 tablespoons of butter in a small saucepan. Saute shallots until translucent.

Add lime juice (or vinegar), wine, and a few basil leaves. Simmer slowly until most of the liquid evaporates.

Remove and discard basil leaves. Add cream. Bring to a boil and remove from the heat. Set aside until salmon is out of the oven.

BAKING

Heat oven to 350°F . Brush the stuffed flowers lightly with olive oil. Place on a lightly oiled baking sheet and bake 10–12 minutes until cooked through.

FINISH SAUCE

Bring cream back to a boil. Turn to low. Whisk in the butter a tablespoon at a time until fully incorporated. Stir in the diced zucchini and remove from heat.

Add salt and a pinch of cayenne to taste. Roll up the remaining basil leaves and snip with scissors into fine strands, letting them fall into the sauce.

SERVING

Spoon the sauce on a warm plate. Place 2 blossoms on each plate and dot with salmon roe. Garnish with a basil sprig. Serve hot.

Chicken Saltimbocca "Scarborough Fair" with Red Wine Chicken Jus

Serves 4

THIS IS A TAKE on that enduring classic, Veal Saltimbocca. The flavor of sage and the other Scarborough Fair herbs complement without overpowering the chicken breast. It's married to a good *dry-cured* ham and the rich tangy flavor of Seattle's Beecher's Flagship cheese. If you can't find Beecher's, substitute a thinly sliced alpine Swiss like Jarlsberg, Emmenthal, or Gruyère.

FOR THE CHICKEN

4	Chicken breasts, skinned and boneless, butterflied (about 12 oz each)
	Salt, pepper, to taste
8	Paper-thin slices of smoky dry-cured ham such as acorn-fed Westphalian, Black Forest, or Italian Speck
8	Thin slices of Beecher's Flagship cheese
¼ cup	Parsley, chppped finely
4 Tbsp	Rosemary chopped finely
4 Tbsp	Thyme, chopped finely
¼ cup	Sage leaves, fresh
3 Tbsp	Neutral oil

FOR THE RED WINE SAUCE

3 Tbsp	Butter, unsalted, divided use
1 Tbsp	Shallot, mined
½ cup	Red wine
½ cup	Chicken stock
¼ cup	Brown sugar
2 Tbsp	Balsamic vinegar
3 Tbsp	Red wine vinegar
	Salt, pepper, to taste

OPTIONAL FOR COOKING

2 Tbsp	Mayonnaise
½ cup	Parsley, chopped finely
¼ cup	Sage, chopped finely
4 Tbsp	Rosemary, chopped finely
4 Tbsp	Thyme, choppped finely

One at a time, place each breast between 2 pieces of plastic wrap, cut-side up, and pound with a meat tenderizer, mallet, or rolling pin until the meat spreads out and is ¼" thick, roughly 7" long and 5" wide.

Remove top piece of plastic wrap and season the cut side of each breast with salt and pepper. Sprinkle with the chopped herbs. Lay a slice of ham on top followed by two sage leaves, and one slice of cheese. Leave last inch uncovered.

Roll up the meat to form a tight spiral, then season the outside with salt and pepper. Can be made ahead to this stage and stored in the fridge wrapped tightly in plastic wrap. Bring back to room temp before proceeding.

MAKE THE SAUCE

In a small saucepan, melt 1 tablespoon butter over medium heat. Saute shallots until translucent. Add red wine and chicken stock. Simmer until the volume has reduced to roughly ½ cup.

Add brown sugar. Simmer 2–3 minutes until the sugar dissolves and the sauce thickens. Stir in the vinegars, whisk in remaining butter, and season with salt and pepper to taste.

COOK THE CHICKEN

Preheat oven to 400°F.

Optional: Coat rolls with mayonnaise and roll in chopped herbs. Cook herbed or regular rolls as follows:

Preheat a large ovenproof skillet over medium-high. Add oil, then carefully lay each chicken roll in the pan. Reduce the heat to medium and cook, turning to sear all sides of the chicken, until they are a nice dark brown.

Transfer pan to the oven and roast for 5–6 minutes until an internal temperature of 165°F. Remove chicken from pan to rest before slicing. Stir any remaining chicken drippings into the sauce.

SERVING

Spoon the sauce on warmed dinner plates, slice each roll in half and place atop the sauce.

Carrie's Summer Corn with Lemon Thyme

Serves 4–8

THIS IS PROBABLY THE simplest dish in this book. But the result is extraordinary. Fresh corn with butter and Lemon Thyme is truly a flavor gift and the pinacle of summer's treasure. The dish was discovered (at least in our household) by Carrie Van Dyck, my wife and partner, without whom The Herbfarm would not have succeeded.

Yes, you can substitute olive oil for the butter, if you must. Believe me, sweet corn and butter were made for one another.

4 ears	Sweet corn, very fresh
2 Tbsp	Butter, unsalted
2 tsp	Lemon thyme, minced
½ tsp	Salt

Preheat oven to 350°F. Put the whole ears of unshucked corn in the oven and roast for 15–20 minutes. Remove. Shuck the ears. With a knife, cut the kernels from the cobs taking care not to cut into the core. Place kernels in a pan with the butter and warm through. Add lemon thyme and salt. Serve this harvest goodness alone or as a vegetable with the main course.

Flavored-Packed Butter Compositions

Each preparation makes about 10 pats from the sliced butter cylinder

WHEN I VISITED the village of Grasse in fabled Provence, France, I was overcome by the intensity of the perfumery fragrances. Butter, like the fats used to extract flower fragrances, is an excellent carrier and keeper of both aromas and flavors. You can capture summer by preserving it in butter, which gives back its goodness as it melts on your food.

CLASSIC PARSLEY-LEMON BUTTER

For Grilled Fish or Steak

8 Tbsp	Butter, softened
2 Tbsp	Parsley, finely chopped
¼ tsp	Lemon juice

Whip the butter in a bowl. Fold in remaining ingredients. Put the butter on plastic wrap or parchment paper. Roll butter into a log. Twist ends of wrap to tighten. Refrigerate or freeze.

NASTURTIUM BUTTER

For Grilled Fish or Shrimp

8 Tbsp	Butter, softened
3 Tbsp	Nasturtium flowers, finely chopped
¼ tsp	Lemon juice

Process as per Parsley Butter.

GARLIC BUTTER

For Fish, Meat, or Vegetables

8 Tbsp	Butter, softened
4	Garlic cloves, minced or grated
¼ tsp	Salt, fine sea
¼ tsp	Lemon juice

Process as per Parsley Butter.

SUN-DRIED TOMATO BASIL BUTTER

For Chicken, Veggies, and Pasta

8 Tbsp	Butter, softened
4 Tbsp	Tomatoes, sun-dried, finely chopped
2 Tbsp	Basil, fresh, finely chopped
½	Garlic clove, grated
¼ tsp	Salt, fine sea
¼ tsp	Lemon juice

Process as per Parsley Butter.

SPICY CHIPOTLE BUTTER

For Steak, Fish, Corn, Chicken

8 Tbsp	Butter, softened
1 Tbsp	Chipotle, powder
1 Tbsp	Jalepeño, pickled, minced
2 Tbsp	Lime juice
2 Tbsp	Cilantro, chopped
¼ tsp	Garlic powder

Process as per Parsley Butter.

HERBAL BUTTERS

Substitute fresh herbs: chives, thyme, mint, or fennel for the parsley in the Parsley Butter.

BUTTER PATS OR SCOTCH HANDS
These innocuous looking wooden paddles have a long history. Yes, they can be used to roll gnocchi, but they were invented to "work" churned butter to remove trapped buttermilk as well as shape the butter.

These days, most of us buy pre-made butter, so the "hands" are workhorses in shaping blobs of butter into fancy shapes. Put a tablespoon of butter in the middle of one of the hands and rotate the other in a circular motion, and—voilà!—have a perfect ball of textured butter. The butter hands need to be soaked in cold water for 30 minutes before use, which prevents the butter from sticking to them. Adopt your pair from an antique store or pick up a new pair online.

Butter Balls Made
with Butter Pats

Sun-Dried Tomato

Nasturtium
Blossom

Parsley-Lemon

Garlic & Parsley

Spicy Chipotle

Make Your Own Fireweed Tea

Makes as much as you want

FUNNY HOW YOU CAN spend your life noticing something, but not truly seeing it. For decades I tramped the meadows and mountains of the Pacific Northwest, noting the fuchsia-colored blooms of fireweed as I passed. It never occurred to me that this tall, somewhat-spindly plant, which thrives in disturbed soil, had any culinary merit. Little did I know.

Fireweed (*Chamaenerion angustifolium*) offers edible green shoots in the spring and leaves from which you can create an impressive black "tea." Found in all northern latitudes of the world—including all of Canada and every northern American state—the plant gained fame as Russian "Ivan Chai." Before the Russian revolution, Ivan tea was as popular as Chinese black tea. The processed leaves look precisely like whole-leaf black tea. When Chinese tea was scarce, unscrupulous tea merchants were rumored to have stretched their stocks by adding fireweed.

Though Russia, Siberia, and east-central Europe still produce the beverage, most of its production is preserved in the time-honored traditions of village life. Making this non-caffeinated beverage requires no special equipment.

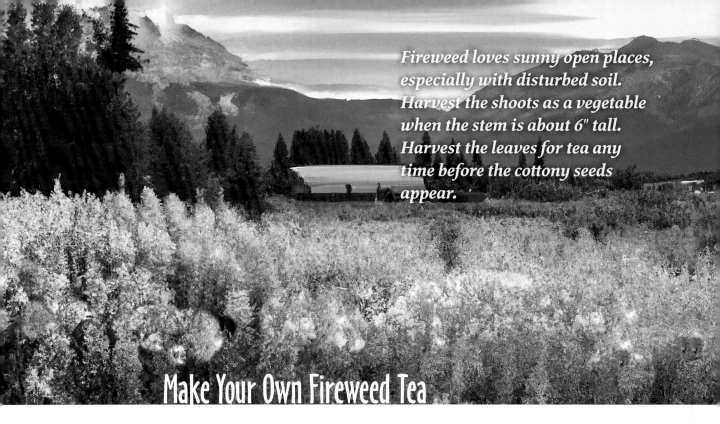

Fireweed loves sunny open places, especially with disturbed soil. Harvest the shoots as a vegetable when the stem is about 6" tall. Harvest the leaves for tea any time before the cottony seeds appear.

Make Your Own Fireweed Tea

HARVEST THE FIREWEED STALKS—Cut the stem just below the last useable leaf. Pick off the leaves from the stem. Discard any leaves that are brown or dry.

WILT THE LEAVES—Allow the leaves to wilt. This may take a few hours or a day.

ROLL AND CRUSH THE LEAVES—Depending on the number of leaves and available time, this can be done by rolling and/or crushing the leaves with one's hands, bashing them with a rolling pin, or other methods you can dream up. It is essential that the cells in the leaves are bruised and ruptured if you are to achieve success.

OXIDIZE THE LEAVES—Let the leaves sit to oxidize and develop optimum taste. The tea turns out best when the oxidizing leaves are at an aromatic intensity: two to 12 hours.

LET THE LEAVES FERMENT—Put the oxidized leaves into a container and place weight on top, pressing firmly so the leaves compact and become more or less "sealed" in the bottom of the container. Allow the leaves to ferment at ambient temperature for 2–3 days, stirring and fluffing 2–3 times a day to prevent mold.

STOP FERMENTATION, THEN

DRY THE TEA—When the leaves have fermented, remove them from the container. Halt the fermentation with heat: either roasting quickly in a hot oven or steaming. Dehydrate the leaves in a low oven or food dehydrator, then store the fireweed tea in an airtight container in a cool, dark place.

Brew as you would any black tea, but add 5 minutes to the steeping time.

Poached Peach with Anise Hyssop & Cucumber Granita

Servers 6

AMONG THE GREAT flavor combinations we've served at The Herbfarm, the pairing of peach and anise hyssop ranks with the classics. The combination was a favorite of Jerry Traunfeld's when he was The Herbfarm chef. Peaches and anise hyssop are in season at the same time. Here we pair the poached peach with a refreshing cucumber granita ice.

CUCUMBER GRANITA

1 lb	Cucumbers, juiced (about 6 oz)
½ cup	Water
½ cup	Sugar
½	Lemon, juiced

PEACHES

6	Peaches, freestone, ripe and perfect
2 qt	Water
1	Bottle white wine, medium sweet such as Riesling, Moscato, or Chenin Blanc
1½ cups	Sugar
1 inch	Ginger, cut into thin slices
8	Anise hyssop sprigs, 6", with leaves and flowers (if any)

TOPPING & GARNISH

6	Small anise hyssop leaves from the top of the plant

What's a Freestone Peach?

Freestone peaches are the easiest to work with for this dessert dish. They have a pit that readily separates from the fruit. The opposite of freestone is "cling," where the pit must be cut from the fruit. Some popular freestones are Red Haven, Redtop, O'Henry, Crest, Fay Elberta, Golden Jubilee, Glohaven, and Loring.

FREEZE THE GRANITA

In a medium metal bowl, combine cucumber juice with water, sugar, and lemon juice. Whisk to dissolve sugar then transfer the bowl into the freezer. Freeze for an hour, then break up the ice chunks with a fork. Repeat every hour until an icy granita forms.

PEELING THE PEACHES

Boil water in a large pot. Set a bowl of ice water nearby.

Cut a shallow "X" through the skin at the top of the peach. Don't cut deeply into the fruit.

With a slotted spoon, lower the peaches into the boiling water. Boil 30 to 60 seconds.

Remove peaches from water and place in the ice water. After a few seconds, the peel will be loose around the shallow "X." At this point the skin will peel easily from the peaches.

POACH PEACHES

Discard boiling water and add the bottle of wine to the same pot. Add sugar, ginger slices, and peeled peaches.

Add water if necessary so that the peaches are barely covered in poaching liquid.

Place pot on stove and bring to a boil; then remove the pot from the heat. Add the anise hyssop sprigs.

Allow to stand until the syrup cools to room temperature.

Remove peaches. Cut a small circle into the bottom of each peach. Carefully work your finger inside to loosen and remove the pit. Return peaches to the syrup, then refrigerate until ready to use.

SERVING

Remove each peach from the syrup. Cut a little slot in the top. Stand an annise hyssop leaf up in the slot.

Spoon the frozen cucumber granita in the bottom of bowls or on a plate. Top with the peach and serve.

Fig-Leaf Ice Cream with Brûléed Figs

Makes 1½ quarts

SOME YEARS AGO, Herbfarm chef Chis Weber found that dried fig leaves have a coconut-like flavor. Since coconut isn't one of the Northwest ingredients in our repertoire, this was an exciting discovery for us. Chris uses the leaves as one of the ingredients for a curry sauce. Why not take the leaves to dessert? So, a late summer dessert served with brûléed figs. The ice cream tastes of coconut and honeydew melon.

ICE CREAM

12	Fig leaves, dried, crumbled into small pieces
1¼ cups	Sugar
6	Egg yolks
¼ tsp	Salt
1¾ cups	Milk
2 cups	Heavy cream

BRÛLÉED FIGS

1–2	Figs per person, halved lengthwise
½ tsp	Sugar, demerara, per fig

ICE CREAM

Place sugar and egg yolks in a bowl. Whisk with an electric hand mixer or wire whisk until the mixture lightens in color.

Add the milk, cream and fig leaves into a medium saucepan. Bring to a boil. Turn off heat and allow the leaves to infuse for 30 minutes.

Strain out leaves. Return flavored milk to the saucepan. Slowly pour the hot milk into the egg and sugar mixture, whisking constantly.

Return the entire mixture to the pan and cook over low heat, stirring constantly, until it thickens enough to coat a spoon.

Strain through a fine sieve into a container. Chill.

Pour chilled base into an ice cream churn and freeze according to the manufacturer's instructions.

BRÛLEÉING THE FIGS

Cut figs in half. Place on a nonflammable plate. Sprinkle demerara sugar on the cut face.

Using a kitchen torch, melt the sugar, moving the flame in circles until the sugar bubbles and browns. Don't worry if a little sugar turns black. After all brûlée means "burnt."

SERVING

Place a scoop of Fig Leaf Ice Cream in a bowl or on a plate. Serve with brûléed figs.

Crustless Italian Prune Plum Tart

Serves 6–8, depending on size of cut wedges

THIS FRUIT TART preparation is simple enough that you can switch between Italian prunes, apricots, peaches, apples, pears, or pie cherries.

The beauty of the dish is how fast the batter comes together. You can mix everything in the same bowl. Its versatility allows you to work with many fruits as they come into season and on the market, though the Italian prune may be the best.

BATTER

¾ cup   Sugar

½ cup   Butter, unsalted, softened to room temperature

1 cup   Flour, sifted

1 tsp   Baking Powder

1 tsp   Cinnamon, ground (preferably "Saigon/Vietnamese," which is more aromatic)

Pinch of salt

½ tsp   Vanilla extract

2   Eggs, whole

FRUIT

14–18   Italian prune plums (depending on size, split in two, pits removed)

You can also use other summer fruits that have a bit of acid and are not too watery.

TOPPING

2–4 Tbsp   Sugar

1 Tbsp   Lemon juice

Your choice to sprinkle on top: Sliced almonds, walnuts, star anise, nutmeg, allspice, cloves—or a mixture of these warming spices

MAKE BATTER

Preheat oven to 350°F.

Spray or butter the inside of an 8-inch springform pan (see tip).

Cream ¾ cup sugar with butter in a medium bowl. Add flour, baking powder, salt, vanilla, and eggs. Mix well.

FILL & TOP TART

Pour the batter into the springform pan. Smooth with a spoon or spatula.

Place plum halves, skin-side up, side by side. Do not press down. Sprinkle with lemon juice and sugar. Use less sugar if the plums are totally ripe and without that sweet-tart firmness.

BAKE THE TART

Place in the oven and bake for approximately one hour. Remove and cool. Unmold.

If you have the time, cover the tart with plastic wrap and store overnight at room temperature. The extra time will allow an even-better integration of the plum juices with the cake batter.

SERVING

Serve plain, with whipped cream, or ice cream.

Tip
An 8-inch pan is the best pan size as it makes for a taller tart. To achieve similar results in a larger pan, use 1½ recipe for a 9-inch springform pan and double the receipt for a 10-inch pan.

First of the winter squashes

Discovered on Orcas Island north of Seattle, the Orcas Pear ripens in September. The flesh is smooth and sweet with a buttery taste.

Autumn

The Feasting Season

YOU FIRST NOTICE IT as a soft chill caressing your cheek on a windless day. A bit of snap vibrates in the refreshed air. Then overhead come the calls of geese, their honks rising excitedly in pitch as they bank over fields and farms before setting down.

The "Feasting Season" has begun. With some luck, summer extends its lease well into September. Now the payoff. Crops we've been tending since spring march to center stage. Plump heritage tomatoes test their sagging vines. Melons, apples, pears, plums, and quince join with

huckleberries, grapes, and saskatoon berries in desserts. Potatoes, corn, winter squashes, and shelling beans announce their entrance. They will stay until spring.

Before the rains come, Eric Fritch reaps and winnows our wheat. We will have bread for another year. And it's the traditional time for harvesting livestock, which keeps the kitchen busy curing hams and featuring fresh cuts and dark-meated fowl. Let's feast.

"Come, ye thankful people come,
Raise the song of Harvest home,
All is safely gathered in,
Ere the winter storms begin."

—Henry Alford (1844)

Master the Taste of Herbs

Become an Herbal Flavor Mixologist

TO BE SKILLFUL IN COOKING WITH HERBS, you should taste the plants in their pure, fresh forms. If your only exposure to oregano has been on a pizza, then it's understandable that the pungent, peppery, sweet-spicy flavor may not be ingrained in your memory. How could you imagine the same herb paired with a firm-fleshed fish? Would you ever be able to conceive of flavoring ice cream with it? Or sprinkling it generously on a melon as a savory counterpoint? Probably not.

Neutral Tasting: Two good ways to taste the true flavors of a plant are shown on the opposite page.

Here Comes the Sun

As a living thing, the flavor and strength of an herb changes—sometimes dramatically—depending on the plant's age and how much sunlight its leaves receive.

The Sun Rule for Herbal Strength

In the Northwest, it takes roughly twice as many leaves in June to equal the flavor strength reached in August.

May
1/4

June
1/2

July
3/4

August
Full

Isolate a Plant Flavor to Understand Its Taste

1 Fresh herbs (Wild Marjoram shown)

2 Pick leaves. Discard large or hard stems.

3 Chop leaves medium to fine.

4 Mix 1 part herb with 3 parts sour cream etc.

5 Let mixture meld 1 hour. Taste on toasted bread.

SAVORY METHOD: This technique works well for oregano, tarragon, rosemary, chives, all basils, borage, chervil, cilantro, dill, fennel, lovage, parsley, sage, sweet cicely, and all thymes.

Herbs You Should Taste with Sugar

SWEET METHOD: Scented geranium leaves, lemon verbena, lemon balm, mints, and most edible flowers are best appreciated when the flavor is drawn out and combined with a bit of sugar. Grind a few leaves with sugar in a blender or mortar and pestle. Dissolve this mix in cold water. Put in the refrigerator for an hour. Strain out the leaves. The result is a fresh green essence of the herb. Dilute it with water and sip like tea. The pureness of cold extraction is wonderful for showcasing plant flavors in ice creams and sorbets.

Hors d'oeuvres: Five Different Devilishly Delicious Eggs

Each preparation makes about 12 deviled eggs (halves)

WE'VE ALL BEEN THERE. You take deviled eggs to a party and they vanish. In fact, they were the first appetizers eaten. Since a hard-cooked egg —when deviled— is a canvas for experimentation, there's no end to the flavors you can make for your guests to relish.

These recipes share the same instructions: cook eggs, peel, cut them in half, *push out the yolk* (instead of using a spoon), and mash or mix the ingredients with a hand mixer. Return the seasoned yolk to the indent in the whites using a small spoon or a pastry bag for a fancier presentation. Garnish as seems appropriate.

DANI'S CURED SALMON DEVILED EGGS

6	Eggs, hard-boiled, halved
2 Tbsp	Salmon, cured and cold smoked
2 Tbsp	Mayonnaise
1 tsp	Lemon juice
6	Drops Sriracha

Salmon caviar, a dollop to top each

Dill, for garnish

RED PICKLED EGGS

6	Eggs, hard-boiled

Boil together:

1	Beet, small, peeled, cut into large cubes
2½ cups	Water
¾ cup	Cider vinegar
¼ cup	Balsamic vinegar
1 Tbsp	Brown sugar
1 Tbsp	Peppercorns, whole

Add peeled, uncut eggs and refrigerate 3–24 hours.

Remove eggs. Cut in two. Proceed as usual.

⅓ cup	Mayonnaise
2 Tbsp	Mustard, Dijon
½ tsp	Curry powder

Salt, pepper, to taste

SPICY DEVILED EGGS

6	Eggs, hard-boiled, halved
2 Tbsp	Mayonnaise
2 Tbsp	Dijon mustard
2 tsp	Honey
2 Tbsp	Chipotle in adobo, chopped fine
1 tsp	Sugar
1 ½ tsp	Garlic, minced
3 tsp	Chili powder

SMOKED DEVILED EGGS

6	Eggs, hard-boiled, smoked*
3 Tbsp	Mayonnaise
1 tsp	Apple cider vinegar
2 tsp	BBQ rub
1 Tbsp	Jalapeños, pickled, diced
12	Jalapeño slices, thin, for garnish

Smoke peeled eggs. Cut in two. Proceed as usual.

*Use the stovetop tenting technique or the bee smoker (see smoked morel dish page 120). Eggs can also be smoked in a lidded barbeque if temperature is less than 180°F. Or use a "Smoking Gun" kitchen tool, which you can find online. Use a mild fruit wood for the smoke. Smoke 30 minutes and no more than one hour.

How to Hard Boil an Egg

There are many variables for a successful hard-boiled egg. But temperature and time are the most important. For consistency always start with eggs at room temperature.

Boiling: Bring a medium pan of water to a hard boil. Add eggs. Keep at a simmer. Remove eggs after 10–12 minutes. Immediately put into a bowl of ice water.

Steaming: Bring water to a boil. Place eggs in steaming rack and steam over the boiling water for 10–12 minutes. Transfer to ice water for at least 5 minutes before removing.

CLASSIC DEVILED EGGS

6 Eggs, hard-boiled

Mayonnaise, sweet pickle relish, yellow mustard, salt and pepper, paprika (sprinkle on top)

Mix to taste, fill, garnish.

Sweet Rub

Dani's
Salmon Eggs

Classic
Deviled Eggs

Red-Pickled
Deviled Eggs

Classic Eggs
End-Cut

Spicy
Deviled Eggs

Smoked
Deviled Eggs

Salmon Head Soup

Makes 6 (8-ounce) servings

1⅓ lb	Salmon heads (1–2 heads)
2 Tbsp	Butter, unsalted
½ cup	Onion, finely chopped (½–¾ onion)
1 Tbsp	Garlic, chopped
1 cup	Carrots, minced (about 2)
¼ cup	Celery, minced (2 stalks)
½ cup	Dry white wine
3″ piece	Leek, thinly sliced
3	Thyme sprigs
3	Parsley sprigs
½ tsp	Black peppercorns, crushed
2 qt	Water

Cut out and remove all parts of the gills under the gill plates. With a large knife or cleaver, carefully split the heads in half. Wash head pieces in cold water. Remove any blood or dark spots, which can taint the flavor.

Smoke on a barbecue until dry, golden, and desiccated. If any char, scrape off all blackened pieces (or discard). Chop into 2 inch-wide pieces to expose the inside meat and fat.

In a large and heavy stock pot, melt butter. Cook the onion until translucent. Add the garlic, leek, carrot, and celery. Cook over low heat until soft and aromatic.

Add wine. Bring to a simmer. Scrape any flavoring from the bottom of the pan. Add thyme, peppercorns, and parsley.

Add the water and fish heads. Bring to a *bare simmer*. Cook for 60 minutes adding water if necessary to keep he heads covered. Strain the stock through a fine-mesh strainer with cheesecloth. Discard heads and solids. Skim off fat.

Season with salt to taste. Serve with chopped chives or green onions on top.

Salmon heads smoking and drying over a low applewood fire. Smoking the head is traditional and adds umami to the soup. Salmon heads are often available from your fishmonger or at many Asian grocery stores.

SALMON HEAD SOUP? Don't be put off by the heads. In the past, creative frugality required people who live with nature to adopt a no-waste "head-to-tail" ethos. Nothing went to waste, which is why fish head soup of one sort or another is found worldwide.

Here in the Pacific Northwest, salmon is the traditional fish for this soup among coastal tribes. The fish were smoked over smoldering alderwood fires. The hard-smoked heads are what endow this stock with its consistency, lending mouthfeel and umami. Fire up your smoker or barbecue to smoke the heads for several hours until the heads are golden and the salmon is jerky like. Alder is authentic. Fruit woods are milder. I use a mixture of alder with a touch of apple.

Serve the soup as a warm sipper or first course. If you like, add rice or pasta to the bowl for a heartier offering.

Nest of Wild Autumn Mushrooms with Sherry-Mustard Sauce

Serves 4

THIS IS A DISH we served for several years in the 1990s. The "nest" of flaky puff pastry holds savory mushrooms and their sauce. In the spring, we'd make a green sauce from wild nettles. Here we move into autumn flavors with a sherry and Dijon mustard accompaniment. Though we made our own puff pastry, I suggest you use frozen premade sheets to save time. If you're up for making your own, check the internet.

PUFF PASTRY CASES

2	¼" sheets puff pastry (or four ⅛ inch sheets. If the latter, glue two sheets together with beaten egg yolk.)
2	Egg yolks, beaten with 1 tsp of water

WILD MUSHROOM FILLING

½ oz	Morels, dried, to grind to a powder
4 oz	Mushrooms, wild, sautéed
1 tsp	Butter
1	Garlic clove, minced
1	Shallot, minced
⅔ cup	Stock, rich
1 tsp	Sugar
½ tsp	Caraway seeds
2 tsp	Soy sauce
1 Tbsp	Madeira wine
½ cup	Heavy cream
Salt, to taste	

SHERRY & MUSTARD SAUCE

2 Tbsp	Butter, unsalted
2 Tbsp	Shallot, minced
2 tsp	Garlot, minced
⅔ cup	Sherry wine, dry
2 cups	Cream
¼ cup	Mustard, Dijon
1 tsp	Paprika, smoked
Salt, pepper, to taste	
Chopped chives or parsley	

PUFF PASTRY CASES

Preheat oven to 425°F.

With a cookie cutter, cut out four 3¼-inch circles from the puff pastry. Do this with cold pastry so that the cut edges don't get crimped. Place them on a parchment-lined baking sheet. Next, cut 4 more 3¼-inch circles. Press a circle in the center of each so that it creates a ½-inch to ¾-inch ring. You'll remove the center after baking.

Brush the top of the first four circles with the beaten egg yolk. Lay the second four exactly atop of yolked circles. Press gently to glue them together. Brush the tops (but not the sides) with egg.

With the back of a knife, score a repeating "V" pattern around the edge of the upper rings.

Place in oven and bake for 20–25 minutes until browned, then further dry the shells in a very low-temp oven for 20 minutes.

MUSHROOM SAUCE/FILLING

Grind the dried morels to powder in a spice grinder or motar and pestle. Melt butter in a medium saucepan. Cook shallot and garlic until translucent. Add stock, morel powder, and mushrooms. Bring to boil. Reduce heat. Simmer 30 minutes.

Add soy, sugar, Madeira, caraway, and cream. Simmer 30 minutes. Season to taste. Add a touch more Madeira.

SHERRY-MUSTARD SAUCE

Melt butter in medium saucepan. Cook shallot and garlic until translucent. Cook 2 minutes, then add sherry. Simmer to ½ volume. Add cream, paprika, mustard, salt, and pepper. Simmer until it begins to thicken. Add parsley. Keep warm or gently reheat before plating.

SERVING

With a small sharp knife, carefully cut out the center lid of the pastry. Hollow out the insides. spoon sauce on plate. Place pastry "nest" in center; fill with the hot mushroom filling. Garnish with chives or parsley.

Celery Root Soup Served in Its Own Bowl

Serves 4

CELERY ROOT—ALSO KNOWN as Celeriac—is the visual ugly duckling of the root vegetable realm. It's easy to imagine the gnarly swelling poking out along a dark forest trail winding toward a witch's creepy house!

The plant's "root" is actually the swollen stem. The vegetable, related to celery, has been cultivated for centuries in Europe, but only landed in the Americas in the nineteenth century.

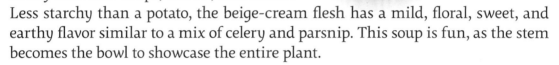

For many years we've fashioned celery root into soups, sauces, and salads. Less starchy than a potato, the beige-cream flesh has a mild, floral, sweet, and earthy flavor similar to a mix of celery and parsnip. This soup is fun, as the stem becomes the bowl to showcase the entire plant.

CELERIAC SOUP

4	Celery roots, large, trimmed and peeled, rubbed with lemon juice. This will become your soup bowl, so use an artistic eye.
4 Tbsp	Butter, unsalted
⅓ cup	Onion, minced
1	Leek, small, white part, thinly sliced
1	Apple, crisp variety with acidity, peeled, cored, and diced
1¾ cups	Half-and-half (or enough to cover the celeriac in the pan)
1	Thyme sprig
1	Bay leaf

Salt, white pepper, cayenne, to taste

Thyme leaves to garnish

Drizzle of olive oil

Nutmeg to grate on top

Preheat your oven to 400°F. Put the prepared celery roots in a deep baking dish. Add 1½ inches of water and cover tightly with foil. Bake until the roots are tender and easily pierced with a paring knife. Depending on size, this will take roughly one to two hours. Remove from the oven and let cool.

Carefully slice off the top inch or so of the celery root. Using a melon baller or small spoon, scoop out the inside of your celery root "bowl," being careful not to pierce the outside. Reserve the pulp (roughly 24 ounces) and hollow bowls separately.

Melt the butter in a large Dutch oven. Add the onion, leek, and apple. Gently sauté until the onions are translucent but not browned. Add the celery root pulp, half-and-half, thyme sprig, and bay leaf. Simmer gently for 10 minutes.

Remove the thyme and bay leaf. Transfer the contents to a blender (in batches if necessary) and purée until silky smooth. If the soup seems too thick, thin it with additional half-and-half, or hot water. Season with salt, white pepper, and cayenne to taste.

Before serving, rewarm the celery root bowls. Fill with hot soup.

Sprinkle on picked thyme leaves, a swirl of olive oil, and a grate of nutmeg.

Cast-Iron Black Cod with Leek Purée & Quick-Pickled Radish

Serves 4

HERE'S A SECRET. In the Pacific Northwest, iconic salmon and halibut are top-of-mind for sport fishers, cooks, and restaurants. But for local devotees like myself, the Pacific Black Cod takes the gold medal. For what's not to love? Black Cod, or "Sablefish," is white-fleshed, mild and flavorful. It's embued with a buttery fatness that tempts with a silken flakiness. It's unlike any other fish I know.

Black Cod fishing boats

A deep bottom dweller, Black Cod are line-caught up the coast into the Gulf of Alaska at staggering depths between 650 and 9,000 feet.

This simple preparation cooks the cod by simultaneously poaching and broiling. A cast-iron pan is necessary to hold and reflect heat.

LEEK PURÉE SAUCE

1 lb	Leeks, white and light green parts, washed and sliced ½″ thick
½ cup	Olive oil, fruity
¼ cup	Stock or water or milk
1 Tbsp	Lemon juice

Salt, pepper and cayenne to taste

BLACK COD

1	12″ cast-iron skillet
1½ lb	Black Cod fillet, thick as you can find, skin on (essential)
2	Shallots, large, sliced, ¼″
1	Bottle of white wine or equivalent from a box

Salt, pepper, and cayenne

LEEK PURÉE SAUCE

Thoroughly wash the sliced leeks. Fill a saucepan with salted water and bring to a boil. Add the leeks and boil until tender, about 5 minutes. Drain and transfer to a blender. Add remaining ingredients and purée. Transfer leek sauce back to the saucepan and keep warm.

POACH-BROILING THE BLACK COD

Heat oven to 525°F with the rack positioned just below the broiler.

Cover the bottom of a cast-iron skillet with shallot slices. Generously season the cod portions with salt, pepper, and cayenne. Place the fish atop the shallots and fill the pan to a bit more than half the height of the fish with the white wine. Broil for 5–6 minutes or until fish skin is crisped and fish is cooked.

Put leek sauce on warmed plates and cod on top. Serve with quick-pickled radishes, regular or daikon (recipe page 208).

Old Salt's Salt Potatoes

Serves 6

POTATOES COOKED IN SEAWATER claim many beginnings. To preserve their stores of fresh water, sailors crossing the Atlantic would cook in saltwater whenever possible. We also know that the fishermen of Portugal, Catalonia, and the Canary Islands would mend their nets on the beach as they cooked small potatoes for lunch in ocean water.

Salted-water cooked potatoes come out perfectly seasoned, with slightly wrinkly skin, and creamy center. Choose tiny yellow, red, or purple potatoes. Leave the skin on. Kosher or sea salt work well here. If you have a stash of interesting salts, make your own saline mix to add a distinctive mineral nuance.

In a medium pot, mix the water with the salt.

Bring the briny water to a boil.

Wash the potatoes. Place in the pot. Cook until tender. Use a paring knife point to test doneness.

Drain the water. Put pot and potatoes back on the stove and heat for another couple of minutes to dry. Then remove from stove and let them sit. The skins will be somewhat wrinkly. The salt frosting will appear like magic and the potatoes will be perfectly seasoned.

Serve just the way they are. Or brown with a little butter or olive oil. Sprinkle with fresh thyme, basil or Italian parsley, if you wish.

4 cups	Water
½ cup	Kosher salt, (or 4 oz mixed salts)
2 lb	Potatoes, bite-sized baby

Mashed Potato Rolls

Yields about 16 single servings. Or two loaves.

WHO HASN'T FOUND THEMSELVES with extra mashed potatoes? These fluffy rolls are just the thing for using them up. The rolls send those leftover spuds to the table in an all-new and delectable form. You can shape this dough—enriched as it is with leftover mash—into rolls, crescents, loaves, or braided bread.

Activate the yeast by adding it along with a pinch of sugar to the warm water. Let sit 5–10 minutes until frothy.

In a large bowl or mixer combine the boiling water, butter, salt, and remaining sugar. Add mashed potatoes and stir until all is incorporated. Add 3 cups of flour and yeast mixture. Knead until flour is incorporated; then add remaining flour a bit at a time until the dough forms. The worked dough should be silky. If shaggy and sticky, add more flour.

Form dough into a ball. Grease bowl with butter. Cover. Let rise in a warm place for half an hour.

¼ cup	Water, warm
1 Tbsp	Dried yeast
2 Tbsp	Sugar, divided use
1 cup	Boiling water
2 Tbsp	Butter
1 Tbsp	Salt
2 cups	Mashed potatoes
5 cups	Flour
1	Egg yolk

Punch down risen dough and knead another minute. Portion dough into 16 rolls, shape and set on a parchment lined sheet pan. Or put in a greased bread pan if making a loaf. Proof an additional 30–60 minutes until doubled in size.

Mix egg yolk with a little water and brush rolls to give them a shine. Bake in a 350°F oven until cooked through and golden, about 18–20 minutes for rolls, or 30–35 minutes for a loaf.

Duck Breast with Apple Cider & Braised Red Cabbage

Serves 2 people generously per duck or 4 with half-breast servings

WHEN **I** WAS A KID, my brother and I would sometimes go duck hunting in the dry potholes of Eastern Washington. The ducks we bagged were invariably mallards, which are leaner than the domesticated varieties found in grocery stores. Since waterfowl season is in the autumn, I associate the rich flavor of duck with the fall. Duck meat is always at home with fruity flavors, so it seems proper to serve it this time of the year with a spiced apple cider sauce.

RED CABBAGE

1 lb	Red cabbage, cored, cut in ¼″ by 1 ½″ strips
1	Onion, medium, diced
1	Apple, peeled, ¼″ sliced
¼ cup	Red wine vinegar
⅛ tsp	Cayenne
4 Tbsp	Butter

Salt, pepper, to taste

FOR THE CIDER SAUCE

2 cups	Apple cider
2 cups	Duck stock (or chicken stock, or beef stock)
1	Cinnamon stick, small
4	Cloves, whole
4	Peppercorns, whole
3	Shallots, large, sliced

THE DUCK

2	Duck breasts, skin-on,

Salt, Pepper, to taste

1 tsp	Neutral oil

MAKE THE RED CABBAGE

Melt 2 tablespoons butter in a large saucepan and sauté the onion until translucent; then add the cabbage strips. Cook, stirring occasionally, 5 minute to soften the cabbage. Add enough water to come half-way up the cabbage. Add apple, vinegar, cayenne, salt and pepper. Cook covered over low heat for 30 minutes. Stir in the remaining butter and adjust seasoning to taste.

MAKE THE APPLE CIDER SAUCE

Combine the cider, stock, spices and shallots in a medium saucepan. Bring to a boil over medium-high heat. Reduce heat to a bare simmer and cook until the volume reduces to 1 cup, about 40 minutes. Cool. Strain through a fine-meshed sieve and discard the solids.

While duck is cooking, reduce sauce in a skillet and cook over medium-high heat until syrupy.

COOKING THE DUCK BREASTS

Preheat oven to 350°F.

Pat duck breasts dry. With a very sharp knife, carefully score the skin of the duck breasts on a diagonal one way and then the other. Be careful not to cut all the way through the skin. Season with salt and pepper, rubbing to distribute it well.

Add the oil to a cold skillet. Place breasts skin-side down in the skillet. Gradually bring up the heat to medium-low to start rendering the fat. Pour off the fat periodically when you see it acumulating in the pan, but keep it for cooking potatoes, etc. When the skin is golden brown and crisp, turn the breasts over then place pan in oven for about 5 minutes.

FINISHING

Remove from oven and check for doneness. Let rest on a cutting board for 5 minutes while you reheat the sauce and cabbage. Slice breasts diagonally ¼-inch thick. Plate duck and spoon sauce on top.

Thyme-Smoked Salmon with Lentils & Horseradish Chantilly Cream

Serves 6

WE INTRODUCED THIS preparation during the restaurant's fifth year. It's a wonderful combination of a light herbal smoke with rich lentils and an enlivening counterpoint from the Horseradish Chantilly Cream. Use the Puy lentil. It originated in Le Puy, France, is farmed here, and packs unparalled texture and taste. Start the dish the day before. Though the list of ingredients may look daunting, there's little last-minute work, making for a great dinner party presentation.

SALMON

2 lb	Salmon, preferably king, skinless, center cut, trimmed and deboned.

FISH BRINE

4 oz	Salt
6 oz	Brown sugar
1	Bay leaf, crushed
1 tsp	Allspice, ground
1 tsp	Mace, ground
½ tsp	Cloves, crushed
1½ qt	Water

HERBS FOR SMOKING

1	Fresh thyme on the stem, handful

LENTILS

1	Bacon slice, small dice
1 tsp	Garlic, minced
¼ cup	Celery root, small dice
¼ cup	Leeks, small dice
½ cup	Yellow onions, small dice
¼ cup	Carrot, small dice
½ oz	Tomato paste
½ lb	Lentils, Puy ("Green French")
6 cups	Chicken stock
1 cup	Apple juice
1	Rosemary sprig, chopped
1	Thyme sprig, chopped
1	Apple, Granny Smith, diced
1 oz	Sour cream

HORSERADISH CHANTILLY

½ cup	Heavy cream
2 oz	Horseradish, freshly grated
½	Lemon, juiced
½ tsp	Honey, mild

BRINE FISH

Combine all brine ingredients in a nonreactive saucepan. Boil. Cool. Refrigerate.

Add salmon portions to the cold brine and weigh down with a plate. Remove from brine after 40 or 50 minutes. Blot salmon dry and rest uncovered on a greased wire rack in the fridge overnight, or dry with a fan if using within a few hours. The surface should feel dry and slightly tacky, not wet and slippery.

COLD SMOKE THE SALMON

Cut into 6 portions. See "How to Smoke on Your Stovetop" on page 120. If fresh thyme is unavailable for smoking, use fruitwood chips or black tea. Don't allow the salmon to cook; refrigerate the pan, rack, salmon, and foil before you begin to keep everything cold.

PREPARE THE PUY LENTILS

In a medium-large pot, render the bacon. Add the garlic, celery root, carrot, leek, and onion. Cook until they are almost brown. Add the tomato paste and stir for several minutes. Then add lentils and stock. Simmer until the lentils are almost tender, 25–30 minutes.

Add the apple juice and herbs and simmer for 15 minutes until the lentils are fully cooked. Add diced apples, heat through, and at the last minute, fold in the sour cream. Salt and pepper to taste. Hold warm, or make ahead and reheat.

MAKE THE HORSERADISH CHANTILLY CREAM

Whip cream to soft peaks. Add horseradish, lemon juice, and honey, and stir to combine. Salt and pepper, to taste.

COOK SALMON

Remove fish from the fridge and allow to warm at room temperature for 30 minutes. Bake salmon on the wire rack in a 350°F oven until just done, about 7–12 minutes. Spoon hot lentils on plates, place salmon on top, and serve with a spoonful horseradish chantilly.

Mom's Farmhouse Turkey Stuffing or Dressing

Makes 2 quarts: One 9″ × 13″ casserole dish (as a dressing) or to stuff one a turkey.

I ALWAYS LOVED MOM'S turkey stuffing. No oysters for us! Our family did the bird with a traditional bread stuffing, which adds drippings as it bakes. I believe this is the only recipe I ever asked Mom to memorialize in her delicate hand-flowing script.

Stuff your bird, or bake this as a side of dressing.

My mother, Lola, learning to truss a turkey from her grandmother. Mom probably raised the turkey herself on their Depression-era farm. Note how turkey breasts have grown during the intervening century.

MOM'S THANKSGIVING STUFFING

14 cups	Bread cubes, cut into ½″–¾″ squares from sourdough, French, Pullman, buns, or Italian loaves (about 2 pounds bread). Don't use bagged store-bought croutons.

Dry at room temp uncovered for two days. Or put in 150°F oven until barely crusted but still soft.

1½ cups	Butter, unsalted
1 cup	Onion, yellow, diced
1 cup	Celery, chopped
1 cup	Walnuts, roughly chopped
20	Sage leaves, fresh
2 Tbsp	Poultry seasoning, store bought or homemade*
1 Tbsp	Salt
1 tsp	Black pepper
1½ cups	Whole milk (Substitute stock only if it is a rich homemade turkey or chicken stock. Store-bought stock's flavor is too watery.)
2	Eggs, lightly beaten
Optional	Fresh chopped sage, parsley, thyme leaves, or rosemary leaves as desired

* HOMEMADE POULTRY SEASONING

4 tsp	Sage, ground
3 tsp	Thyme, ground
1 tsp	Marjoram, ground
2 tsp	Rosemary, ground
⅛ tsp	Nutmeg, ground
1 tsp	Pepper, white or black

Combine ingredients. Can be used as a poultry rub, too.

The amount of this stuffing is sufficient for a large turkey. Do not stuff a turkey tightly, or it will impede the roasting. Bake extra stuffing in a casserole.

Preheat your oven to 350°F.

In a large skillet, melt the butter and sauté the onion for 1 minute, then add the celery. Cook 10 minutes, being careful not to burn the onions.

Put the bread cubes (hold back one cup) in a large mixing bowl. Pour the onion mixture over the cubes.

Sprinkle on the remaining dry ingredients and add the milk (or chicken stock). Mix well with your hands.

If the stuffing seems too wet, add in the reserved bread cubes.

For a side dish of dressing, spread the mixture evenly in the prepared casserole dish—bake for 30–50 minutes until the top is golden and crisp.

Remove from oven. Finish with fresh herbs.

Best served warm. If made ahead, reheat gently in an oven or with short blasts in a microwave.

Store leftovers in a covered, airtight container.

Spaetzle & Co.

Makes 8 cups of finished spaetzle. One cup per serving is typical.

I **THINK WE SERVED** spaetzle only a couple of time at The Herbfarm, though Carrie remembers the version with Chestnut Flour (substitute ¼ of the total flour).

Why? I suppose because it is a somewhat rustic dish. But the "pasta" is quick and tasty when finished—perfect for home.

Think of Spaetzle as the child of gnocci and pasta, but easier to make. In fact it is a loose batter pushed through the round holes of a colander into boiling water. If you want to "go pro," you can find nice, inexpensive spaetzle makers online. This basic recipe is versatile. You can add anything you want to the batter from soft, chopped herbs to powdered mushrooms or other flours.

THE SPAETZEL

8	Eggs, whole
1⅓ cup	Milk, more as needed
4 cups	All-purpose flour
1½ tsp	Salt
6 Tbsp	Butter, unsalted

Salt, pepper, nutmeg, to taste

FOR FRYING AT THE END (OPTIONAL)

Fresh basil or Italian parsley, a loose handful

3	Garlic cloves, chopped

Olive oil as needed

Salt, pepper, to taste

PORK CHOPS

2	Pork chops, bone-in, thick-cut

Salt, pepper, to taste

2 Tbsp	Neutral oil
2 Tbsp	Butter, per chop (one when chop goes in oven; one to whisk into pan juices)

MAKE THE SPAETZEL

Whisk together all wet ingredients. Gradually whisk in flour. Season well with salt, pepper, and nutmeg.

Adjust the amount of flour as needed; dough texture should be between dough and pancake batter, barely falling off a whisk. If too stiff, add a little more milk.

Let batter rest for a few minutes. Meanwhile, bring a pot of salted water to a boil. Set a colander on top.

Using a rubber spatula or plastic bowl scraper, push the batter through the colander into the water.

When spatezel floats, cook another 2–3 minutes, then spoon into a bowl of ice water. Spaetzle will shrink in size. Drain and rinse well, twice. If not frying immediately, toss with some neutral oil to keep it from sticking.

To serve, heat butter in a frying pan and sauté until it begins to brown. Toss with the optional ingredients.

COOK THE PORK CHOPS

Preheat the oven to 375°F.

Throughly dry chops. Season generously with salt and pepper. Put 2 tablespoons of oil in a ovenproof skillet on high heat. Add chops. Sear until brown. Flip and sear the other side and the edges. Top each chop with a tablespoon of butter.

Transfer skillet to oven and roast until internal temperature in the thickest part reads 135°F. Remove and let rest for 10 minutes. Internal temp will rise to 145°F, medium rare.

To serve, combine pan and meat juices. Whisk in a tablespoon of butter. Drizzle on top of the plated pork.

Pan-Seared, Oven-Roasted, Double-Cut Porkchop with Spaetzel and Saged Apple Balls (recipe for balls on page 210)

Black Pepper Chanterelle Ravioli with Corn Jus

Makes 4 servings

CHANTERELLE MUSHROOMS APPEAR in the Northwest beginning in late August. The wild foragers prize the mushrooms for their fruity flavor and woodsy aroma. They harmonize beautifully with fresh corn. If you're "foraging" for chanterelles at the grocer, look for those of light color running into dark yellow. Don't buy brown ones. Feel them: if they are rain-soaked, choose the smallest ones. If you must use wet chanterelles, use one-and-a-half times as much by weight. Don't use dried chanterelles; they have little flavor.

MAKE PASTA DOUGH

Put all of the dough ingredients in the bowl of a food processor. Pulse until it has the consistency of bread crumbs. Flour a work surface and knead until smooth. Form ball. Brush with oil. Wrap and let rest at room temp for 30 minutes or overnight in the fridge. Return to room temp before rolling pasta.

BLACK PEPPER DOUGH

2½ cups	Flour, "00" or bread flour
4	Eggs, large
1 Tbsp	Extra-virgin olive oil
2 Tbsp	Pepper, freshly ground

MUSHROOM FILLING

8 oz	Chanterelles, minced
1 Tbsp	Extra-virgin olive oil
2 Tbsp	Shallots, finely minced
2	Garlic cloves, minced
1 Tbsp	Parsley, Italian, chopped
⅛ tsp	Black pepper, ground
5 oz	Comté, Gruyère, or fontina cheese, grated
1	Egg yolk, lightly beaten

CORN SAUCE

2 Tbsp	Extra-virgin olive oil
1	Yellow onion, chop fine
2	Garlic cloves, minced
½ cup	White wine, dry
1½ Tbsp	Sherry, dry
3 cups	Chicken stock
2 cups	Corn, fresh kernels
¼ tsp	Espelette or cayenne
¼ cup	Cream, heavy
1 Tbsp	Basil or chives, chopped

MAKE THE RAVIOLI FILLING

Add oil to a medium skillet. Sauté chanterelles 5 to 10 minutes until expelled liquid dries. Remove a few of the nicest small mushroom to use as a garnish.

Add shallots, garlic, parsley, and pepper. Cook for 3 to 4 minutes. Remove from heat and mix in the cheese. Let cool, then add the beaten egg yolk to the chanterelle and cheese mixture. Mix well. Season with salt, to taste. Chill until needed.

MAKE CORN SAUCE

Heat olive oil in a medium saucepan. Add onion and garlic. Cook until soft, 5–10 minutes. Add the wine and sherry. Cook until almost dry. Add the stock, corn, and espelette (or cayenne). Bring to a boil, reduce heat, and simmer 15 minutes. Take off heat and cool a bit; then purée the sauce in a blender until silky smooth. Return to the pan, add the cream, bring to a boil before reducing to a bare simmer. Cook until it thickens. Add the herbs. Season with salt and pepper, to taste.

ROLL PASTA. MAKE THE RAVIOLI. COOK. SERVE.

Pass dough through a pasta machine according to the manufacturer's instructions. Finish with the thinnest setting. Cut rolled dough into two strips of equal lengths and widths. Brush one of the strips with egg wash (2 egg yolks and 1 tablespoon water). Spoon tablespoons of filling in the middle of one strip of pasta leaving 1½" between each mound. Cover with the second half of dough, press out air pockets, and cut around the filling.

Bring a large pot of salted water to a boil. Cook batches of the ravioli 6 to 8 minutes. Carefully remove with a slotted spoon. Serve with the corn sauce and a sprinkle of chopped herbs.

Shoestring Potatoes A.K.A. Julienne Fries

Serves 4

MATCHSTICK, SHOESTRINGS, FRENCH, and steak fries. Each size has its place and fans. But thin Julienne cuts can't be matched for sheer speed of preparation and crunchy goodness. Unlike their larger brethren, these skinny minis need only be fried once.

4 lb	Russet potatoes (about 4), peeled or not, your choice
3 Tbsp	White vinegar
2 quarts	Neutral oil for frying
	Salt, to taste
	Lots of paper towels

With a mandolin, *carefully* slice ⅛" × ⅛" or even ¹⁄₁₆" juliennes from russet potatoes. Rinse in a bowl of cold water with a splash of white vinegar. Pat on paper towels until *thoroughly* dry.

In a heavy deep pot, heat 2 quarts of oil to 400°F. Cook potatoes in 4 batches until golden. Allow the oil to return to 400°F before cooking the next batch. Drain well on paper towels, salt, and serve.

Quick-Pickled Radish: Easy as 1–2–3!

Makes 5 cups pickling solution

THIS QUICK PICKLING recipe is called upon all the time at The Herbfarm. It pickles all sorts of vegetables, fish, and even berries. The formulation is easy to remember: 1 part vinegar, 2 parts sugar, and 3 parts water.

Combine liquids and dissolve sugar. Add mustard seeds, bay leaf, juniper berries, or whole allspice, to taste.

The thinner the slice, the faster the pickling. Submerge radishes in pickling solution, and let stand at room temperature. Thinly sliced radishes are ready as soon as 30 minutes; spiral-cut daikon, 40 minutes; 2 hours for beets; 45 minutes for onions.

Refrigerate for up to 2–3 weeks in their pickling liquid.

This amount (left) will pickle roughly 40 radishes.

40	Radishes
3 cups	Water
2 cups	Sugar
1 cup	White vinegar

Carrots Glazed with Pear Brandy

Serves 4

STEVE MCCARTHY CAPTURES Oregon in a bottle. His Clear Creek Oregon Pear Brandy is the pristine essence of the Bartlett pear, giving these carrots and your taste buds a saunter through the orchard.

1 lb	Carrots, medium size, peeled	With a small paring knife, trim carrots into 2″ lengths. Pare to an enlongated olive shape (optional).
1 cup	Water	Place carrots in a shallow pan. Add water, butter, and honey. Bring to a boil and simmer until carrots are tender and the water has evaporated. Roll around to coat each piece. Add brandy, cook 1–2 minutes.
2 Tbsp	Butter, unsalted	
2 Tbsp	Honey	
2 Tbsp	Pear brandy, Oregon or other	
Salt, pepper, to taste		

Brussels Sprouts with Shallots

Serves 4

I SHUDDER TO REMEMBER the Brussels sprouts of my childhood. Mom boiled and tortured the little veggie balls into mushy blobs. Entering the house, it was clear when sprouts were on our nightly menu: the place reeked of sulfur fumes. Luckily times change. Everyone will gobble up these toothsome little "cabbages," which are so easy to prepare.

18 Brussels sprouts	Bring a large pot of salted water to a boil. Add the brussels sprouts and cook for 4 minutes. Remove sprouts and shock in ice water. Drain sprouts and cut each in half lenghtwise.
2 Tbsp Butter	
1 Shallot, minced	
2 Tbsp Water	
Salt and pepper	Melt butter in a skillet. Add the shallots and sweat over medium heat for 1–2 minutes. Add the sprouts and water. Continue cooking for 4–5 minutes, turning sprouts often. Season with salt and pepper, to taste.

Herbfarm Rosemary Shortbread

Makes about 24 shortbreads

THESE HERBAL SHORTBREADS swell with memories of the original Herbfarm kitchen and era. Chef Bill Kraut, who worked with me in the kitchen, brought the rice flour to the recipe. This, I believe, is the "secret" to the success of the preparation.

1 cup	Butter, room temp	Preheat oven to 375°F. Line 2 baking sheets with parchment.
½ cup	Sugar	
1½ Tbsp	Rosemay, fresh, finely minced	In a mixer, cream butter until light in color. Mix in sugar, salt, and rosemary, then add flours. Dough will be soft. Wrap and chill for 1 hour.
1½ cups	Flour, all-purpose	
⅓ cup	Rice Flour	
¼ tsp	Salt	

Flour a board. Roll out dough to ¼" thick. Cut into 1½" × 2" shapes. Put on baking sheets; bake 10–12 minutes or until golden. Store in airtight container. Pair with desserts or enjoy on their own.

Saged Apple Balls

Makes 40–50 balls

WINE-POACHED FRUITS ARE easy and versatile. They can accompany dessert as well as make excellent friends with savory dishes such as duck, rabbit, and pork. The fresh sage is essential, imparting a sweet pungency. No fresh sage? Substitute cinnamon, rosemary, bay, or pepper.

1½ cups	Red wine	In a small saucepan, combine sage, wine, and sugar. Simmer gently for 15–20 minutes.
¾ cup	Sugar	
8	Sage leaves, fresh	
4	Apple, Granny Smith	Peel apples. Cut out balls with a small melon baller. Simmer balls in the reduced

liquid for 5 minutes. Don't cover the pan. Transfer the balls into a container. Cover with the liquid. Refrigerate overnight.

To serve, remove balls from liquid. In a skillet, reduce a bit of the liquid until it is syrupy. Add balls, toss to coat.

White Chocolate–Dipped Ground Cherries

As many as you have the ingredients for

WHAT TASTES SOMEWHAT like a grape crossed with tomato and is typically more tangy than sweet? Why, the ground cherry (*Physalis pruinosa*). This not-well-known crop, a relative of the tomatillo, is easy to grow in your own garden and can be found in some farmer's markets in late summer and early autumn. It is also known by other names, including husk cherry, husk tomato, husk berry, golden berry, or cape gooseberry.

The slight tang of the ground cherry is amazingly harmonious with the vanilla-like flavor of white chocolate. I don't recall when we first began dipping the fruity orbs in the white chocolate, but the combo is a classic. When pulled back and left attached to the fruit, the husk makes for an easy-to-handle bite with an artistic flair.

Ground cherries

Pure white chocolate (check ingredients to be sure there are no other fats or oils)

Gently melt white chocolate in a double boiler (pan over simmering water) until it melts. Pull chocolate on and off the heat as needed. White chocolate has a very low melt point. Don't let temperature exceed 125°F!

Pull back husk on the fruits and dip, leaving some of the ground cherry showing. Allow to cool on a parchment paper-lined baking sheet. Store cool in an air tight container. Serve to "yums" and raves.

Caramelized Herbal Pumpkin Ice Cream

Makes 1 quart

WE USED TO GROW an acre of pumpkins. Not so much for the restaurant, as for the amusement of children and "big kids." It can take a stretch of imagination to figure out what to do with the leftover orange fellows. How about Caramelized Pumpkin Ice Cream with Rosemary and Thyme?

ICE CREAM

1½ cup	Half-and-half
2½ cups	Cream
¼ cup	Sugar, for the milk mixture
3	Rosemary sprigs, 4″–6″
2	Thyme sprigs, 4″–6″
1 cup	Sugar to caramelize
5	Egg yolks
½ cup	Pumpkin purée, homemade or canned
Salt, pinch	

MAKE THE ICE CREAM

Put half-and-half, cream, and ¼ cup sugar in a medium pot. Add the herbs and bring to a simmer. Remove from heat and steep 30–45 minutes. Remove herbs.

In separate pot, melt the sugar over medium-high heat until it caramelizes. Don't stir. When melted sugar is a medium-deep golden color, slowly add the herbed milk, stirring with a wooden spoon. Cook on medium to dissolve any unmelted pieces of the caramel. Strain the mixture.

In a medium bowl, whisk up the egg yolks with the pumpkin purée and salt.

Slowly add the hot caramel-milk mixture, stirring constantly.

Return the mixture to the pan and cook on medium heat, stirring constantly, until the mixture thickens to coat the back of a spoon.

Remove from heat. Strain through a fine strainer. Cool and refrigerate for an hour or overnight.

Pour chilled base into an ice cream churn according to the manufacturer's directions.

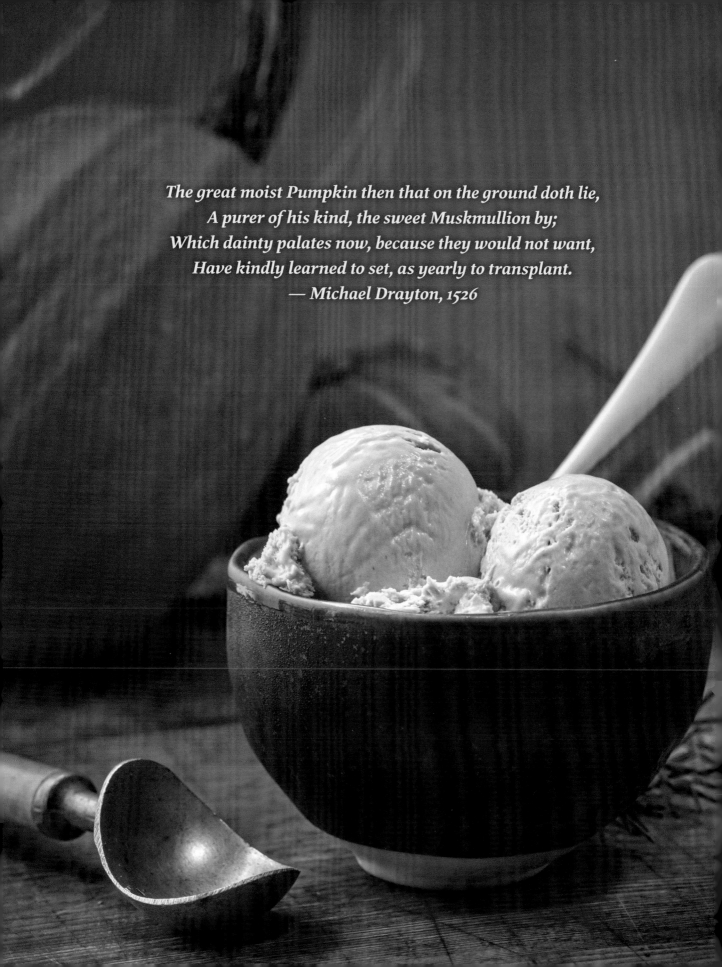

The great moist Pumpkin then that on the ground doth lie,
A purer of his kind, the sweet Muskmullion by;
Which dainty palates now, because they would not want,
Have kindly learned to set, as yearly to transplant.
— Michael Drayton, 1526

Red-Wine Poached Pear with Gorgonzola-Walnut Ball

Serves 4

RED WINE-POACHED PEARS are a winter classic. I've served some version of this for holiday desserts for many years. Consider this "recipe" only a jumping-off point. The pears can be served classically with a syrup of reduced poaching liquid. Add a sprig of mint to the plated pear for color and flavor counterpoint. Or you can hollow out much of the pear; then use a pastry bag to stuff it with your choice of flavored, slightly sweetened cream cheese. The Gorgonzola-walnut mixture below is such a stuffing. The possibilities are endless.

When shopping for poaching pears, be sure they are slightly underripe. Bosc, Anjou, and Comice are the standard autumn pears. If you're lucky enough to discover tiny Sekel pears that aren't too ripe, you can create a mini version of this pear dessert.

In bowl: Sekel Pears
Left: Bosc Pear

GORGONZOLA-WALNUT BALLS

¾ cup   Cream cheese
½ cup   Gorgonzola cheese crumbles
½ cup   Mascarpone cheese
2 tsp   Brandy, Cognac, or pear grappa
1 Tbsp   Extra-virgin olive oil, fruity
⅛ tsp   Cayenne
Salt, pepper, nutmeg, to taste
1 cup   Walnuts, roasted, chopped

In a large bowl, combine the cheeses, brandy, olive oil, cayenne, and a grating of nutmeg. Scoop 1 tablespoon of cheese mixture and drop in a bowl with the walnuts. Roll it around until the cheese is completely covered. Refrigerate. Bring to a cool room temperature for serving.

WINE POACHING LIQUID

4–5 Cups   Wine, red
1¾ cups   Sugar
1   Bay leaf
1   Star anise, crushed
1   Cinnamon stick, 4″
2   Cloves
4   Peppercorns, black
1   Lemon, Juiced

The amount of poaching liquid will depend on the size of the pears and the width and depth of the container for the pears. Whole pears will require doubling the recipe.

POACHING LIQUID

Put wine and sugar is a large pot. Bring to a boil. Tie the herbs and spices in cheese cloth or put in a large teaball and add to the mixture. Simmer 30 minutes until well infused.

FOR POACHING 4 LARGE PEARS

Peel pears, slice them in half (top to bottom) and core with a small melon baller. Add the pears to the hot poaching liquid and simmer for 10 minutes. Allow to cool in the liquid. Store in the fridge for a minimum of 2 hours or better yet for 2 days.

It's Nutty—Hazelnut Cheesecake

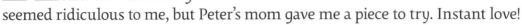

Serves 8

HARD TO BELIEVE, but I was in my teens and had never heard of cheesecake until Peter Haskell, a neighbor kid, said he was having cheesecake for dinner. The idea seemed ridiculous to me, but Peter's mom gave me a piece to try. Instant love!

This version salutes the famous nut of the region: the hazelnut or filbert. We also have a wild version. This woody shrub, not really a tree, hides its nuts under its leaves. But the sleuthing is worth it mid-to-late summer.

HAZELNUT BOTTOM CRUST

Combine the chopped hazelnuts, all-purpose flour, powdered sugar, and salt in a mixer. Add cubes of the softened butter and mix well. Add water, a bit at a time, while mixing until the dough comes together into a ball. Wrap the dough in platic wrap; flatten it to a thick disk, and let it rest in the refrigerator for an hour.

When ready to use, remove it from the fridge and let it warm for 10 minutes. Heat oven to 350°F. On parchment, roll the dough until it is a larger circle than your 8" springform pan: 10"–11". Place your springform top on the dough and cut the dough into a circle. Transfer it to the buttered bottom of the springform. Press the dough gently to remove any gaps between it and the sides of the pan. Prick all over with a fork; prebake in the oven for 10 to 11 minutes. Remove. Let cool a bit.

HAZELNUT CRUST

1 cup	Hazelnuts, raw
1⅓ cup	All-purpose flour
½ cup	Powdered sugar
Salt	pinch
½ cup	Butter, softened, diced
2–3 Tbsp	Water

FILLING

1 cups	Hazelnuts, raw
1 Tbsp	Extra-virgin olive oil
¼ tsp	Lemon zest
¼ tsp	Rosemary
2 lb	Cream cheese (four 8-ounce packages), room temperature
1¾ cups	Sugar
4	Eggs, whole
1½ tsp	Lemon juice
½ tsp	Lemon zest, grated

SAUCING (OPTIONAL)

Blueberry, strawberry, sea-salted caramel, huckleberry, chocolate, Nutella, and heavy cream

MAKE THE FILLING

Spread nuts in a large ovenproof skillet and roast at 325°F until lightly browned, 8–10 minutes. Remove from oven.

Wrap nuts in a towel and then rub to remove the skins. Heat the olive oil in the skillet; add the nuts, the lemon zest, the rosemary, and a large pinch of salt. Cook, stirring constantly, for about 2 minutes. Chop the nuts coarsely with a nut chopper or food processor.

With a mixer, beat the cream cheese with the sugar until it is light and fluffy. Add the eggs one at a time, mixing well before adding the next. Fold in the chopped nuts and lemon juice and zest. Pour batter into the 8-inch springform pan. Smooth the top.

BAKE

Heat oven to 325°F. Wrap the bottom of the pan in foil so it can't leak. Set the pan in an ovenproof baking dish. Pour boiling water around the pan, so it comes about halfway up the sides. Bake for 1½ hours until a cake tester comes out clean. The center should still jiggle slightly. If not, it is overcooked. Turn off the heat. Prop the oven door open 2 inches and leave the pan untouched for an hour as the cake finishes gently cooking in the cooling oven.

Foragers: Look for the wild beaked hazelnut in the Northwest woods.

Drying our Roy's Abenaki Flint corn for the 100-Mile Dinner

Winter

Photo by Paul Houser

Winter

A Low Sun Rising

WINTER. It's the darkest and the coldest of the seasons, but with chill, and the possible snowfall comes the holiday season, giving us wonderous moments for cozy retreat, hibernation, and family time.

With candles lit and hearth aflame we nibble on preserved fruits, fresh game, and cured meats. The earthy delights of Sunchokes, Douglas fir, and cranberries melding deliciously with oysters, caviar, and the rich, umami infused by truffles.

Delighting in camaraderie as we indulge in sweet luxuries of soufflés, tarts, and cookies galore as the ovens fill the house with such savory vapors.

Toasting to friends and family with homemade eggnog or mulled wine, we reminisce, knowing that the light and warmth of spring will return to us soon.

This table has been a house in the rain,
an umbrella in the sun

—— Joy Harjo

Winter Food Friends

WINTER IS A TIME to enjoy farm and nature's fare in the warmth of your home. Most winter foods are the harvest of the growing season, but frosty weather enlivens greens left in the field, giving them a sweet and vibrant flavor found at not other times of the year.

Great Pairings for Winter Fare

Chicken	Garlic, lemon, Italian parsley, chives, tarragon, oregano, rosemary, coriander, savory, sage
Duck	Star anise, ginger, Sichuan pepper, orange, lemon, lime, 5-spice, basil, rosemary, sage, thyme, bay, coriander
Turkey	Sage, rosemary, thyme, bay, Italian parsley, marjoram, garlic, lemon
Beef	Thyme, black pepper, onion, rosemary, sage, basil, Italian parsley, horseradish
Pork	Sage, rosemary, mustard, mustard seeds, cumin
Lamb	Thyme, rosemary, pepper, Italian parsley, mustard, garlic, mint
Fish	Chervil, dill, fennel, French tarragon, garlic, Italian parsley, rosemary, English thyme, lemon thyme, shiso
Salmon/Trout	Chives, dill, garlic, citrus, spearmint, mustard, Italian parsley, pepper, shallots, thyme, balsamic vinegar, sorrel, watercress
Halibut	Garlic, lemon, Italian parsley, shallots, thyme, sherry vinegar
Shellfish	Lovage, paprika, Italian parsley, pepper flakes, shallots
Crab	Basil, chives, lemon, oregano, thyme, rosemary, Italian parsley, sage, onions, mustard, and citrus. Avocado is magical.
Mussels/Clams	Lovage, Italian parsley, garlic, pepper, chili peppers, bay, chives, lemon, cayenne, saffron
Oysters	Shallots, pepper, Italian parsley, lemon, leeks, chives, chervil, vinegar, caviar

Potatoes	Garlic, onion, rosemary, thyme, pepper flakes, tarragon
Squashes	Bay, chives, cumin, garlic, hot peppers, marjoram, oregano, rosemary, savory, thyme, ginger root
Pumpkin	Spices: cinnamon, nutmeg, cloves, ginger, cumin, chilis, cayenne, allspice, vanilla, pepper
Corn	Basil, bell peppers, chili pepper, dill, garlic, peppers, onions
Peas	Mint, basil, chives, garlic, onion, butter, cream, ham, tarragon
Mushrooms	Garlic, caraway, chives, marjoram, rosemary, bay, onion, extra-virgin olive oil
Breads	Anise, caraway, coriander, dill, marjoram, oregano, rosemary, thyme
Cheese	Basil, chives, curry, dill, fennel, garlic, marjoram, oregano, sage, thyme
Pasta	Basil, oregano, thyme, rosemary, Italian parsley, sage, Parmesan
Eggs	Basil, dill, garlic, oregano, Italian parsley, tarragon
Greens	Garlic, olive oil, green onions, chili sauce, yellow onions, ham/bacon, red wine vinegar, balsamic vinegar
Soups	Bay, tarragon, lovage, marjoram, parsley, savory, rosemary, thyme
Salads	Garlic, marjoram, oregano, rosemary, chervil, Italian parsley, chive
Fruit	Candied angelica, anise, cinnamon, coriander, candied ginger, lemon verbena, mints, nutmeg, rose geranium

A Treat & Greet for Guests

Cheese to Please

CHEESE IS THE **GREATEST** greet and nibble for a party. The world's cheeses offer you a seemingly endless array of flavors and textures. Artisan cheese—like fine wine—speaks of a particular place and time. As they say in the wine world, a fine cheese expresses the "terroir" of its home.

Some cow cheeses, like Gruyère, Emmentaler, and Appenzeller, capture the sunshine and green grass of high Alpine meadows. Other cheeses speak to dry hillsides and garrigue where only goats can fare.

There is no such thing as Swiss Cheese . . . only cheese from Switzerland. Yet the name, like cheddar, has been co-opted into a banal and shrink-wrapped factory product for the American grocery story.

Shown here are some real cheeses to delight you and your guests. They're among hundreds of choices from which you can explore the journey from grass to milk to luscious fare.

A Mixed Board of Cow, Goat & Sheep Cheeses

BUILD YOUR CHEESE BOARD with a range of selections from mild to punchy and from softer to more aged. Offer your guests other flavorful nibbles to accompany their enjoyment of the cheeses:

MEATS: Salami & Prosciutto di Parma

FRUITS: Grapes, sliced pears, dates, figs, dried apricots

ANTIPASTO: Olives, cornichons, Piquillo peppers

NUTS: Marcona almonds, walnuts, candied pecans

SWEETS: Jams, preserves, jellies, honey

BREADS: And, of course, plenty of bread and crackers!

A Moovable Feast

❶ Cascadia Creamery Sawtooth, Washington
❷ Beecher's Flagship Reserve: Washington
❸ Parmigiano Reggiano: Italy
❹ Stilton: England

A Few Other Cow Cheeses
Saint-Nectaire: France
Cascadua Creamery Cloud Cap: Washington
Alpine Tommes: Switzerland & France
English Cheddar, esp. from Neal's Yard
Rogue Creamery (various blues): Southern
Oregon

Have a Cow

Revel in Chèvre

❶ Laura Chenel Fresh Goat: California
❷ Cypress Grove Purple Haze, California
❸ Humboldt Fog: California
❹ Twin Sisters Farmhouse (cow): Washington
❺ Beemster Goat Gouda: Holland

A Few Other Goat Cheeses
Quillisascut Farmstead Curado: Wash.
River's Edge Up in Smoke: Oregon
Rove de Garrigues: France
Robiola Tre Latti (cow/goat/sheep: Italy
Tieton Farmstead Venue (goat/sheep: Wash.

Got Your Goat

Ewephoria

❶ Central Coast Ewenique: California
❷ P'tit Basque: Spain
❸ Idiazabal: Spain
❹ Young Manchego: Spain
❺ Locatelli Pecorino Romano: Italy
❻ Roquefort Papillon Black Label: France

A Few Other Sheep Cheeses
Pecorino Toscano: Italy
Torta del Casar: Spain
Rodolphe Le Meunier Tomme Brulee: France
Queijo di Évora: Portugal
Robiola Bosina: Italy

Counting Sheep

Frothy Douglas Fir Eggnog

Holiday Greetings Fir Yew!

Serves 4

A **CUP OF EGGNOG** evokes my childhood. Christmas wouldn't have been complete without a punchbowl of the sweet eggy rich goodness with warming spices. Usually, Dad made the festive concoction whose beginnings harken back to the middle ages. My brother Bob and I often drank our share in front of our real, wood-burning fireplace. Home sweet home.

This Northwest version is a fun alternative to the standard eggnog. In the spirit of the holiday season, it's infused with woodsy Douglas fir. Add alcohol to all or part of each batch for parties and visiting guests.

1 quart	Milk, whole
1½ cups	Douglas fir needles, chopped
4	Eggs, yolks and whites separated
½ cup	Sugar
¼ tsp	Cinnamon
¼ tsp	Nutmeg
	Salt, pinch

OPTIONAL

¼–½ cup alcohol such as brandy, rum, bourbon, sweet sherry, or a dark stout beer

Whipped cream for top with a grate of nutmeg and/or a sprinkle of cinnamon

In a medium saucepan, combine milk and fir needles. Bring to a simmer and cook for 15 minutes. Remove from heat and add spices. Cover, and let infuse for another 15 minutes.

While infusing, whisk the egg yolks and sugar until thick and light in color. Pour milk infusion through a fine sieve into the egg yolk mixture, whisking constantly. Return to saucepan and gently cook, stirring constantly, until mixture thickens and will barely coat the back of a spoon. Remove from heat, strain again, and chill.

To serve, whip egg whites to moderately stiff peaks and fold them into the eggnog. Add alcohol, if using. Ladle into mug. Serve with a stir-stick of fir and a dollop of whipped cream.

OR YOU CAN MAKE IT GREEN

If you grind the fir needles with the sugar, you can impart a green tint to the eggnog.

Yule Tree Mulled Wine

Serves 6–8

AMAZINGLY, **OLD LATIN** texts and mosaics from excavated villas show that mulled wine has been drunk in Rome since the second century. As the heating and spicing of wine became common, the Romans spread the practice across their empire. Though the empire collapsed over 1,500 years ago, the tradition of a warming spiced wine never waned. In keeping with the spirit of the Yuletide, we devised this version which we season with citrusy and woodsy Douglas Fir needles.

The combination of simmering the wine plus the addition of water makes for a nice winter warmer for entertaining.

1	Bottle fruity red wine
½ cup	Water
1 cup	Sugar
1 cup	Douglas fir needles, chopped
½	Cinnamon stick, broken
4	Cloves, whole
3	Cardamom pods, crushed

Douglas fir sprigs and lemon slices for garnish

In a medium saucepan, combine all ingredients except garnishes. Over medium heat, stir to dissolve sugar. Raise temperature to boil; then reduce the heat to low. Simmer 10 minutes. Remove from heat. Let steep an hour.

Strain out solids and reheat (but not boil) to serve and add garnishes.

MAKE SUGAR-FROSTED NEEDLES AS A DRINK GARNISH

Why not frost the wine's stir-stick garnish to give it a wintry twist?

In a small bowl, lightly beat 1 egg white with a teaspoon of water. Put 2 cups of superfine sugar in a separate bowl.

Use a small brush to paint the needles with the egg white mixture. Hold the needles over the bowl of sugar and sprinkle sugar with your fingers to coat.

Place on a wire rack and let dry at room temperature for 30 minutes or overnight. Carefully store in an airtight container until needed.

Beggar's Purses Filled with Caviar

Makes 6 first-course servings

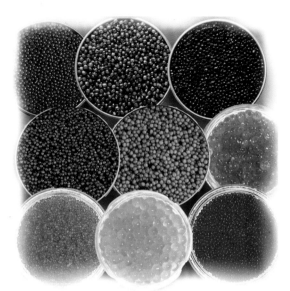

THE 1980S AND 1990S were a major culinary apprenticeship for me. Not only was I dining at great restaurants in Europe, but also at what I found as the most magical restaurant in America: The Quilted Giraffe in New York. Their signature beginning was a little crepe purse filled with caviar. This is the original version without the supplemetal edible gold leaf on top!

1½ cups	Whole milk, more as needed
2	Eggs
1 cup	Wondra® or instant flour
1 tsp	Salt
1 Tbsp	Unsalted butter, warm and melted
12	Chives, fresh, blanched and shocked
¼ cup	Crème fraîche
6 oz	Caviar, your choice
¼ cup	Clarified butter, melted

Whisk milk, eggs, flour, and salt until entirely incorporated. Add 1–2 additional tablespoons of milk as needed until the consistency of thin pancake batter. Add the melted butter. Strain to remove lumps. Preheat a small nonstick skillet on medium. Brush with clarified butter. Pour a scant ¼ cup of batter into the pan and swirl pan quickly to spread the batter. Cook until set, 30–45 seconds. Turn over the crepe and cook for 10 seconds. Crepes should be paper thin and white. Repeat to use all of the batter.

Put a teaspoon of crème fraîche and a tablespoon of caviar in the center of a crepe. Pull up edges to form a bundle. Tie shut with a chive. Brush top of beggar's purse with clarified butter just before serving.

A Visit to the Caviar Bar

Sturgeon—The word "caviar" is synonymous with sturgeon. Sturgeon caviar can be wild or farmed. Different subspecies create a range of flavors, colors, and the bead size of the eggs. Ossetra, Sevruga, and Beluga are the stars of the sturgeon world and come in various grades. As wild stocks of sturgeon become threatened, new hybrids that breed in captivity offer alternatives but are still expensive. $$$$

Paddlefish—I love this wild native caviar from Montana. The high-quality black caviar is much like sturgeon roe. Paddlefish yield medium-sized caviar grains   firm in texture and providing a strong   ocean flavor with a bold, earthy finish and gray-colored beads like osetra. $$$

Salmon—Here in the Pacific Northwest, salmon caviar reigns as the top choice for all-around gourmet enjoyment. Its bright orange color and briny pop make it the most popular "Ikura" caviar in Japanese Sushi restaurants. Salmon Ikura can be created from all of our Pacific species, but Keta (Chum) and Sockeye salmon are popular and available. $$

Other Caviars—Technically, only sturgeon qualify for the name caviar. But many fish offer delightful alternatives. Trout roe is a beautiful gold. Flying fish eggs are tiny and pop in the mouth. Lumpfish roe (red or black) is priced such that you should feel free to spread it on toast or toss it in omelets or risotto. $

Crepe in 6"–7" pan

Add sour cream and caviar

Pleat crepe and tie with a chive

Prawn & Rutabaga Bisque with Thyme & Paprika

Yields 3 Quarts: 12 8-Ounce Servings

AMONG THE WINTER field vegetables, rutabaga is certainly the least-known and most underrated. As an ancient marriage between an unknown cabbage and turnip, it has a distinct behind-the-scenes earthiness that lends character to dishes like this winter farm-inspired shrimp bisque.

3 lb	Prawns, jumbo, peeled and deveined
2½ cups	Rutabaga, peeled, diced, divided use
2	Celery stalks, diced
1	Carrot, diced
1	Yellow onion, diced
4	Garlic cloves, peeled
1	Bay leaf
¾ cup	White wine, dry, not oaky
¾ cup	Heavy cream
4 Tbsp	Unsalted butter, divided
4 cups	Fish stock (canned "Bar Harbor," or clam nectar)
4 cups	Chicken stock
2 Tbsp	Smoked paprika
2 Tbsp	Cornstarch
2 Tbsp	Thyme, fresh leaves, divided use

Salt, pepper, cayenne to taste

Melt 2 tablespoons of butter over low heat in a four-quart pot.

Add the celery, carrot, onions, garlic, and all but 1 cup of the rutabaga. Cover pan and cook until the vegetables are soft but not browned. Add a bit of water if necessary to finish softening without coloring.

Add the wine and bay leaf and simmer, uncovered, until reduced to a quarter cup.

Add fish stock, chicken stock, and three-quarters of the prawns.

Add half of the thyme leaves. Simmer everything for 10 or 12 minutes; then add cream and simmer for 10 minutes more. Add the paprika. Remove bay leaf.

Bring a small saucepan of lightly salted water to a boil. Add remaining shrimp and poach until just tender, about 2–3 minutes. Remove shrimp and add the remaining rutabaga. Simmer until soft but still has some "tooth" to it. Remove rutabaga set both aside, reserving the blanching water for thinning the soup if needed.

Transfer to a blender and blend until the bisque base is silky smooth, thinning with the reserved water as needed. Return to the pot and bring to a simmer.

Mix the cornstarch with a little water. Drizzle it into the simmering soup, stirring until it thickens. Add cooked shrimp and blanched rutabaga to warm them. Season with salt, pepper, and cayenne to taste.

Portion soup into bowls. Garnish with a sprinkle of the remaining thyme leaves.

Homemade Oyster Crackers

Yields 1 sheet pan of crackers per recipe

YES, YOU CAN make your own oyster crackers at home. They won't save you any money, but they are richer with real butter, and you can create fanciful shapes of nearly any size. These crackers are a great addition to almost any chowder or soup. They're also excellent on their own as snacks.

1⅛ cup   Flour, all purpose
1 tsp   Salt, Kosher
½ tsp   Sugar
1½ tsp   Baking powder
2 Tbsp   Unsalted butter, cold, cut into cubes
1⅛ cup   Water, cold

Heat oven to 350°F. In a large bowl, whisk together the dry ingredients.

Cut in butter with a pastry cutter or work with your fingers until the butter is incorporated and the mixture is like a coarse meal.

Add water. Stir with a spoon until everything comes together. Add more water or flour a tiny bit at a time if needed to make a dough. Cover ball and let it rest 20 minutes to fully hydrate.

Roll out dough on a well-floured surface to a tad thicker than ⅛ of an inch. Be sure the surface and the cutter are well-floured.

Cut dough into desired shapes. Transfer to a parchment-lined sheet pan. Leave a little space between crackers. Any resulting scraps can be rolled out again.

Bake crackers 20–25 minutes. Bottom edges will show color when done. Remove from oven to cool. Crackers can be stored in an airtight container for several weeks.

Seasoned Oyster Crackers

You can also season these crackers for snacking. Heat oven to 250°F. Pour 4 tablespoons of neutral oil in a bowl and add 1 to 2 tablespoons of dried ranch powder plus ½ teaspoons each of garlic powder and pepper. Pour over crackers and stir until coated. transfer to a parchment-lined sheet pan and bake for 15–20 minutes, stiring half way through. Cool and snack!

Be Creative! Control Your Own Shapes and Sizes

Square
Cut with ravioli wheel

Triangle
Cut with pizza wheel

Circle
Stamped with round cutter

Long

Oysters with Sabayon au Gratin

For 12 oysters

FOR TWENTY-FIVE YEARS I hosted glittering multicourse Christmas dinners at our home. Families grow and shrink. Eventually some relatives could no longer attend on Christmas evening. So we switched to a Christmas Eve fête.

The Italianesque "Feast of Seven Fishes" became the inspiration and theme for the Christmas Eve gathering. For this dinner, we ate these local oysters cooked under a gratinéed sabayon. Even a person who had never met an oyster that they liked exclaimed, "Delicious! This is the best oyster I've ever had!"

4 oz	Unsalted butter
12	Oysters, small or medium sized, shucked with all juices
1	Leek, medium, white part split and washed, thinly sliced
8 oz	Spinach, stems removed, coarsely chopped
1 oz	Clarified butter, melted
2	Egg yolks
2 Tbsp	White wine or Champagne

Coarse rock salt for stabilizing oysters in the oven and on service plate

Salt, white pepper, cayenne to taste

Note: *Slightly* over-season with the cayenne—the extra heat will meld with the whole oyster bite.

Melt butter in a medium skillet and sweat the leek. Add spinach and stir until entirely wilted. Season the mixture with salt and pepper.

Put the rock salt in a shallow baking dish. Place the bottom oyster shells, cup up, on the salt. Divide the spinach mixture between the 12 oysters.

Poach the oysters in the reserved oyster juice for one minute only to tighten them. Place the oysters back in their shells atop the spinach mixture.

SABAYON

Put the egg yolks and white wine in a medium metal bowl and whisk briskly over simmering water until it thickens to the ribbon stage. Move the bowl back and forth so it doesn't get too hot and curdle the eggs.

Remove from the heat. Whisk in the clarified butter and season with salt, pepper, and cayenne to taste.

Spoon the Sabayon over the oysters, covering each entirely.

When ready to serve, place under the broiler for 1 to 2 minutes until browned on top. Browning will not take long, so be vigilant!

Remove from oven. Serve oysters stabilized on the plate with salt, as necessary.

Put shells on a salt bed. Place greens in shells.

Put oysters on greens. Top with sabayon. Then broil.

Ron's Best Rosemary and Bay Leaf Yukon Gold Potato Gratin

Serves 8

I'M AN UNREPENTANT POTATO NUT. There are two "tricks" when making this dish. First, we pack flavor into it by first steeping the herbs in the simmering dairy before adding the potatoes. To save time, prepare the flavored dairy first while you go about prepping the potatoes and the other ingredients.

Secondly, when you cut the potatoes, each slice frees some of the potato's starch. Don't wash the slices! This potato starch dramatically thickens the dairy when you precook the sliced potatoes in the herb-infused dairy. Then, as it bakes in the oven, the slices will come together, creating a rich and unctuous dish. These potatoes taste even better the second day!

2 lb	Yukon Gold Potatoes, peeled (or not, your choice)
4 Tbsp	Unsalted butter
½	Yellow onion, peeled and minced
1	Bay leaf, ideally fresh
4	6" sprigs fresh rosemary
1½ cups	Half-and-half
½ cup	Sour cream
2 cloves	Garlic, minced (about one tablespoon)
⅛ tsp	Cayenne pepper or 10 or 12 drops of Tabasco®. A pinch of pepper flakes are also nice.
2½ tsp	Salt
½ tsp	Black pepper
1	8" × 10" baking dish or equivalent

Preheat oven to 350°F. Melt the butter in a 4-quart saucepan. Add onion and cook until translucent. Add the rosemary and bay leaf. Sauté the herbs in the butter for 1 minute. Do not allow the onion to brown.

Add half-and-half. Bring to a boil. Remove from the heat and let the herbs infuse their flavor while you prep the potatoes (10–15 minutes).

Peel the potatoes. Slice in half lengthwise. Then slice each half crosswise in ⅛" slices. Do not rinse or place in water!

Remove the bay leaf and two of the rosemary sprigs. Strip the needles from the remaining two rosemary sprigs and leave the needles in the infused half-and-half. Return the pan to the heat. Bring to a simmer. Add the garlic, cayenne, salt, and pepper. Stir in the sour cream.

Add potatoes and cook over medium-low heat, stirring potatoes carefully, until the liquid thickens and the potatoes are softened and partially cooked, about 10 minutes.

Spoon the potatoes and sauce into a buttered baking dish, pressing on the potatoes to smooth the top. Wipe the inside rim of the dish to clean the exposed edge. Add a couple of tablespoons more of half-and-half if the top potatoes are not mostly covered and moist.

Place in oven and bake for about 45 minutes until the top is medium brown and little crusty pieces have formed at the pan edge. Cool 20–30 minutes before cutting.

Circle
Pastry punch or cookie cutter

Scoop
Large spoon

Wedge
Knife & then spatula

Square
Knive & move with spatula

Pheasant with Caramelized Honey & Thyme

Makes 1 pheasant

THERE USED TO BE A GAME FARM not far from The Herbfarm when we were in Fall City. We served pheasant several times a year. The original version of this recipe removes the breasts of the bird the night before. The remaining carcass and legs (full of tendons) are then simmered overnight in a slow cooker with alliums, red wine, carrots, celery, bay, and thyme for a rich stock and thus a sauce of real depth.

Since most of us don't cook that way anymore, I suggest you roast the whole bird. You can then remove the legs and carve or slice the birds in the kitchen or at the table. This recipe also works for lean game birds such as wild turkey or quail.

PHEASANT BRINE

8 cups	Water
½ cup	Salt, Kosher
2 Tbsp	Sugar
1	Bay leaf

FOR THE PHEASANT

2	Pheasants, whole
2 Tbsp	Butter
Pepper, to taste	

CARAMELIZED HONEY THYME

1 tsp	Thyme leaves, fresh
½ cup	Honey
½ cup	Red wine vinegar
1 cup	Pheasant stock or reconstituted chicken demi-glace to the strength of homemade stock

Salt, pepper, to taste

BRINE AND DRY THE BIRDS

Bring the water and brine ingredients to a boil. Let cool. When cool, submerge birds for 4–5 hours. Don't brine any longer as the birds will become too salty.

Remove birds from brine. Pat dry. For extra-crispy skin refrigerate uncovered overnight.

MAKING THE HONEY-THYME SAUCE

Place honey in a small saucepan. Add thyme and cook over medium heat until honey turns dark and begins to caramelize. Add vinegar and mix well.

Add stock and simmer over very low heat until the sauce reduces, thickens, and will coat the back of a spoon. About 20–30 minutes. Adjust seasoning and serve warm over pheasant.

ROASTING THE PHEASANTS

Preheat oven to 450°F. Bring the pheasant to room temperature. Butter the bird, smearing it all over. Season with pepper.

Roast the pheasant uncovered for 20–30 minutes until the skin browns slightly. Remove from oven and reduce oven temp to 350°F. Give the oven a good 15 minutes to reach this lower temperature.

Return birds to oven and roast uncovered for 30–40 minutes, or until the internal temp of the thigh is 155°F. Juices should show just a bit of pink. Do not overroast or the meat will be dry.

Let the pheasant rest for 10 minutes. Slice breasts and serve with the Caramelized Honey and Thyme Sauce.

Douglas Fir old-growth logging on the Chehalis River, 1903

Know Your Douglas Fir

Douglas fir (*Pseudotsuga menziesii*) needles are flat, fairly soft, and pointy without being sharp or prickly. The back of the needle is lighter than the top. Each needle has a very skinny attachment to its branch. The newest light-green spring growth has little flavor. The rest of the year the needles taste citrusy and woodsy—ideal for sorbet.

Douglas Fir was featured at the 11th International Botanical Congress held in Seattle in 1969.

Doug Fir Sorbet

1 cup	Sugar
3 cups	Water
4 cups	Douglas fir, fresh, 4–5″ tips
¼ cup	Lemon Juice
½ cup	(Opitional: Sparkling wine/Champagne)

In a medium pan, bring sugar and water to a boil. Add fir tips, stir, simmer 1 or 2 minutes, then remove from heat. Add lemon juice. Steep 1 hour. Strain mixture through a fine strainer. Add sparkling wine, if desired. Chill, then pour into an ice cream churn and freeze according to the manufacturer's instructions.

For an icy granita, freeze the mixture in a bowl and scrape with a fork every hour to beak up the ice into large crystals.

Serve with a fir tip sprig.

Readers of a certain age will remember Euell Gibbons's immortal phrase, "Ever eat a pine tree? Many parts are edible!" from a TV ad for Grape Nuts. For years I wondered which "food" was meant to benefit from that comparison, Grape Nuts or pine trees; to this day I've ingested plenty of one and none of the other. Thanks to The Herbfarm, however, I have eaten fir tree, in a Doug Fir Sorbet memorable for its bracing resiny vapors. It was like swallowing a Northwest breeze.

— *Kathryn Robinson, SeattleMet*

> "**Memorable for its bracing resiny vapors. It was like swallowing a Northwest breeze.**"

A Taste of Trees: Douglas Fir Sorbet

Serves 8

THE NOTION THAT DOUGLAS FIR could flavor a sorbet or other dish was hatched in 1985 when Canadian friend Dr. Nancy Turner mentioned that the Coast Salish tribes would make a tea of the needles When we first served this sorbet, it was an instant hit, a classic, and a good idea subsequently adopted by many Northwest restaurants. Not only do we serve "Christmas Tree Sorbet" most years at The Herbfarm, but it is de rigueur as part of my holiday dinner for family at home at the "Mark Twain Table" (see memoir for details).

Needless to say, Douglas Fir needles are a Northwest ingredient available in near-endless quantities. Very refreshing and unique, you can also fashion this dessert or palate cleanser from Alpine Fir, Noble Fir, and Balsam Fir.

Caramelized Pear Tarte Tatin with Blue Cheese Mascarpone

Serves 6

LEGEND HAS IT that the original inspiration for desserts of this sort was an accident. Two sisters ran a restaurant in France. Stephanie Tatin did the cooking. During one busy lunchtime service, a customer requested a caramelized apple pie. In her rush to fill the request, she forgot to add the pastry before baking. Not knowing what to do, she pulled the pie from the oven and put dough over the apples. When the pastry was golden, she turned the dish upside down. The Tarte Tatin was born.

TARTE PANS OR RAMEKINS

| 3 | 6" cast-iron mini skillets |

TARTE TATIN PASTRY

2 cups	Flour, all-purpose, more for dusting
1½ tsp	Salt
1 cup	Unsalted butter, cold, cut into small cubes
1	Egg yolk
2 Tbsp	Water, cold

TARTE TATIN PEAR FILLING

5–6	Pears (Bartlett, Bosc), peeled
9 Tbsp	Unsalted butter
⅔ cup	Sugar
1 tsp	Salt

BLUE CHEESE MASCARPONE

8 oz	Mascarpone cheese
5 oz	Soft blue cheese such as Gorgonzola Dolce
1 tsp	Salt
2 Tbsp	Yogurt or heavy cream, optional

MASCARPONE DIRECTIONS

Mix and beat all ingredients until smooth and integrated but still able to hold a shape. Adjust consistency as needed with yogurt or heavy cream.

MAKE THE PASTRY (OR BUY IT)

(You may substitute store-bought puff pastry)

Combine flour and salt in large bowl. Add butter and work with fingers until butter is pea-sized.

Beat egg yolk and water and add to the flour mixture.

Work until the dough comes together. Press dough into a ball and refrigerate for 30 minutes. Remove from fridge 20 minutes before rolling out. *Do not roll out until the filling is ready.*

PREPARE PEAR FILLING

Peel and cut pears in half lengthwise; then again into quarters. Core the quarters with a melon baller. Then cut each quarter again in half (8 slices per pear).

Melt the butter, sugar, and salt in a large saucepan. Cook on medium-high heat until the butter bubbles. Add pear wedges and cook, stirring occasionally until the sauce turns a deep amber. Remove from heat and let cool.

Butter the tarte pans. Carefully arrange pear wedges in a neat array, skinny end toward center. Try not to leave any spaces. Place on a sheet pan.

ROLL PASTRY AND BAKE

Preheat oven to 375°F. Flour a surface and rolling pin. Cut pastry ball in thirds. Pat the dough into a flat round. Roll until it is just shy of ¼" thick.

Trim pastry rounds ¾" larger than the pans. Lay the pastry over the filled pans and tuck extra *inside* around the pears. A fork may help ease it in.

Transfer to the oven and bake until the pastry is crisp and golden, about 25 minutes. Remove and let cool 15 minutes before carefully inverting tarts. Tidy up any pears that have moved. If desired, cut each tart in half to create 6 servings. Serve with the Mascarpone Blue Cheese.

The Elusive Oregon Truffle

Makes 1½ Quarts

IN 1987, A MAN appeared at the restaurant as I was preparing food. From the paper bag, he gently poured out about twenty little brown spheres. The room was filled with a distinctive woodsy kerosene aroma. These were my first Oregon truffles. An underground fungi, native truffles are now better known, with many enthusiasts seeking them in second-growth Douglas Fir stands. The most sought-after are the white and black. This ice cream is a great way to showcase this unique wild flavor.

BLACK TRUFFLE ICE CREAM

1	Oregon black tuffle, large or 2 medium
1¼ cup	Sugar
6	Egg yolks
1¾ cup	Milk
Pinch	Salt
2 cups	Heavy cream

Grate the truffles into the cream. Refrigerate overnight or longer.

Whisk yolks with sugar until they lighten in color.

In a medium saucepan, bring the milk to a boil. Slowly pour the hot milk into the egg mixture while whisking vigourously. Return pan to low heat. Stir with a spatula or wooden spoon until the mixture thickens to coat the back of a spoon. Add the cream. Strain into a bowl and chill. Churn in an ice cream machine then freeze until set.

Truffle ice cream tastes like malt. Though it is made with black truffles, the result is cream colored.

Dogs or Pigs?

Traditionally in Europe, truffles were sought using female pigs. The pigs seek truffles because they emit pheromones similar to male pigs.

However, pigs also love to eat truffles. Imagine trying to pull a 200-pound sow away from a truffle!

Here in Oregon, truffles were initially harvested by recognizing the habitat and noticing where voles and squirrels were digging. The truffle hunter then used a four-tine rake to pull back the forest duff to reveal the harvest. Now more and more people are training dogs for the search. Though their sense of smell isn't as acute as that of pigs, dogs truffle hunt for fun.

A day's harvest of Oregon white truffles

Raspberry Soufflé with Rose Geranium Crème

AS WE TRAVELED the world and visited fine restaurants Carrie and I would always order the magical soufflé that usually required deciding well ahead of time and a willingness to wait to the very end for delivery.

Simple yet elegant, soufflés have a reputation for being hard to pull off. I was definitely nervous the first time I made them for guests. But really, as long as the eggs are truly at room temperature, and they are beaten to a nice peak, soufflés are fairly foolproof.

RASPBERRY SOUFFLÉS

Makes twelve 3-oz ramekins

3 Tbsp	Unsalted butter, melted
¼ cup plus 2 Tbsp sugar, divided use	
4	Egg whites, room temperature
1½ cups	Thawed frozen raspberries
1½ Tbsp	Cornstarch

Preheat the oven to 425°F. Middle rack.

Butter each ramekin, then evenly coat with 2 Tablespoons of sugar. Set aside.

Press the raspberries through a fine-mesh strainer with a rubber spatula to yield ½ cup raspberry purée.

ASSEMBLE SOUFFLÉS

Combine cornstarch and raspberry purée. Whisk out lumps. Over medium-low heat, whisk until smooth, continue cooking, stirring constantly with rubber spatula until quite thick about 3–4 minutes. Transfer to a large bowl and whisk to cool slightly.

Whisk the whites on medium-high speed until they are foamy. Whisk in the sugar in a steady stream until the whites are glossy and hold fairly firm peaks. Gently fold the whites into the base one third at a time.

FINISH AND BAKE

Spoon the mixture into the ramekins to the top. Smooth to create a slightly domed top surface. Place in the oven on a lined sheet pan. Pour boiling water into the sheet pan to cover the bottom for steam. If your oven has steam, set to 50. Bake for 8–10 minutes until the top rises an inch or so and is golden.

Serve immediately. Instruct your guest to use their spoon to pierce the top and pour 1–2 oz of room temperature herb-infused crème anglaise right down the center.

ROSE GERANIUM CRÈME ANGLAISE

Makes 1¼ cups

1 cup	Whole milk
3½	Tbsp sugar
½ cup	Rose geranium (or mint, or anise hyssop) leaves, loosely packed
4	Egg yolks, at room temperature
Food thermometer	

INFUSE THE MILK

Over medium heat in a 2-quart saucepan heat milk until scalding but not boiling. Turn off heat, submerge the rose geranium leaves in the milk. Cover and let stand for 15 minutes. Pour through fine strainer, pressing on the herbs to extract maximum flavor.

COOK THE ANGLAISE

Whisk egg yolks and sugar in a stainless steel bowl. Gently whisk in ¼ cup of the hot milk mixture. Place bowl with hot milk over pot of simmering water (double boiler) gently whisking in the tempered egg yolk mixture until 175°F. (The eggs will curdle if you exceed 180°F). It should coat the back of a spoon. Remove from heat and whisk rapidly to cool. It will continue to thicken as it cools. Strain once more. Use immediately or cover and refrigerate for up to 5 days.

SERVE

Serve at room temperature. If too thick, whisk in a bit of milk until the right consistency.

Herb and Goat Cheese Soufflé

Makes about 10 eggshell soufflés

ADD **A** BIT of frivolity to your dinner! While the best results for high-rising soufflés are from ramekins with straight sides, as you see, eggshells work well too. Empty the eggs. Gently rub inside of the shell with your finger to remove the membrane and any stray bits of shell. (I have had success without removing the membrane too). Gently rinse the shells and set upside down on a clean paper towel to dry.

12	Large brown eggshells, topped, emptied, and cleaned
5 Tbsp	Unsalted butter, divided use
3 Tbsp	Fine bread crumbs
3 Tbsp	Flour
¼ cup plus 2 Tbsp Whole milk	
¼ cup	Goat cheese, plain
3	Large eggs, separated
½ tsp	Cream of tartar
A cardboard egg carton bottom	
2 Tbsp	Fresh, finely chopped oregano
½ tsp	Kosher salt
Pinch of black pepper	

Preheat the oven to 425°F.

Empty 3 eggs for their shells and separate the yolks from the whites. Empty the other 9 shells and reserve contents for future use.

Wet the cardboard egg carton thoroughly; set on a lined sheet pan.

Melt 2 tablespoons of butter. Swirl it around the inside of an egg. Pour off excess into the next shell and repeat until all are buttered. Then dust insides with bread crumbs and set in wet carton.

MAKE THE SOUFFLÉ BASE

Melt 3 tablespoons of butter in a medium saucepan, whisk in flour. Cook, stirring, on medium-low heat for 2–3 minutes (don't let it brown). Whisk in the milk until the sauce thickens, about 2–3 more minutes.

Remove from heat and stir in goat cheese to melt. Stir in egg yolks, herbs, salt, and pepper. Transfer mixture to a large, shallow bowl.

WHIP THE EGG WHITES

Whisk egg whites and cream of tartar on medium-high speed until firm peaks.

Gently fold the whites into the base one third at a time.

FILL AND BAKE

Fill the eggshells to the tops using a piping bag or a small spoon. Immediately bake for 6-8 minutes, or until the tops are puffed, golden brown. They should be set but moist in the centers. Transfer to egg cups and serve immediately.

Easy Soufflé Secrets

· Room-temperature eggs will whip better than cold. Put in bowl of warm water to warm them up from the refrigerator.

· Make sure there is no egg yolk in the whites (it will prevent them from whipping properly).

· Try substituting thyme for oregano, anise hyssop for rose geranium, or toss some chopped mint into the raspberry soufflé batter.

· Before you start set up your serving items— egg cups, saucers, small spoons. You want to get the soufflés to the table as quickly as you pull them from the oven.

· Cooking 4–5 soufflés at a time makes it easier to pull out of oven at perfect rise.

· To test, sacrifice one soufflé by pulling it out of the oven and "cracking it open" with two forks. The middle should be set and be glossy and soft.

Egg Cracker or Topper:
You can order these online.

Green Walnut Nocino Tart

Serves 8: Makes an 8" tart

GREEN WALNUTS SEEM an unlikely food or makings of a unique liqueur. Yet, practically since opening day at The Herbfarm, they've found their way into our repertoire, including pickles for salads. The most beloved transformation of the unripe nut is the liqueur Nocino. Though credited to Italians, many European cultures made such a beverage in the past. Make your own or shop around for a local or Italian bottling. All are different. This nocino tart is both lovely and a delicious treat.

PASTRY

6 Tbsp	Unsalted butter, cold, cut into small cubes
1½ cups	Flour
¼ cup	Sugar
1 pinch	Salt
1	Whole egg
1	Egg yolk

TART FILLING

⅔ cup	Nocino liqueur, purchased or homemade*
3	Whole eggs
1	Egg yolk
½ cup	Heavy cream

GARNISH

| 8 | Walnut halves to top the finished tart |

Optional: a sprinkle of coarse salt for the top

Optional: whipped or ice cream

*Traditional Homemade Nocino

Pick 25–30 green English walnuts before the inner nut shell hardens. Cut in quarters. Mix 35–40 ounces of vodka with 5 cups sugar. Put in a 64-ounce mason jar and shake well. Add walnuts. Add a little cinnamon or clove if you wish, but very little as the walnut liqueur should end up smelling of walnuts. Put in a sunny place and mix and turn 2–3 times per week. After 60–70 days, strain. Bottle liqueur and age 2 months or up to a year for best results.

MAKE THE PASTRY

Cut butter into pieces and add them to the flour, sugar, and salt in a bowl. Work with your fingertips until the butter is pea sized.

Mix in the whole egg and the yolk just until combined. Don't overwork. If the dough is not coming together, add a touch of vodka or gin to moisten (makes a flakier dough than with water).

Squeeze firmly into a ball. Cover with plastic wrap and let rest an hour or more in the refrigerator before using.

BLIND BAKE THE TART SHELL

Heat oven to 400°F. Lightly butter and dust your 8" tart pan pan with flour. Roll dough into a 10" circle, and ⅛" thick. Carefully lay the dough circle over the tart pan. Tuck it in and press it all around into the sides. Fold the dough over the rim and trim it ¼" above the edges of the pan. Pierce the base all over with a fork. Cut a foil circle and cover the bottom of the tart shell. Bake about 15 minutes then remove the foil and bake 5 minutes more. Remove from oven.

MAKE THE FILLING

Preheat oven to 325°F. In a medium pan, boil the nocino until large bubbles form and it becomes the thickness of honey or maple syrup.

Whisk together the eggs, egg yolk, cream and ⅓ cup of the nocino reduction. Nocinos vary greatly in sweetness. Taste the mixture and add sugar if you think it needs it.

Fill the tart shell with part of the mixture. Set it in the oven on a middle rack. Now ladle or pour in more filling until it reaches the brim.

Bake 20–25 minutes. Check for doneness by lightly shaking the pan; remove it when it is still wobbly in the center but no longer liquid. Garnish with walnut halves and cool on a rack. Carefully unmold. Serve with the remaining nocino reduction as a sauce.

Ark of Taste

Blue-Foot Chicken

Pellegrini Bean

Down on Our Farm

KEEPING IT CLOSE TO HOME. Since opening the restaurant in 1986, The Herbfarm has actively farmed. We were among the first to foster this direct involvement between the earth, kitchen, and our guests.

What began as a modest (though thoroughly charming!) kitchen garden now involves multiple acres. The kitchen crew spends a few hours a week at the farm working with our farm team.

As the years have passed, we've delved into rare and exotic plants, maintained endangered crops, and discovered our "forever favorites." Many of our special crops are on the Slow Food Ark of Taste.

Roy's Calais Flint Corn

Ozette Potato

The Story of Herbfarm Dinner "Themes"

SINCE THE FIRST MEAL at The Herbfarm, each day's luncheon or dinner has had a named theme. In the early days, these were usually poetic evocations of the season, such as "A Summer's Afternoon" or simply "A Visit to Our Farm" for the Uzbek Republic Puppet Theater (used to traditional

crusty whole-grain loaves, they didn't like our soft Pullman loaves. This sparked a change in our bread which continues today.)

Soon, like galactic gases gathering into planets, the themes coalesced into storybooks. Each ran for two or three weeks and featured—much like a theater—marquee posters of the current "performance" at the entrance and similar artwork for the menus and personalized welcoming greetings in small silver frames.

Over time, some of these events became annual affairs dear to the hearts of guests. Others started well but wore out their welcome.

As the themes became more specific guests loved, to "collect them all!". Each year the actual menus for the recurrent themes were different. So, a guest who loved mushrooms for instance, could dine during A Mycologist's Dream menu theme year after year and never see the same dishes presented. Mother Nature dictates which mushrooms appear when but the preparations varies. This provides the chefs freedom to respond to the best that nature provides at the time honoring the focused seasonality that is a basic tenet of The Herbfarm.

The themes provide the "frame" for the foods of field, pastures, wilds, and sea from which the kitchen draws and creates the ever-changing nightly meal.

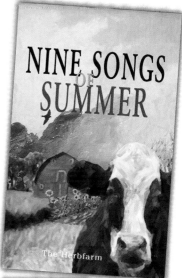

The Holly & the Ivy

Super Cattle in Seattle

The Great Basil Banquet *Ran each August for over 10 years until the novelty of basils wore off.*

The Moon & the Stars

A Menu for Truffle Treasure

The Spring Forager

A Walk in the Woods

The Chambers of the Sea *Every course contains seafood*

A Menu for a Copper King

Salmon Nation

The Native Forager

The Iron Sommelier

A Journey into June

Christmas on the Farm

An Herbfarm Thanksgiving

A Testament to the Tomato *"We love tomatoes. But not in every dish."*

A Menu for Uber Tuber *Who knew there were so many kinds of potatoes and ways to cook them?*

A Witch's Brew

An Autumn Sketchbook

An Exultation of Vegetables *Vegetarians loved it. The general public still wanted animal protein.*

SOME CURRENT & PAST DINNER THEMES

Makin' Bacon *Heritage pastured pork*

A Taste of Trees *Probably our most-creative menu. I loved it. But people couldn't wrap their minds around trees giving fruits, nuts, syrups, flavored barks, and smoking wood.*

A Menu for Two Hearts *All decked out for Valentine's week.*

The Spring Forager

Birds of a Feather

The Hunter's Table

The Fundamental Root

The Harvest Table

A Menu for Red Heads *Red wines paired with each course.*

An Indian Summer

Knife, Fork, Smoke *Cooking with fire, coals, and smoke.*

A Mycologist's Dream *One of the first themed dinners. Explored native mushrooms. Very popular.*

June's Silver Spoon

Odd Bins & Cellar Treasure

Nine Songs of Summer

A Menu for a
Mycologist's DREAM

The Herbfarm Restaurant

Mists blue the sky
from salted shore to high land meadow.
With punctured cries, a distant crow
departs his spartan post. Fallen leaves
and forest duff gain voice, recounting
in deep-down, dream-like whispers—
"Time. Time. It is time! The mushrooms
await!"

THOUGH THE NORTH PACIFIC COAST
OF NORTH AMERICA IS BLESSED WITH
MUSHROOMS throughout the year, *autumn is
high season* for abundant and esculent fungi. Since
1986, we have featured an annual mushroom feast,
bringing the flavors of the forager's basket to the
comfort of our table.

In this spirit, we once again present "A Menu
for a Mycologist's Dream." With one of the best
seasons ever for wild mushrooms, we keep our fingers
crossed; the ever-changing nightly menu will be
woven with whatever wild mushrooms nature offers
up each day, supplemented as needed with local
mushrooms gathered fresh from a local farm.

Experience and taste the [...] and enduring
flavors of autumn mus[...] [wi]th friends and
family for a nigh[...] [...]mber.

Reserve [...]

A MENU FOR
A Mycologist's Dream
SUNDAY, OCTOBER 21, 2001 · 4.30 O'CLOCK

From the Gatherer's Basket
Coral Mushroom Tempura
Oyster and Angel Wing Stew with Lovage
Morel Mushroom and Caraway Thyme Soufflé
1997 ST. INNOCENT BLANC DE NOIRS

Matsutake Flan and Alaskan Spot Prawns
With Roasted Matsutake and Pea Sprouts
2000 ELEMENTAL CELLARS MELON, DEUX VERT VINEYARD

Chanterelle & Cauliflower Mushroom Consomme
With Delicata Squash Ravioli, Leek, and Quince
2000 CHATEAU STE. MICHELLE-DR. LOOSEN 'EROICA' RIESLING

Seared Duck Foie Gras
With Celery Root and Potato Blintz,
Blue Chanterelles and King Bolete Mushroom Sauce
1994 WILLAMETTE VALLEY VINEYARDS PINOT NOIR, O.V.B.

Green Grape & Lemon Verbena Sorbet

Northwest Lamb Loin
Oven-Poached in Olive Oil & Thyme
With Lobster Mushroom, Butterball Potatoes,
Golden Beets and Chard Gratin
1994 CHATEAU STE. MICHELLE ARTIST'S SERIES MERITAGE

Sally Jackson Sheep Cheese & Quillisascut Curado
With Autumn Greens

Festival of Harvest Fruit
Sekel Pear Edulis
Triple Ginger Cake with Pumpkin-Bay Ice Cream
Caramelized Apple Soufflé with Rosemary Custard Sauce

Brewed Coffees, Teas & Infusions

A Selection of Small Treats
VINTAGE 1875 BARBEITO MALVAZIA MADEIRA
Herbfarm Multigrain Rolls · Herbfarm Herbed Focaccia
Chive and Calendula Butter Coins

Mycologist's Dream

EXPLORING THE WILD MUSHROOMS OF THE NORTHWEST.
FORCEPOINT / OPTIV CELEBRATING PARTNERSHIP
3 NOVEMBER 2016

Pine Mushroom Trilogy
• Crab & Matsutake Salad on Toast with Nasturtium & Shiso.
• Matsutake Chawanmushi, Green Tomato, Steelhead Roe.
• Tempura of Papa Cacho Potato, Matsutake Purée, Chives.
TREVERI CELLARS SPARKLING GEWÜRZTRAMINER, YAKIMA VALLEY

Poulet Bleu Pour Vous
• Crisped Bun of Blue-Footed Chicken, Sweet Potato, Shiitake, Tarragon.
• Soup of Blue Footed Chicken and Wild Cauliflower Mushrooms.
2014 DELILLE CELLARS CHALEUR BLANC, COLUMBIA VALLEY

Hail the Bolete
Wood-Roasted Autumn Bolete, Oca Cooked in Pear Juice,
Dried Oregano Flowers, Crispy Fontina Cheese.
2010 FACELLI WINERY SANGIOVESE, COLUMBIA VALLEY

Pastoral Triptych
• Smoked Pork Collar "Ham", Yellowfoot Mushroom Sauce.
• Lamb & Coriander Sausage, Fermented Radish, Saffron Milk Caps.
• Bison Tartare with Celery, Foie Gras, Pickled Cherries.
• Warm Mushroom Pretzel.
2012 RED LILY VINEYARDS TEMPRANILLO, APPLEGATE VALLE[Y]

Chanterelle Salad
Autumn Greens, Pickled Golden Chanterelles, Winter Squash, Seed Granola

Root & Fruit
Layers of Carrot and Quince Jams, Rose Flavors, Carrot Lassi Ice Cream
2013 FINN HILL SÉMILLON ICE WINE, ROSEBUD VINEYARD

Coffees, Native Beverages & Teas
Coffees, Teas, and Historic Bark & Root Decoctions of the American West.

Harvest Tastes
• Huckleberry Pate de Fruit
• Bay Meringue with Pumpkin • Dark-Chocolate Chile-Puffed Quino[a]
• Corn Macaron with Corn White Chocolate Ganache.

House-Churned Holstein Butter • Woodoven Rye Boule with More[l]

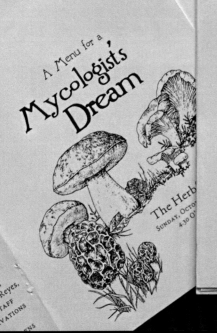

A Menu For
A Mycologist's Dream
OUR 10TH YEAR · SATURDAY, OCTOBER 26, 1996

A Brace of Wild Mushroom Soufflés
Wild Hedgehog Mushroom Soufflé
Wild Boletus Mushroom Soufflé
With Jerusalem Artichoke Chips
HERBFARM HERBAL CHAMPAGNE COCKTAIL · 1991 ARGYLE BRUT

Vegetable and Seafood Mushrooms
Pacific Spot Prawn and Lobster Mushroom Skewer
Cauliflower Mushroom and Fennel in a Jingle Bell Pepper
1995 AMITY VINEYARDS PINOT BLANC

Pacific Halibut Wrapped in Braised Leeks
With a Matsutake Mushroom Broth
1995 EYRIE VINEYARDS OREGON PINOT GRIS

Foie Gras with Morels and Delicata Squash
And a Cider Glaze
1991 APEX GEWÜRZTRAMINER ICE WINE

Grape, Rosemary, and Lemon Verbena Sorbet

Breast of Muscovy Duck
With Chanterelle Mushrooms and Quince
Accompanied by an Onion Timbale,
Historic Anna Ozette Potatoes and Autumn Vegetables
1994 DOMAINE SERENE EVENSTAD RESERVE PINOT NOIR

Autumn Greens
And Local Farmstead Cheeses

Pear Edulis
Poached Pear with a Hazelnut Mousse
And a Chocolate-Hazelnut Sauce

A Selection of Small Treats
Petit Fours of the Season
VINTAGE 1900 D'O LIVEIRAS MALVAZIA MADEIRA

Herbfarm Rosemary Bread
Parsley-Pineapple Sage Butter Coins
Starbucks Coffees · Choice of 17 Teas

A Menu for the FUNDAMENTAL ROOT

The Herbfarm

A Menu for the Chambers of the sea

A Menu for TWO HEARTS

Herbfarm Re...

A Menu for a

June's Silver Spoon

INTIMATIONS OF SUMMER ENVELOP THE NORTH PACIFIC COAST.
9-COURSE DINNER AT THE HERBFARM • 26 JUNE 2016

Edge of the Sea
Beef Tartare with Sea Vegetables and Smoked Laminaria Kelp.
Sidestripe Shrimp, This-Morning's-Egg Omelette, Chives.
Leek-&-Oyster-Filled Squash Blossom, Montana Paddlefish Caviar.
BLUE MOUNTAIN OKANAGAN BRUT, BRITISH COLUMBIA

Keep Clam
Salad of Savoy Cabbage and Geoduck,
Nasturtium, Chrysanthemum Leaves, Dried Mackerel Sauce.
2014 IDILICO ALBARIÑO, YAKIMA VALLEY

Sea Wing
Skate Wing with Rockfish Mousse, Grilled Fava Beans with Lovage.
2014 DELILLE CELLARS CHALEUR ESTATE BLANC, COLUMBIA VALLEY

Grain & Goat
Farro Ancient Grain with House-Churned Goat Butter,
Nodding Onion, Fermented Radish, Lemon Verbena Oil.
DOMAINE SERENE ROSÉ "R," DUNDEE HILLS, OREGON

Lamb Afield
Sage-and-Rose Roasted Saddle of Cattail Creek Lamb,
Grilled Lamb Tongue, Oregon-Olive-Poached Lamb Tender,
Spiced Mustard, Black Currant-Sage Sauce.
2013 OWEN ROE YAKIMA VALLEY RED MERITAGE

Morel Rising
Morel & Caraway Soufflé, Summer Savory Béchamel.

Pound Town
Grilled Lemon Thyme Pound Cake, Anise Hyssop Cherries,
House Yogurt, Almonds.

Berry Serenade
Roasted Blueberry Rice Pudding, Black Pepper & Rosemary Sablé Breton,
Strawberry-Wild Elderblossom Sorbet.
2013 ANDREW RICH ICE GEWURZTRAMINER, CELILO VINEYARD

Coffee, Teas & Native Beverages
Lamb Licks

Accompanying Dinner
• House-Churned Holstein Cow Butter
• Wood-Oven Seeded Sourdough Loaf • Herbfarm Epi

The Chambers of the Sea

A DISCOVERY OF THE SEASCAPE OF THE PACIFIC NORTHWEST
THE HERBFARM • SUNDAY, 28 APRIL 2013

Edge of the Sea
• Poached Pacific Oyster, Tiny Root Vegetables, Champagne-Chervil Cream.
• Smoked Togiak Herring Mousse, Dilled Horseradish, Quinault Steelhead Roe.
• Sea Air Baguette, Albacore Tuna, Elderberry Capers, Oregon Olives, Lovage.
• Giant Alaskan Octopus, Olympic Peninsula Saffron Arancini, Chive Aïoli.
TREVERI CELLARS SPARKLING PINOT GRIS, COLUMBIA VALLEY

Crab Pool
Bellingham Bay Dungeness Crab, Green Garlic Custard, Spring Radish,
Turnip, Foraged Wild Greens, Warm Lemon Thyme Vinaigrette.
2011 DOMAINE DROUHIN OREGON CHARDONNAY, ARTHUR, DUNDEE HILLS

Three Clams and a Squid
Squid Ink Penne with Three Native Clams (Razor, Geoduck, Manila),
Herbfarm House-Cured Coppa, Fennel Fronds.
2010 SWIFTWATER CELLARS NO. 9 SÉMILLON, WAHLUKE SLOPE

The Wild Chinook
Herb-Smoked Columbia River Spring Chinook Salmon, Mustard Seeds,
Grilled Spring Onions from Our Farm, Vichyssoise Sabayon.
2008 L'HERBE SAUVAGE PINOT NOIR, BALCOMBE-CROFT VINEYARD, OREGON

Vestal Sturgeon
Wood-Grilled Columbia River Sturgeon, Oregano,
Wild Mushroom-Potato Mille-Feuille, Nettles & Parsley as a Vegetable,
Sturgeon Marrow-Black Trumpet Mushroom Bordelaise Sauce.
2008 BRIAN CARTER CELLARS TUTTOROSSO, SUPER-TUSCAN-STYLE RED

Meadow Bloom
Ancient Heritage Cow's Milk Camembert Cheese,
Shower of Spring Flowers, Herbfarm Honey.

Pearls in Half Shell
Sorrel Tapioca, Buttermilk Granité, Spearmint Meringues.

Baba au Rhubarb
Spring Baba Soaked in Foraged Botanicals of Western Juniper,
Wild Ginger, Elderflower, and Orange Balsam Thyme
With Rhubarb-White Chocolate Yogurt Sauce
Accompanied by Rhubarb Stalk Sorbet with Walnut Tuille.

Coffees, Native Beverages & Teas
Choice of Coffees, Teas, Herbal Infusions,
And Historic Bark & Root Decoctions of the American West
2010 KIONA RED MOUNTAIN CHENIN BLANC ICE WINE

Sea Treats
Smoked House-Churned Holstein Cow Butter
• Nori Focaccia with Seaweed Salt • 8 Grain Rye Loaf

A Fete for the Sun

SUNDAY, AUGUST 12, 2001 • 4.30 O'CLOCK

Treasures of the Tide Pool
Montana Paddlefish Caviar on Chive Flan
Morel and Marjoram Fritter
Mint-and-Lovage Roasted Mussels
1997 ST. INNOCENT BLANC DE NOIRS

Corn and Side-Stripe Shrimp Soup
With Chanterelles and Perilla
2000 DR. LOOSEN RIESLING, EROICA

Herbed Quillisascut Goat Cheese in Zucchini Blossoms
On Warm Sungold Tomato & Basil Salad
2000 AMITY VINEYARDS PINOT BLANC

Herb-Smoked Columbia River Sturgeon
With Fennel-Apple Marmalade & Walnut Watercress Sauce
1998 ARGYLE 'NUTHOUSE' CHARDONNAY

Santa Rosa Plum-Lemon Verbena Sorbet
In Minted Melon Soup

Lavender-Grilled Squab
With Blackberry Sauce, Confit-Chard Strudel,
Golden Beets, Baby Turnips, and Round Carrots
1998 ELK COVE PINOT NOIR, LA BOHEME VINEYARD

Salad of Green Beans, Purslane, Nasturtium, and Tarragon

Festival of Fruits
Raspberry-Rose Geranium Ice Cream Sundae
White Donut Peach Roasted with Hazelnuts and Anise Hyssop
Apricot Souffle with Cinnamon-Basil Sauce

Brewed Coffees, Teas & Infusions

A Selection of Small Treats
VINTAGE 1875 BARBEITO MALVAZIA MADEIRA
Herbfarm Multigrain Bread • Sourdough Rosemary Bread
Chive & Calendula Blossom Butter Coins

One-of-a-Kind Dinners

FROM TIME TO TIME, we've had the opportunity to create a one-off dinner with a special theme. These were challenging and fun, as we explored a specific niche in the world of food and wine. Or raised funds for special causes (Katrina; Japanese tsunami; Christchurch earthquake).

"Dine at a Level Seldom Experienced" took us via the Victoria clipper to Vancouver Island for a multi course affair at The Sooke Harbour House.

One year we packed up and were off to the James Beard House in New York City for "A Northwest Passage"—a joint affair with chef Fernando Divina. The meal came off with aplomb. Of the many unique events, these are among the most memorable.

A Madeira Party

An authentic re-creation of the last great Madeira tasting of the nineteenth century

NEARLY FORGOTTEN TODAY, the fortified wines of Madeira were by far the most popular drink of Colonial America. Unlike Port, the process of aging Madeira stabilizes it so that it never goes bad. I began collecting vintage eighteenth- and nineteenth-century Madeira not long after we opened the restaurant.

At the end of the meal, we'd serve an elegant sip of the ancient brew. Guests were enchanted by the story each bottle held, genie like, in its bottle (see menu on page 85).

When Mannie Berk of the Rare Wine Company proposed we re-create the great dinner documented by S. Weir Mitchel in 1895, I jumped at the chance. Re-creating the original nineteenth-century menu proved quiet difficult. Wild canvasback ducks were a daunting quest. For the terrapin soup, we finally got the turtles, frozen, from the Carolinas. After a formal tasting of fourteen nineteenth-century bottles, we enjoyed dinner matched with madeiras and the thematic napkins printed in sepia of a Madeira map. We topped off the evening with the legendary 1900 Barbeito Malvasia Madeira.

"We Pledge Our Lives, Our Fortunes, and Our Sacred Honor"
Founding Fathers toast the Declaration of Independence with Madeira

The Last Supper of the Twentieth Century

A grand dinner and experience for the turn of the millennium with wines from three centuries

The wood and brass New Year's bells are engraved: This bell was RUNG AT MIDNIGHT to welcome the twenty-first century at the last supper of the twentieth century.

YOU ONLY GET ONE SHOT when celebrating the passing of 1,000 years. For this event we installed a barrel of reserve Cabernet and set up a bottling station. Just before midnight, guests wrote their memory capsules and began filling their engraved, gold-foiled, deeply etched magnum bottles. As midnight struck, we rang our souvenir brass bells and sang "Auld Lang Syne." The big bell next door at Boehm's Chapel sounded, resonating with gentle hope. We somehow managed to silkscreen souvenir napkins with every date since the year 1,000. At the finish of the meal, we offered up the rarest of Madeiras: the 1795 Barbeito Terrantez Madeira.

DYSPHAGIA *When I opened this 1795 Madeira and imbued its aroma, my vision was overwhelmed with a wonderful, intense chartreuse light.*

An Evening with Mario Andretti

A dinner with the greatest race car driver of all time

NOT EVERY DINNER need be a serious food and wine event. Some are just plain fun. To raise funds for the arts, Mario Andretti brought some of his Napa Cabernets. The Hedges added to the selection for this dinner. Guests got checkered flag napkins. Mario told storvies. The next day he took interested guests to the local speedway to ride, white knuckled with him in a Porsche. At 60, Andretti was then off to race at Le Mans.

In Search of Umami—The Beautiful Taste

IF YOU'RE LUCKY, YOU get one or two mentors in life. Jon Rowley was my culinary guide. With the ambling gait of a contemplative bear, Jon wandered through the American food scene, bringing Copper River Salmon, Totten Inlet Virginica oysters, Shuksan strawberries, Walla Walla onions, and profound peaches, to the table. Though a common term now, Jon's goal was to see "umami" in a dictionary and in print. These days, the main use of the word expresses a savoriness. Jon's ideal, though was the ancient Japanese meaning, a more profound and philosophical relation to nature and food.

There are two meanings in Japanese for "umami":

旨味

A term used in modern times by food technologists for a so-called "fifth taste" (savory, pungent, meaty), or the chemical basis for that taste (monosodium glutamate). This savory sensation is most easily found in shiitake mushrooms, kombu kelp, and dried yellowfin tuna flakes.

An older philosophical/cultural meaning probably has roots in Zen Buddhism.

The ancient definition of umami does not easily translate into English.

Japanese who attempt translating umami use words such as "taste," "flavor," "deliciousness," and "essence," yet will say, "but that's not it." Most Japanese experience frustration trying to convert umami into English.

A food has umami when it optimally transforms, when it reaches its peak of quality and fulfillment.

Before that point a food has the potential for umami. After that point the food has lost it — umami "goes away."

In Shinto and Zen Buddhist religions, each food's natural flavor, color, shape, and aroma comprise a gift from nature, to be enjoyed and revered. This combination of qualities represents a food's umami.

Umami involves all the senses: sight, smell, touch, hearing, and taste. Umami awakens positive emotions.

Umami has cultural, spiritual, and even mystical aspects. Education, experience, and understanding elevate and refine tastes, and perception, and enjoyment of umami. Umami contains a promise of pleasurable

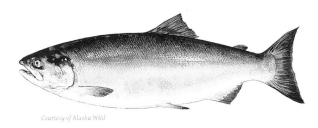

Courtesy of Alaska Wild

UNTIL THE 1980S, Copper River Salmon was canned and not eaten fresh. Seeing the quality of this fish, Jon Rowley convinced a few fishers to treat the fish gently, bleeding and icing them at sea. The "catch of the day" was then rushed to air cargo in Cordova, Alaska, and flown overnight to Seattle.

The result was sensational. Chefs and customers clamored for this firm, fat, red flesh with a rich oil content you could actually feel with your fingers.

These days the price is dear. Some think it a scam. But frankly the best salmon from the Copper River run can't be topped.

outcomes. Umami conveys beauty. A sense of anticipation enhances umami.

Umami does not exist unless we have the experience and understanding to perceive it.

Seasonality and ripeness are essential umami elements. If picked too soon, a food may never achieve umami. Umami usually implies proximity to a growing area. Umami will "go away" if grown, harvested, handled, prepared, or served with neglect or disrespect.

Setting, preparation, and presentation enhance our perception and appreciation of umami.

Umami usually implies the naturalness of food with minimal use of seasonings or accompaniments.

"EAT THEM BY SUNDOWN" should be the rule for the luscious Shuksan strawberry. The glistening berry is dark red all the way through. A single bite will define "strawberry" for the rest of your life.

Because of their fleeting shelf life, the Shuksan is a secret shared only by home gardeners and a few commercial accounts. Eat them by sundown to lose yourself in umami.

TO SEE JON ROWLEY SLURP A HALF-SHELL OYSTER is to witness a man transported to another place. First, he looks at the plump briny meat, smells the oyster, and then with one practiced move slides it, quivering, to his welcoming mouth. "You must chew the oyster a bit," he admonishes. "This frees the flavor, with every river estuary having its own unique terroir."

Jon calls the minerally Virginica oysters from Totten Inlet "the best oyster on the planet." He should know. As America's own Brillat-Savarin, he's been an oyster worshiper around the world.

"Tell me what you eat, and I will tell you what you are."
—Brillat-Savarin

Raise your own hens for a palate of colors.

Guests always enjoy fresh eggs from our very own free-range chickens.

The 100-Mile Dinner

A Nine-Course Dinner with All Food, Wine, and
Beverages Grown, Raised, and Produced within a
Maximum of 100 Miles from The Herbfarm

THE 100-MILE CIRCLE Nothing can be used outside this circle*

Squamish, British Columbia	Shy of Astoria, Oregon	Shy of Neah Bay
Lake Chelan & Wenatchee	Willapa Bay on the coast	Strait of Juan de Fuca
Western edge of Yakima	Most of the Olympic Peninsula	Cowichan Valley on Vancouver Island, British Columbia

* All measurements are "as the crow flies," not highway miles.

The Ultimate Quixotic Challenge: A Total 100-Mile Dinner

Is it even possible to create a grand 9-course dinner with every molecule made or found no more than 100 miles of the restaurant? We donned our field clothes and chef's jackets to find out. And we fell down the rabbit hole.

NEAR AS I CAN remember, the nascent mullings for a total 100-Mile Dinner started with a couple in Vancouver, British Columbia. For one year, they would consume only food from within 100 miles of their apartment. No more olive oil, rice, citrus, warm-climate nuts, or frozen or pre-packaged foods. But they did exclude some treats they felt they couldn't live without such as chocolate, lemons, and coffee.

The Herbfarm had long since sourced and cooked with only regional foods. After so many years we had become comfortable in this culinary voice.

But had we stretched the search for local terroir to the limit? What if we also made *all of those hidden ingredients* that no one gives a thought too?

Could we make our own salt, vinegars, baking powder, cheese, or cultured cow butter? Or goat butter? If any existed, was there 100-mile wheat to mill to make crusty sourdough bread?

So, in 2008, we began the quest. We didn't completely nail it that first year. It was a journey. Rennet for making age-worthy cheese eluded us until we tried an old artisan way. So much common knowledge and old techniques have been lost. Here's what we've found.

Lower Mainland, BC

Olympic Peninsula   Yakima, Lk. Chelan

Columbia River

The 100-Mile Dinner

Where (Truly) Every Last Molecule of Food & Beverage
Comes from No More than 100 Miles from Our Dining Room.
At The Herbfarm • 6 September 2015

Salt made from Rosario Strait seawater. Vinegars are fermented from local wines and apple cider.

Ancient Ways

Slow-Roasted Lummi Island Reef-Netted Chinook Salmon,
Applewood-Smoked Holstein Yogurt, Pickled Crab Apple, Fennel Pollen, Ice Lettuce.
2011 VENTURI-SCHULZE BRUT NATUREL, VANCOUVER ISLAND, CANADA

Salmon were harvested in the traditional reef-netting manner off of Lummi Island. Fermented the Yogurt here in milk we smoked. Grew all of the other ingredients.

Directly imported this great sparkler from our friends on the lower portion of Vancouver Island. The Herbfarm is the only place to enjoy it in America.

Used fig leaves from our fig tree to imbue the flavor of coconut into the base of this "curry". Raised all of the other ingredients on our farm.

Fig Leaf Curry

Sugarpie Pumpkin, Zucchini & Onion "Curry" created with
Fig Leaves, Peppers, Garlic, Basil, and Green Coriander Seed.
2014 LOPEZ ISLAND SIEGERREBE, PUGET SOUND AVA

Barnacles harvested for us by Nick Jones. Barley from Nash Huber in Sequim. All other items we grew.

Barley Corn

Olympic Peninsula Barley Risotto with Fresh Sunflower Seeds,
Lopez Island Gooseneck Barnacles, Leeks, Fresh Bay Leaf.
HERBFARM 100-MILE PALE ALE: WATER, BARLEY, YEAST, HOPS

Sourced barley from the Skagit Valley, sprouted and kilned in Arlington. Then took the grain and sous vided some at 155F and dried it to create "Vienna" malt and roasted some to 20 Lovibond as an adjunct. Grew the Cascade hops at The Herbfarm. Got the water from Lynwood Artesian Well #5. Brewed it with Whitney Burnside of 10-Barrel Brewing.

Grew this historic potato that was left by Spanish explorers on the Makah Nation lands in 1791. Got the seed starts in 1994, and have been raising it ever since.

Farm & Field

Historic Ozette Potatoes Roasted in Yakima Riesling Seed Oil,
Green Grapes, 5-Herb Sauce Made With Local Cured Lamb.
2012 WILRIDGE ESTATE BIODYNAMIC NEBBIOLO, NACHES HEIGHTS

Raised 6 kinds of heritage tomatoes, the romaine, and the mint.

Transition in Tomato

Tomato-Water Granité, Fresh Tomato, Romaine, Mint.

Pruned Pinot Noir vines 1 mile from restaurant. Ducks & livers from Puyallup. Picked berries and went to Lake Kacheess to get the Vanilla Leaf.

Quack!

Grapevine-Grilled Moulard Duck Leg,
Roasted Puyallup Valley Foie Gras, Huckleberry-Wild Vanilla Leaf Sauce,
Candied Eggplant from Our Farm.
2012 TSILLAN CELLARS ESTATE RESERVE SYRAH, LAKE CHELAN

Sourced the fourth stomach of an unweaned calf from Bellingham. Cleaned, salted, and cured the stomach. Soaked pieces in mild vinegar made from apples to extract the rennet enzyme. Sent rennet to Blacksheep Creamery in Centralia who made the cheese for this dinner.

Grew Roy's Calais Flint Corn the previous year for this menu. This is the corn Squanto gave to the Pilgrims. Dried, shucked, and ground the corn in a stone mill. Served with honey from one of our 6 hives on the farm.

Old Maids & Milk Maids

Herbfarm Blacksheep Creamery 60-Day-Aged Sheep's Milk Tomme,
Half-Popped Heritage Flint Corn with English Thyme, Our Beehive Honey

25-Year-Old Balsamic from the Cowichin Valley. Hazelnuts from Bellingham. Peaches from Wenatchee.

Plum

Bleeding Heart Plums Roasted with Woodruff Butterscotch, Rye Crumble.

Peaches & Vinegar Cream

Vancouver Island Balsamic Vinegar Ice Cream,
Crunchy DuChilly Hazelnuts, Rose Geranium-Peach Sorbet
2013 BENSON ESTATE LATE-HARVEST VIOGNIER, LAKE CHELAN

For baking powder, took white ash from our wood oven and dripped water through it to make lye. Created a fruit fermentation and bubbled the CO_2 through the lye to create Potassium Bicarbonate. Dried liquid in a Dutch Oven. Chiseled out the "stone" and ground it to dust.

100-Mile Plant Infusions
Final Thoughts: Small Sweets

Wild yeasted sourdough captured from the air. Wheat from Kevin Tevaldi on his farm in Arlington.

With Dinner Woodoven Skagit Valley Wheat Bread • House-Churned Butter

We always make our own butter in house.

It All Started with Salt

After initially simmering the salt, we use smaller pans for the final reduction where the flakes and crystals form.

Carrie Van Dyck fetches salt water from the Saratoga Passage. A van load of this water became the salt for the first 100-Mile Dinner.

Chef Weber examines the dried and flaky finishing salt that forms on top of the reduced brine.

TWAS NO SALT. LOCAL, THAT IS. And that would be a problem. So we grabbed some 5-gallon Jerry cans and toted water back from Lummi Island. Chef Chris took up the challenge of simmering the water down to 20 percent, where the supersaturated water began creating salt. When we ran out of salt, Chris drove to the Sound at 3 a.m. for more water. His sea salt was ready in time to make dinner the next day. We also learned to reuse our vegetable blanching water twice to preserve this precious ingredient!

Some things we learned by making our own Sea Salt from local waters

When you make sea salt by simmering sea water, you get **two kinds of salt**. The first are crystals that fall to the bottom of the pan. The second is the fleur de sel. The crystals are best for cooking. The fleur is a finishing salt best sprinkled atop a dish.

Location makes a difference. Tidal flushes in the Strait of Juan de Fuca create a salty minerality. Water from the south Puget Sound hints at kelp and low tide; a true sense of place.

Seasonal yield: you get more salt from water in the summer than winter. In the rainy season, river flows dilute the top 30–40 inches of the sea.

In the summer, expect to get 3.2 ounces of salt per gallon. In the winter the yield will be about 2.8 ounces.

Almost Forgot the Acids

SOMEHOW IN OUR headlong rush to ready for the first 100-mile dinner, we forgot the need for acid in cooking. And, of course we couldn't use lemons or commercial vinegar.

We needed to act fast!

I remembered that the huge tanks of wine at Four Monks were said to turn to vinegar in just a few days. By pumping air through the wine, the Acetobacter vinegar bacteria operate overtime chewing alcohol to acid.

But how to do this on short order?

I rushed to the pet store to purchase an aquarium pump. I toted bottles of biodynamic Madeleine Angevine wine from Puget Sound's Bainbridge Island Winery. Et voilà! Those bottles became our first 100-Mile Vinegar in just three days!

Making vinegar fast with an air pump.

Some of the 100-Mile Acids We've Created for the Restaurant

Grape Wine Vinegars *All varietals of grapes.*
Apple Cider Vinegar *Juice of heritage cider apples*
Malted Grain Vinegar *Barley wort beer*
Douglas Fir and Spruce Tip Vinegar
Green English Walnut Vinegar

Verjus *Unripe grapes provide an acid zing*

Balsamico *Aged in progressively smaller wood barrels with their estate-grown grapes at Venturi Schulze in the Cowichan Valley of Vancouver Island.*

Fat of the Land

Fats and oils from things within 100 miles? We began with butter.

To Make Your Own Butter

- *Chill heavy cream, ideally non-homogenized and high fat content, for a day.*
- *Whip or churn the cream until it thickens and breaks.*
- *Strain off buttermilk liquid.*
- *Wash butter with cold water. Slap it against counter to squeeze out all the remaining liquid.*
- *Shape, wrap, store.*

Draining and working the skim milk from the butter.

Finished butter ready to portion and shape.

TO COOK A 100-MILE Dinner, we needed cooking fats and oils Though there are now olive orchards and oil created in Oregon, they fall well outside of our 100-mile circle. Oregon's olive oils today are excellent, and we use them in the restaurant. But wish as we might we'd have to find other fat sources in the local area for our 100-Mile Dinner.

Butter was the easiest target. Anywhere dairy animals were kept, people made their own butter. Even today, without the daily restraint of the 100 miles, we still make cultured butter nightly for guests' dinner service. It just tastes better.

Housemade 100-Mile Fats

Cow butter Most butter is made from cows. The milk of different breeds tastes different and has more or less butterfat. Jersey or Guernsey cow milks are the richest in fat.

Goat butter A white goat butter I enjoyed at Asador Etxebarri in the Pyrenees was an epiphany. So I ordered a farmstead cream separator Eastern Europe. With anticipation, we separated local goat milk. But the yield of cream for butter was not enough volume.

Sheep butter Sweet, rich, soft buttery flavor. MORE?

Lard Rendered pig fat. A real workhorse available in quantity.

Tallow Rendered cow fat

Chicken fat "Schmalz," rendered chicken fat

Goose fat One of the best

Duck fat Rendered duck. Great for sautéing potatoes and root vegetables and general cooking.

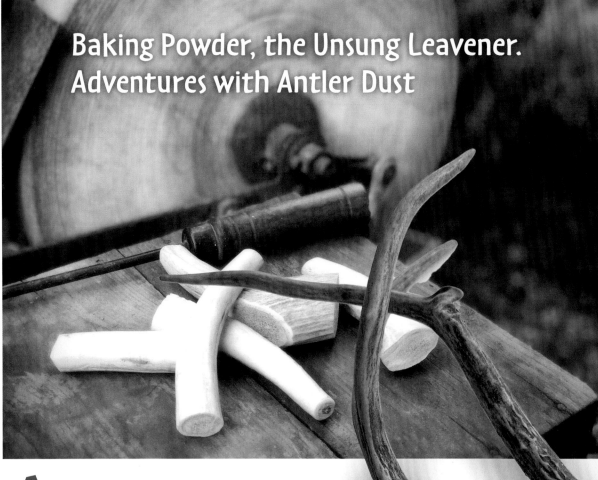

Baking Powder, the Unsung Leavener. Adventures with Antler Dust

AFTER CHEF **CHRIS AND** I finished dining, we were chatting with René Redzepi at his Copenhagen restaurant, Noma. I mentioned I was stumped by making baking powder with only 100 mile ingredients.

"Hmmm," mulled René. "They say that in the old days, people used reindeer antlers." Reindeer?

On the plane home, I thought about reindeer. We DO have mule deer in PNW. I found a piece of antler and used a sander to create powder. I split a batch of cookie dough in half.

One half got baking powder. The other the antler dust.

With no expectations, I tasted the baked goods. Amazingly, the deer dust cookies tasted better! And the thin cookies stayed fresh for days.

But antlers are harder than bone. I tried unsuccessfully to find others to grind them. No bites. Looking for another solution which I found in a 200-year-old book. Wood ash.

From the Ashes

TODAY WE TAKE BAKING POWDER for granted. But visit a cook's kitchen before 1856 and cakes and other baked goods were leavened with sourdough, yeast, or a substance called "'saleratus."

Having seen the futility of making enough mule deer antler powder, I uncovered a book outlining a nineteenth-century farmstead method for creating saleratus baking powder. It involved wood ash turned to lye.

To make your own 100-mile leavener, you must first collect white wood ash and sift out the charcoal bits. Drill an old bucket with many holes in the bottom and fill it with ash. Drip water through the ash and catch it below. After two passes of water, replace the ash and pour the previous water through your brew. Now simmer down your lye water. Put it in an old pan (it will be ruined). Bubble carbon dioxide from an active fermentation through the lye. Bake in the oven until it is a wet paste. Dry this and grind to a powder. Now you can use your homemade saleratus for 100-mile baked goods. Or buy a can of regular baking powder!

Baking Our Daily Bread
Raising Our Own Bread Wheat

Farmer Eric Fritch reaps our acre of wheat with his old combine. He grows the special wheat for us. The harvest is just enough to make rustic bread for a year.

"**OKAY. YOU CAN GO,**" sighed the man. The perplexed border control agent had wondered why someone would drive to southern Vancouver Island for common flour. After all, flour was to be had everywhere.

Well, yes.

But not for 100-mile flour of a special variety. Chef had gone for some special wheat that once was the workhorse for crusty bread all across Canada. Renan. In fact, it was also called the "Canadian Wheat." Now rarely grown, it made one of the finest whole wheat loaves.

Driving to Canada every year for a 100-mile wheat was impractical.

But then the Washington State University Bread Lab launched. The Bread Lab breeds and field trials thousands of grain varieties in the Skagit Valley near the British Columbia border. Their emphasis is on wheat that can be milled and made into whole-wheat breads. And, most importantly, it must be delicious. Since none of these special wheats were commercially raised, Dr. Steve Jones gave us 50 pounds of Renan starter seeds. Eric Fritch of Chinook Farms in the Skykomish Valley seeded and harvested an acre of half Skagit–1109 and half Renan wheat. Each year, our one acre provides just enough grain for us to house-mill wheat for The Herbfarm's dinner service.

Our mill stone grinds the grain to flour.

Dr. Steve Jones helped found the Bread Lab, where researchers test thousands of wheat varieties each year.

What Is Bread?

Bread is simple.
It basically has four ingredients
- **Flour:** Any flour—whole wheat, rye, oats, buckwheat, cornmeal, rice flour.
- **Water**
- **Leavener:** sourdough or yeast
- **Salt:** Whole-wheat makes a more wheat-y and substantial bread. That's what we use, From these basics, a whole range of breads with different flavors and textures can be crafted.

How Sweet It Is

HOW DO WE SWEETEN the 100-mile food? Luckily sugar is regularly made from Yakima sugar beets. So that part was easy. There are other natural native flavors to work with also.

Tapping our native bigleaf maples to gather the clear, slightly sweet liquid.

Bigleaf Maple Syrup

Yes, our abundant bigleaf maples can be tapped for their sap. In fact, a century ago there was a thriving maple syrup industry on Vancouver Island. But Eastern sugar maple syrup priced the local craftsmen from the market.

I tapped a few trees and reduced the sap to a tiny amount. But not nearly enough to use in the restaurant.

A bit different than eastern maple syrup, the bigleaf syrup production was revived on a tiny scale in the 70s. Now an enterprise on the Skagit River links hundreds of trees via tubing to a vacuum. They craft fine 100-mile syrup.

Honey from Our Hives

Few know that the vast majority of store-bought honey isn't local but comes from China. For our 100-mile needs, we just had to go two miles down the road to our farm. Here, for a few years, David Nold tended seven hives and extracted the sticky goodness for us. Bees not only make honey, they are critical for pollinating crops for our harvests.

David Nold frees the honeycomb from its frame. It will be heated and spun to liberate the honey.

Say Cheese
100-mile Cheese
with Animal Rennet

"NO ONE'S EVER ASKED FOR ONE" said the small custom butcher skeptically. "You want what?"

"An abomasum, the fourth stomach of a calf, lamb, or kid goat," I replied. "And it can't have eaten grass."

I needed the stomach to make rennet. Without this key component—used for centuries—we could never make 100-mile hard cheeses. Soft cheese, yes. But not cheese that could coagulate the milk and be compressed to make "real cheese."

The enzyme, chymosin, lines the last stomach. It curdles the casein of its mother's milk separating the curds (solids) from the whey (liquid) All rennet derives from male dairy cattle, who have no use at a creamery.

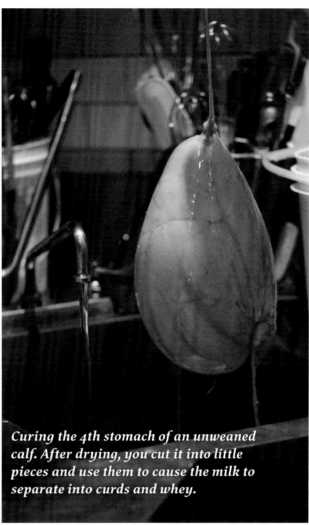

Curing the 4th stomach of an unweaned calf. After drying, you cut it into little pieces and use them to cause the milk to separate into curds and whey.

Surprisingly, much of the flavor of famous cheese derives flavor from the rennet. Beloved cheeses such as Parmigiano Reggiano, Pecorino, Roquefort, Stilton, and many others would taste differently if made without animal rennet.

With the precious stomach in hand, it was back to the restaurant. I rinsed and dried my prize. I blew it up like a balloon, tied it shut, and refrigerated it to further dry. After a few days, I cut the stomach open and cleaned up the inside. Then I cut it into little pieces, each ready, with a touch of vinegar, to coagulate and separate milk into curds and whey. A local creamery filled the molds and pressed them to form the cheese.

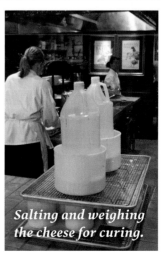

Salting and weighing the cheese for curing.

100-Mile Beer: Drinking the Regional Terroir

ONE FINE JULY DAY in 2015, Chef Chris and I met Whitney Burnside in a garage in northern Seattle. Whitney had been an extern at The Herbfarm before falling for fermentation. This garage was her pilot brewery. She was becoming a professional brewer.

After several years of decoding 100-mile food, we now felt comfortable in brewing our own beer and wine with ingredients solely from west of the Cascades.

Skagit Valley Malting had opened just south of the Canadian border. They were key in roasting local barley to varying degrees. I had secured 28 pounds of pale-roasted Copeland barley.

Together we heated our water (toted from an artesian well) to 151°F, added the grain, and brewed it one hour before "sparging"" the mash at 168F. 'We inoculated the fermentation with Hales Foundation 1988 yeast.

After primary fermentation was complete, we added a little sugar to the batch to restart fermentation. We bottled it to create the carbonation during the second fermentation. I made labels.

This was the first 100-Mile beer. As I learned to brew, I roasted my own additions.

The first 100-Mile Beer, which was brewed in a garage. Me with a mere handful of the dozens of beers I brewed with local ingredients. Beer offers bountiful possible kinds.

Other Beers

AFTER MAKING THE FIRST 100-mile beer, I became possessed. I made beers no longer produced; beers with herbs; a series of mushroom ales, a truffle brew, and simple beers as might have been made in a farmhouse in Norway. Here are a few of them.

Eric Fritch of Chinook Farms raises a quarter of an acre of NZ–151 (Fritz) barley for us. I made 4 nano batches of 100-Mile beer just for him. Each is slightly different. He liked "Summer's Well," so that became the 100-Mile Beer for that year.

Franklin's Old Ale
Rosemary IPA
Obadiah Parson's 1790 Brown Tavern Ale
Northwest Mycological Series
   MacMorel Scottish Ale
   Porcini Porter
   Golden Chanterelle Golden Ale
   Candy Cap Mushroom Brown Ale
Finish Sahti Spruce Beer (with Douglas fir)
Old Goat Doppelbock
Pumpkin Stout
Wet Hops (from our farm)
Persian Lady Apricot Ale
Black Braggot Apricot Cider Ale
Oystercatcher with Oysters
Polish Links
Lichtenhainer Polka Smoked Wheat Beer

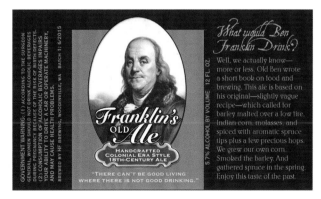

One of my favorite brews is a re-creation of an ale that would have been served in the nineteenth-century downstairs tavern in Philadelphia. The recipe is from notes written by Ben Franklin. I like to imagine the bricked walls with fire burning and Franklin and Washington toasting with this brew. I even refermented some of it in authentic seventeenth-century beer bottles.

The One-Mile Vineyard Project: A Year in the Vines

CAN YOU MAKE PINOT NOIR wine near Seattle? We were about to find out.

Just up the hill from The Herbfarm is a south-facing slope of land . Steve Snyder had planted 2,200 Pinot vines in 2005. Based on the weather, some years the vines ripened. Most years they didn't.

The previous year I'd run into Steve. "I'm throwing in the towel, he announced. All work and no pay."

"But, Steve," I exclaimed, "the vines are just reaching maturity!"

Here's the deal I proposed " We do all the work this year to keep the vineyard in shape. Our pay will be the harvest which we will make into wine"

The 1-Mile Hollywood Vineyard in its dormant phase. Note how tall the old vines are. Each vine must be pruned to its bottom catch wires All 2,200.
Jack, Chris, Carrie, and I spent a month taking out the old shoots in anticipation of the new year's growth.

Steve accepted adding that he would give us advice and instruction so as not to ruin his pruning. January pruning is critical to ensure we keep the best fruit-bearing shoots for this year.

Pinot Noir fruit clusters are surprisingly small.

AWARD-WINNING WINEMAKER BRIAN CARTER was our technical advisor. He advised us when to pick the grapes and did the lab work every two weeks. We learned about many aspects of vineyard work as well as the chemistry of the fermented juice.

It was a daunting task

Tending a vineyard is backbreaking work. This Pinot Noir vineyard had been planted so that the fruiting zone was only 18" from the ground to capture the low heat and help ripen the fruit. It meant that much of our work was done stooping over. Ouch!

These days a crew of specialists usually tends to all the vineyard tasks.

In total, we made 14 (fourteen!) passes through all of the vines.

Though I wanted to wait two more weeks, the weather was changing! We gathered a crew and picked the grape clusters on October 14. The juice of the crushed grapes went directly into two and a ½ oak barrels. It fermented for fourteen months. After the light-Burgundy style wine was bottled, we named our One-Mile wine 'Ephemere'.

The vineyard was threatened by birds. Flocks of crows in particular descended on the vines and threatened to eat everything. We bought a bird netting applicator.

Bottling day

Reflections on Working at The Herbfarm Restaurant

1990
Jerry Traunfeld

I first met Ron and Carrie while I was teaching at The Herbfarm; They would invite chefs to come to The Herbfarm to teach a class. To me, it was this fantasy place. The gardens were incredible, just amazing. They put unbelievable resources into having every kind of herb, for sale or for use in the kitchen. Nobody had those resources then.

Ron and Carrie had a distinct style based on their experiences traveling in France. Very European. And yet very much grounded in the Pacific Northwest. Rooted, really. Inspired by *The Auberge of the Flowering Hearth*, yes, but completely at home in Woodinville, Washington. It was such a work of love for them. It wasn't ever, "How do we make the most profit?"

The premise of the restaurant was that every dish we made had to feature one culinary herb. As chef, it was up to me to fit into that. And that's what I ran with. Before I started, Ron had certain dishes he had created—the salmon cold-smoked over basil wood, for example—and I adapted them and did my own variations. It was a really nice creative process. In seventeen years, I made that dish over and over again and over again. It evolved into many versions because that initial idea of Ron's, cold-smoking salmon over basil wood, was just so solid.

Today you probably can go to Olive Garden and they'll have fresh fennel or fresh oregano. It's not that we invented anything. Chefs like Deborah Madison and Alice Waters were both using culinary herbs in imaginative ways back then, like in desserts and things. But we really went to town with it.

Herbs and foraged wild plants. Ron was the foraging guy. You know, when he was a kid, he was foraging through the woods on his own. These wild plants came up earlier than anything in our gardens so he really wanted to put these things on the menu. Every spring we offered the Spring Forager's Menu, where every course had wild ingredients in it. It seemed so off the wall at the time, but it's become such a trend in finer dining restaurants, the whole Noma thing. But there was Ron, way, way early.

It's now legend how Ron and Carrie, whose only restaurant experience was understanding the delight of a perfect meal in a perfect setting, were able to turn an out-of-the-way garage into a nationally acclaimed dining destination. Ron understood their restaurant as an expression of its environment. Before everyone else, he dreamed up a magical place serving lingering multicourse menus, growing herbs and vegetables from its own gardens, supporting local producers, foraging for wild ingredients, and championing our emerging wine industry. His and Carrie's creation, The Herbfarm, was about giving people pleasures of a moment and memories of a lifetime. I was so lucky to be a part of it.

2001
Carrie Van Dyck

When we opened in Woodinville, we were finally being "just a restaurant." What I mean by that is that in Fall City, in hindsight, we were technically a restaurant all along, but I never thought of us that way. We were an educational facility. We offered hundreds of classes on cooking, growing, crafting, and medicinal use of herbs. We manufactured, we sold retail, we sold mail order, we grew plants, we offered educational garden tours as part of every meal. We'd host the microbrewery festival and thousands of people would come to sample all these different artisanal beers, but there was always a serious educational forum going on throughout the festival. Same with the wine festival. We were so many entities in one. Could we tear off one piece and have it succeed?

While we did still have a farm in Woodinville, it was not on the same property as the restaurant building. It was a mile up the valley. There wasn't any room in Woodinville for those other activities. Ron probably always thought of The Herbfarm as a restaurant. Well now, we were finally going to discover if we could survive being "just a restaurant."

It seems that we did survive the challenge!

The Herbfarm is now (and has been since the early 2000s) one of only fifty restaurants in the United States to receive a 5 Diamond Award from AAA. Chris Weber, chef and now owner/chef, was at one time the youngest chef among his 5 Diamond peers. He was almost twenty-one when he started as commis in The Herbfarm kitchen.

2007
Chris Weber

I was used to working in a "standard restaurant." Chef is always telling you what to do, but you're in control of your station, of every order that comes in, of how you cook the food. But you don't have control over how many diners are there or when they show up.

At a regular restaurant, the guest sits down, orders a drink, reads the menu, orders their dinner and fifteen, maybe twenty minutes later, they expect it to show up. You don't know how many of what items will be ordered and you don't want to waste food so you have to do your prep as you go. Dishes are generally much simpler. And you can get slammed if lots of people arrive at the same time. Or if more people than expected order one certain item off the menu.

It's completely opposite at The Herbfarm. We have total control over how many diners are coming. We know who they are, when they're coming, what they won't eat. All of a sudden, the nuance becomes the part that's unknown. You shift your attention to the details, to fine-tuning everything you're doing every day.

Jerry drove me crazy. I was a young cook, looking forward to learning. I had always worked for chefs who let you know exactly what they wanted and exactly how they wanted it and they let you know if you didn't do it the way they wanted.

The way we got slammed was when Jerry would come at three o'clock in the afternoon and tell you he wants something different than we had planned or prepped for based on previous day's events. That's where I had no control. That's when the workload increased and the pressure was on. Fine dining is prep heavy.

What I learned from Jerry was the importance of spontaneity, of waiting till the last minute for the best ingredient. While I say he drove me crazy, it's because he made me work harder than I thought I could work in a way I didn't know you had to.

At The Herbfarm, with a fixed menu and a single seating, people expect to see great food on the table within five to ten minutes. Cooking at The Herbfarm is more like catering that way. Everything has to be perfectly prepped and ready to go when the guests sit down. It's all about dialing in the execution, so it happens quickly. What you're delivering is an experience as well as a meal.

I'd started working at The Herbfarm just as Jerry was preparing to leave after seventeen years at the kitchen helm. I saw a bit of struggle in transition as Ron and Carrie tried to find the right replacement for him. I left for a few months and returned in fall 2008 as lead line cook. I felt like I had a good relationship with Ron, who was often in the kitchen chatting about this or that ingredient or technique, always trying to push the edges.

When I became sous-chef, Carrie, Ron, and I started having regular meetings, which was kind of unusual, since meeting with the owners wasn't really part of the job description. One night in 2010, they invited me to join them for dinner on one of The Herbfarm's "dark nights." During that dinner, they asked me if I wanted to take over as chef. Surprised the hell out of me. I was twenty-four years old at the time and did not see that coming. I was born the same month The Herbfarm served its first meal in that garage in Fall City, so maybe this is where I was meant to be.

2015
Carrie Van Dyck

It was 2015 and The Herbfarm was winning awards and had lots of national and international press coverage. We were fully booked with waiting lists most every night. We were in our prime. I suggested to Ron that we start to think about selling the restaurant and not wait until the quality declined because we got too old. "Now's a really good time to get out of here so The Herbfarm can stay at the top," I said.

It only took me four more years to convince Ron that selling to the right person was the best way to preserve what we built and continue the life of The Herbfarm into the future. We can't all live forever. We found a chef/buyer, but our landlord did not honor his prior agreement for a lease extension. That deal fell through and we ended up in court to win that extension. But finding the right buyer was hard, because running The Herbfarm requires a hands-on, hardworking team of people to keep it at the level we were running. Ron and I each put in eighty to ninety hours each week. I was in the office at 8 a.m. and still in the dining room at 1 a.m.

We knew that the best owner would be our very own chef, Chris Weber, and other Herbfarm employees, but he was not quite ready to take on that large of a "challenge."

When the pandemic hit in 2019 and we were forced to close the restaurant, I told Ron that rather than reopening, we would wind it down and retire. That was when I finally got Ron 100 percent on board with trying to find The Herbfarm's new owner. During that time, when we seemed to have to reinvent ourselves for survival every few months, Chris saw the versatility that ensures survival and began to realize that a good business pays for itself over time. Along with his sous-chef, Jack, we all reached an agreement, finally turning over the reins in March 2021. Wow, what a ride!

2023
Chris Weber

The Herbfarm is now in its third generation. I think that says a lot. It's not like three is going to be the last generation is how I see it. Typically, restaurants don't get to this point without continuing for quite a bit longer.

When I came to The Herbfarm in 2007, it was evident that my experience here would be filled with firsts. It is where I have spent most of my adult life, which means it has heavily influenced (both directly and indirectly) who I am, how I think, and what I prioritize. Perspective is a word that means a lot to me, and I think that is something I have been taught throughout my tenure.

There has always been an element of personal investment required for people to be successful here. Ron and Carrie epitomized this—to the extent of having the discipline to take risks and pursue the impractical. It takes a lot of hard work to make every evening seem effortless. I appreciate their tenacity now more than ever. I can hear the same conversations we had over the years echoed in conversations I have with what will be the future generation of this restaurant.

Ron said to me once that a person needs to find three things in their work: mastery, autonomy, and purpose.

In 2023, after Ron's passing, Carrie created a scholarship in his name for local hospitality students to further their education and influence by becoming interns with us. This scholarship will be used to offset costs associated with pursuing a career while also being a student: transportation, childcare, tuition. It is one of the most characteristically generous ways that Ron and Carrie have, and will always, support making this industry a more interesting place. I'd like to think that my relationship with The Herbfarm is unique, but I fully recognize that the statement itself isn't; there are decades of people who hold the same sentiment about their time at The Herbfarm. I find a great deal of purpose in the responsibility of continuing that.

The Ron Zimmerman Scholarship
for work and study at The Herbfarm Restaurant

SEATTLE COLLEGES FOUNDATION

Help us sustain Ron's incredible, irrepressible joy in living, learning, and caring for the people and places around him.

The new Ron Zimmerman Scholarship will help talented students in the culinary programs at Seattle Central and South Seattle Colleges intern for a quarter, with pay, at The Herbfarm Restaurant, learning beside Chef Chris Weber and other extraordinary team-members. The Scholarship will also offset other living expenses so students can drink the full measure of this potentially career- and life-shaping opportunity.

Ron and his wife Carrie Van Dyck co-founded The Herbfarm Restaurant in 1986. Known for exceptional cuisine that celebrates nature, the changing seasons, and the freshest local ingredients, the restaurant is garlanded with honors. These include the "best-of" lists of Zagat, Wine Spectator and Forbes, plus twenty-plus years of AAA Five-Diamond Awards — the only Washington restaurant with this distinction. The Ron Zimmerman Scholarship will pass the flame to a new generation equally committed to culinary adventure, conscientious stewardship of the earth, and the warm conviviality of the table.

To contribute in Ron's honor: www.seattlecolleges.edu/herbfarm. *Or* ▶▶▶

In Memoriam

Ron Zimmerman 1948–2023

Chris Weber
A romantic, skeptic, brother, pioneer, mystic, a man of routine and adventure, dreamer, friend, stranger, mentor: a man as contrasting as the Cascades and coast from which he was born.

Bill Nicolai
Ron Zimmerman's career as a restaurateur began with meals he used to prepare at home, memorable dinners. The excellence of his cooking and presentation was so profound it resulted in a world-renowned restaurant. My life was altered for the better simply by knowing him.

Jerry Traunfeld
It's now legend how Ron and Carrie, whose only restaurant experience was understanding the delight of a perfect meal in a perfect setting, were able to turn an out-of-the-way garage into a nationally acclaimed dining destination. Ron understood their restaurant as an expression of its environment. Before everyone else, he dreamed up a magical place serving lingering multicourse menus, growing herbs and vegetables from its own gardens, supporting local producers, foraging for wild ingredients, and championing our emerging wine industry. His and Carrie's creation, The Herbfarm, was about giving people pleasures of a moment and memories of a lifetime. I was so lucky to be a part of it.

John Payne
I was the executive sous-chef for Jerry Traunfeld for about five years in the early 2000s, and it was some of the hardest, most rewarding work of my life. Every day with Ron was a new discovery and adventure.

Bill Edwards

I knew Ron for almost fifty years. We spent the first twelve, along with Bill Nicolai, as a close creative team that built one of the most iconic outdoor companies of the seventies, Early Winters. And after that, I watched as he and Carrie created The Herbfarm restaurant and elevated it to atmospheric heights in the world of cuisine—not to mention, of course, an enormous wine cellar of quality, breadth, and depth.

With this homage, I pay my respects to my incomparable friend, an exemplar of inspiration in this world. I have never known a more inquisitive, creative, and generous man than Ron Zimmerman.

Thank you, my friend. It has been a very precious gift to know you. You will remain in my heart and memory forever.

Mitch Stroum

I was listening to the radio sometime in 1992 when I heard about The Herbfarm. A crazy story about a one-day window to call in and get reservations for their coming season. I thought how good could this restaurant be? I was hooked. Called in and the lines were swamped. I persisted and finally got through. Probably to Carrie. She went over the dates and different menus. I picked Basil Banquet. Fall City had limited seating (thirty-two seats) and only one table for six in the entire restaurant. I reserved the table for six and off we went on a twenty-five-year love affair with The Herbfarm. Jerry Traunfeld is a fabulous cook and got his first standing ovation on our first dinner from our table of six, which included two other Seattle Chefs. The Fall City Herbfarm was a very special place. Empress trees (I had to have one) and walking on Filbert shells . . . that intimate space was heaven. We were there the day after the fire and at the ground-breaking for Woodinville and dinners in between. As frequent diners, we introduced friends and family to Ron and Carrie over the years. To say they had an impact on our lives would be fair. Silver water goblets, cabbage leaf chargers, candle lamps, and many bottles of Madeira made it back to our house. We always enjoyed Ron's rhymes in the little silver frames that welcomed us. Some time ago, after dinner at The Herbfarm, Ron and I were discussing some current event or something. He said, "Well, I won't we around to see it." It went right over my head, but it stuck. Here we are now. Cheers to you both. Love Melany & Mitch.

Jessica Chen

Ron was unlike anyone I've ever met. Filled with curiosity, knowledge, and generosity, he was truly one of a kind. His acts of kindness and hospitality were what brought me to work at The Herbfarm. Honored to have worked for him, but even more, to know him. He was the definition of a student of life, always learning and asking questions. He had a story for everything. A life well lived and a legacy I'm proud to be a part of. Thanks for the memories, Ron. You're already missed.

Fernando Divina
Truly, one in a million. Grateful for having collaborated with Ron and Carrie for the classes taught at The Herbfarm and at our collective debut at the James Beard House with Ron, Carrie, and Jerry Traunfeld. From the earliest shared moments of engagement, Ron "saw" me as one hopes others might, and as a result, we shared unique indigenous and gastronomic food discoveries that served to inspire and nurture our celebrated shared foodway in a most enlightened, gratifying way only had in the manner of the likeminded. Condolences to family and friends as we grieve his passing, celebrate his life mightily, and acknowledge the evanescence of Ron while we endeavor to uphold his legacy at the cutting edge of rugged excellence.

Adams Bench Winery
Such a kind and authentic person. Always remember in the very early days of the pandemic, my husband was in search of an onion at PCC and there were none. Ron Zimmerman saw him and they chatted. Later that same evening, a beautiful, labeled box of onions arrived on our doorstep, left by Ron.

Carrie Oliver
Ron, you believed in and encouraged me to continue to think differently, to seek knowledge (to geek out over it, actually), and you taught so many of us to look beyond the obvious and well-worn. Your contribution to humanity and the world of food is unparalleled. Thank you for being such a generous person, and as Adams Bench Winery said above, kind and authentic. Wherever you are now is lucky to have you. Carrie, my thoughts are with you, you two made magic together.

Tim Lockwood
I am so sorry to hear of Ron's passing. It was a true honor to work with him at The Herbfarm, where his impishness and passion was prevalent in all he did.

Bryan-David Scott

Many great laughs together. Watching your face when you tasted one of our new coffees was fun. I sipped some of the greatest wines ever at your hand. We encouraged and inspired each other. You are missed.

Collene Cordova

Very sobering to hear of his passing. Ron was one of a kind and so mischievous. He once tricked me into eating rabbit. That rascal, first and last time I'd eat a bunny. Carrie and Ron taught me more in three years than in any other job I've had. I still, to this day, believe that every customer service skill I have is because of them, and I never tell anyone "no problem." The Herbfarm, hands down, was one of the best places to work because of the people, the atmosphere and them, not to mention that occasional dishes were brought upstairs to be enjoyed by the office staff. Cheers, Ron, to a life well lived.

Acknowledgments

FIRST, **I** WANT to thank my husband, Ron Zimmerman (the author), for having written and designed such a thoughtful and beautiful book with a great story. I am sure he left it unfinished so I would have a project to keep me occupied after he left. Learning about the publishing world was quite new to me. Along the way, I reached out to many people who were so kind and generous offering advice, knowledge, and assistance. This list is not complete because we aren't done yet!

James of Culinary Book Creations got Ron restarted on this book and has provided support and advice both to Ron and to me.

Thanks to Nancy Leson, who supported and directed me in so many ways. Becky Selengut, who shared her knowledge of how to publish from an author's perspective and connected me to her agent, Sharon. Sharon Bowers, who, without ever having met me, was so generous with her time and advice and contacts.

Dan and Xuan Osser laboriously tested and edited every single recipe. Julie Hearne helped add a recipe that Ron didn't get to do himself. She also connected me to the writing team, Schuyler Ingle and Joyce Thompson, who helped massage the memoir Ron wrote into a cohesive whole.

Ubon Leonard, Angela Dubois, and Tysan Dutta, all three of whom are longtime friends and my first marketing team. They offered untold support in so many ways. I even learned the difference between a Tag and a Hashtag thanks to Ubon!

Most of the photographs in this this book were taken by Steve Hansen, who is not only a great photographer but has been so helpful in styling, propping, and adding those extra pictures that make this book so lovely.

Bob Hise was Ron's first art department hire at Early Winters, and he followed us to The Herbfarm where he employed his graphic, construction, and drawing skills to all levels. For this book, he provided the pencil sketches.

Scott Chilcutt appeared from my Early Winters past and took the lead in getting this book out to the public in ways I just didn't know how to do—a blog, Facebook, Instagram, emails, and more—an amazing contribution to the success of this book.

Ron always did everything graphic for The Herbfarm, for our family dinners, or just for fun. So, being totally Adobe InDesign ignorant, I particularly appreciate all the support and direction from David Blatner, who has repeatedly gone above and beyond not only coaching me but rolling up his sleeves and digging in to solve the myriad details of going from bytes to paper.

For both moral and legal advice, I have to thank my good friend David Nold, who, with his wife Casandra Mack, helped me stay on course through these strange waters. And Casandra provided artwork and art critique throughout.

Lastly, Chris Weber, chef and owner of The Herbfarm Restaurant, has been a friend, advisor, contributor on many levels, helping me ensure that Ron's writing and recipes were true to The Herbfarm and doable in-home kitchens.

And to all who purchased a copy of *The Spirit of The Herbfarm Restaurant* before I even had a publisher: thank you for believing in me and in honoring Ron. I hope you will use this book and enjoy the anecdotes Ron wrote for you.

Thank you with all my heart.

Happy Reading and Cooking and Foraging.

Carrie

—Carrie Van Dyck (the other half)

PS: A special thanks to Nicole Frail, my contact at Skyhorse Publishing. While the contract I had to sign gave full control over everything to the Publisher, she honored her word and gave me great leeway to honor Ron's (or what I thought were Ron's) vision for his book from cover design, to layout, to order of pages, to artwork, down to the color of the ribbons. Thank you so much for everything.

General Index

Recipe Index

Metric Conversions

If you're accustomed to using metric measurements, use these handy charts to convert the imperial measurements used in this book.

Weight (Dry Ingredients)

1 oz		30 g
4 oz	¼ lb	120 g
8 oz	½ lb	240 g
12 oz	¾ lb	360 g
16 oz	1 lb	480 g
32 oz	2 lb	960 g

Oven Temperatures

Fahrenheit	Celsius	Gas Mark
225°	110°	¼
250°	120°	½
275°	140°	1
300°	150°	2
325°	160°	3
350°	180°	4
375°	190°	5
400°	200°	6
425°	220°	7
450°	230°	8

Volume (Liquid Ingredients)

½ tsp.		2 ml
1 tsp.		5 ml
1 Tbsp.	½ fl oz	15 ml
2 Tbsp.	1 fl oz	30 ml
¼ cup	2 fl oz	60 ml
⅓ cup	3 fl oz	80 ml
½ cup	4 fl oz	120 ml
⅔ cup	5 fl oz	160 ml
¾ cup	6 fl oz	180 ml
1 cup	8 fl oz	240 ml
1 pt	16 fl oz	480 ml
1 qt	32 fl oz	960 ml

Length

¼ in	6 mm
½ in	13 mm
¾ in	19 mm
1 in	25 mm
6 in	15 cm
12 in	30 cm